THE MYSTIC SEAPORT
ALL SEASONS
COOKBOOK

EDITED BY CONNIE COLOM

ILLUSTRATED BY SALLY CALDWELL FISHER

INTRODUCTION BY SALLY McBEE

PUBLISHED BY MYSTIC SEAPORT MUSEUM STORES
MYSTIC, CT.

Net income earned from the The Mystic Seaport All Seasons Cookbook will go toward supporting the programs at Mystic Seaport Museum, a non-profit educational institution.

For additional copies of the The Mystic Seaport All Seasons Cookbook, use the Order Blank in the back of the book or write directly to: Mystic Seaport Museum Stores
Mystic, CT 06355

or for credit card orders:
Call (203) 572-8551

Suggested retail price: $13.95 + $3.00 for packing and shipping charges. (Connecticut residents add State Sales Tax.)

The Mystic Seaport All Seasons Cookbook may be obtained by organizations for fund-raising projects or by retail outlets at special rates. Write to the above address
for all of the details or call the above number.

ISBN 0-939510-06-5

First and second printing 1988

CONTENTS

PREFACE

Because Mystic Seaport Museum recreates the quintessential 19th century New England setting, one might expect a cookbook bearing the Seaport's name to include such traditional fare as chowders, johnnycakes, beans and brown bread. Indeed, those recipes are included here, gleaned from family recipe boxes which have been handed down for generations. Other recipes in this collection reflect the contributions of ethnic groups that settled in New England, complementing the region's cuisine with French Canadian Pork Pie, authentic Italian Tomato Sauce and Portuguese Sweet Bread.

There are no limiting stereotypes which can be applied to a Mystic Seaport Cookbook. As the foremost maritime museum in the United States, the Seaport has a membership drawn from all over the country. This cookbook reflects such geographic diversity with the inclusion of Sausalito Crab Dip, Savannah Pralines and Texas "Chowder."

Adventuresome sailors, having sampled exotic fare in foreign ports, have contributed recipes flavored with their special memories. Among them are Tahitian Marinated Fish, Turkish Nut Dip, Bahamian Hummingbird Cake and Chicken in Mexican Mustard Sauce.

Treasured traditional recipes and unusual new ones have made Christmas Memories Cookbook popular during the holiday season. In this latest collection from Seaport members, you will find additional treasures contributed with hopes that they will please you, your family, and guests through all the seasons of the year.

Enjoy!
Connie Colom

P.S. A word about ingredients . . .

Captain's Choice — you may notice the use of Seaport Stores' own line of delicious jams and jellies suggested in several recipes. You may, of course, substitute another superior quality product if Captain's Choice is not readily available.

Cilantro, coriander (also called Chinese Parsley) — the fresh leaves of this herb are used extensively in Mexican and Southwestern dishes, as well as in Mediterranean cooking, and are known as cilantro; in Indian and Oriental cuisine the same herb is called coriander. Cilantro's distinctive smell and flavor diminish greatly when cooked or dried; therefore, it is usually added to a dish towards the end of preparation or as a garnish.

Butter — for uniformity in testing, butter was used in almost all recipes. You may prefer to substitute margarine and may do so successfully except in those instances where "no substitute" is specifically indicated.

Recipe Contributors

**A special thank you to all the Members of Mystic Seaport
who made this cookbook possible.**

Carol Aageson
Aimee Altin
Mary Lou Andrias
Nancy Cloos Babin
Clara K. Balhatchet
Alice H. Barrows
Harriet Barry
Mrs. Helen W. Bement
Helen Benedict
Barbara Bergman
Sharon K. Birmingham
Camilla Bertsche
Barbara Blackwood
Laurie Blefeld
Connie Boehm
Jeannie MacDonald Booth
Bonnie & David Bosworth
Anne & Lewis Branscomb
Louisa Broadbent
Florence Brown
Van Brown
Ann Callahan
Mr. & Mrs. Willliam Campbell
Pat & Sev Carlson
Ann F. Carroll
Donna Valery Catalano
Paul Cerullo
Kay Chapin
Florence M. Chapman
Mary G. Chapman
Mrs. Warren W. Chapman
Holly Chase
Patricia Sullivan Chew
Susan Chipman

Marjorie Christianson
Caroline Colom
Jessica Colom
Nancy Combs
Carol M. Connor
Victoria C. Cooke
Patricia W. Cornish
Patricia & John Coward
Mrs. Robert B. Crane
Norman G. Cubberly
Donna Currie
Mrs. D. Weston Darby, Jr.
Virginia B. Darrow
James A. Day
Mary E. Derosier
Ann Sloan Devlin
Cindy Devlin
Beverly DeClementi
Violet Dolson
Louise Duret
Eleanor Earle
Michael M. Edwards
Joanne Erickson
Doris Jean Estes
Mrs. D.M. Farrell
Joy Fast
Janice Fitton
Helen Katz Freedman
Joyce French
Dorothy Frew
Jean Fryer
Harriet F. Gidley
Barbara Gilderdale
Barbara T. Gould

Fred Griffith
Douglas Marsh Griswold
Nancy Horn Grubin
Arden Gustafson
Denise Guterman
Linda Haegele
Pam & Robert Hagberg
Alison W. Hannan
Kathleen Hanning
Kay Hansen
Mary B. Harding
John Harker
Margot M. Harley
Ann Parsons Hehre
Samuel J. Hicks
Ann H. Holmes
Mary Hudecek
John E. Hunter
Dottie Jalbert
Rachel Jasenak
Joy C. Jastremski
Catherine Jensen
Arthur V. Johnson
David G. Johnson
Lulu & Dick Kiley
Lois Klee
Rebecca A. Kraimer
Linda B. Krause
Betsy Lancaster
Leslie Larson
Beverly T. Lathrop
John L. Lathrop
Frannie Lawler
Virginia Leavitt

Mrs. J.M. Lightfoot
Patricia Lindholm
C.V. Lyon
Mrs. Ronald W. MacDonald
Michael McBee
Phyllis McBee
Sally McBee
Ellen H. McGuire
Judy McGuire
Leslie Ann McKenna
Donna Magner
Carol Maloney
Kathleen Manning
Jeanne Martin
Mary Martin
Jo Merrill
Lois M. Moore
Anne F. Morris
Karen Mott
Evelyn B. Nelson
Lillian Newcomer
Patricia Newton
Mrs. Robert E. Niebling
Trudy O'Connell
Grace M. Olsen
Mrs. Donald W. Olson
Deborah S. Palmer

Mark J. Palmer, Sr.
Amy Morgan Parker
Harriet Patterson
Irene M. Patterson
Jean H. Peabody
David W. Peterson
Sarah J. Phelps
Connie Poynter-Fink
Theodore Pratt
Barbara Raho
Sarah Hyatt Reid
George Richards
Mrs. Donald W. Robinson
Robert L. Rosbe, Jr.
Nancy Rymut
Mrs. John P. Samuels
Louise E. Scaramuzzo
Jane Schaefer
Mrs. Paul Schoonman
Peter A. Schweitzer
Jan Scottron
Fran Scully-Power
Anne I. Seal
Annamary Searles
Grace S. Smith
Lorelei Smith
Dorothy N. Somers

Lolly Stoddard
Jackie Stolz
Sophie E. Szopa
Dorothy Tower
Joan Truesdale
Mr. & Mrs. Jerry Turner
Joan Tyree
Marie F. Underwood
Patricia & David Varholy
Andrea Vizcarrondo
Bonnie Vuilleumier
Kathleen Waggoner
Roberta Warren
Charlotte Watrin
Lawrence W. White
Virginia Earle Whitehouse
Sally Wilbur
Roderick O. Williams
Jacqueline Williston
Jayne R. Woods
Frances M. Worsley
Margaret H. Wright
Sue Yacovino
Mary Zastrow
Liz Arellano

Those interested in learning further about the evolution of gastronomy in the United States may enjoy reading Eating in America by Waverly Root and Richard de Rochemont, Connecticut Firsts by Wilson H. Faude and Joan W. Friedland, and It's An Old New England Custom by Edwin Valentine Mitchell, all of which were invaluable research sources for parts of this book.

INTRODUCTION

Everyone has a favorite season at Mystic Seaport.

Perhaps for you it's spring, when the first robins beckon us back outdoors and the air smells just, well . . . springlike! (Are there truly any words to capture that glorious earth-in-bloom fragrance?) Spring is, of course, rebirth, and with it comes to Mystic Seaport a renewed commitment to its preservation of our past, evident in a hundred small ways.

In spring, exhibit doors, shutters and hatches, recently closed against winter's chill, are propped invitingly open to the newfound warmth. Visitors may observe a weaver, bathed in a shaft of April sunlight, meticulously threading a loom, or harken to the ring of the shipsmith's hammer echoing roundly through Seaport streets. The windows at Buckingham House might be thrown open just as the cook is taking a steaming kettle from the open hearth, leaving the breezes to waft delicious aromas where they may. Ships' carpenters, happy again to be in shirt-sleeves, go about their work with a lighter step and a whistle.

A benediction, this spring stuff. A reawakening. The <u>Joseph Conrad</u>, the <u>L.A. Dunton</u>, <u>Brilliant</u>, all the Seaport ships ride quietly on a gentled river, and once again, all seems "right with the world."

But wait: maybe it's summer you like best, that no-hats, no-jackets, triflingly short season we New Englanders try to snatch like a brass ring. Though most Seaport exhibits are open year-round, it is surely summer weather that swells attendance and sparks enthusiasm.

Outside activities abound, as visitors delight in such demonstrations as sail-setting and furling, whaleboat rowing, and horse-drawn carriage rallies. The <u>Charles W. Morgan</u>, America's last surviving wooden whaleship, welcomes guests to tred her time-worn decks under sunny skies, while inviting them to imagine themselves alone on a fearsome sea in what, by today's standards, appears to be a rather unwieldy craft. A short distance away, the Village Green plays host to summer concerts as chanteymen and folk musicians entertain crowds ringing the bandstand on balmy evenings.

We try hard to "get it all in" while the season lasts. Inveterate outdoorsmen, we plunge into a marathon of sailing, picincking, and vacationing with a joyful abandon that, finally, can only propel us headlong into . . .

Fall. Yet when it has arrived, who would trade the charms of this season? Like spring, a New England fall defies definition; we would say simply that if you haven't experienced one, you need to.

Mystic Seaport is a perfect spot to begin. To sit on a Seaport riverbank on an October afternoon is to gain a sense of wonder, timelessness, and serenity. Can anything really be so beautiful? The vista across the river, a line of elegant 19th century homes and tranquil woodlands, is a scene that has changed little in the last hundred years; viewed agianst the flaming autumn foliage, the panorama is breathtaking, a sparkling memory to recapture by the fire knee-deep in December.

And, yes, December, January, and February must come, a time when we truly are knee-deep in snow, slush, and cold. A harsh mistress, our New England winter, downright uncompromising at her worst, yet how often she proves us fickle.

What other season can match Mystic Seaport's beauty at Christmastime, when its stately evergreen, atwinkle with tiny lights and festive red velvet bows, welcomes travelers along Greenmanville Avenue and visitors at the front gate? Winter sightseers find the Seaport a whirlwind of activity, as Lantern Light Tours, the Star of Bethlehem Show at the Planetarium, and the singing of carols throughout the village bring a taste of an authentic American Christmas of the the 1800s. What with wreaths adorning every doorway and costumed guides spinning tales of yore, a December visit to the Seaport is always a merry adventure.

Spring, summer, fall, winter . . . the seasons in New England are as distinct from one another as brandied fruitcake and fresh strawberry pie. We chose to create an all-seasons cookbook because as our seasons change with such clarity, so do our foods; we eat differently in every season to accommodate the enormous swings in both temperature and lifestyle. These 400-odd recipes, culled from our members' personal files, demonstrate just how well we have learned to adapt our eating habits to our time of year.

Mystic Seaport, an institution dedicated to preserving our seagoing heritage, is proud to offer this selection of recipes, family recollections, and highlights from New England's culinary history as a means of preserving other valuable memories upon which tradition is built: namely, remembering the foods we enjoy in season and passing down the many ways we like to prepare them.

We hope that no matter where you live — and in whatever ways your seasons change — you will take pleasure in trying these recipes all year long.

Sally McBee

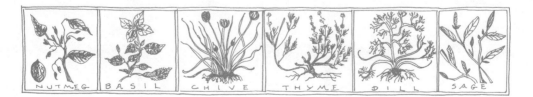

SPRING

SPRING

Br-r-r! Mystic Seaport's sailing classes begin in early March, and participants sometimes find themselves guiding their Dyer Dhows around lingering patches of ice in the Mystic River, a reminder that spring is a perennial latecomer to our New England coast. Our peripatetic spring weather also reminds us that there's still time (and necessity!) to serve family and friends a hearty Chicken Gumbo or a warming Sausage and Artichoke Pie before the daffodils bloom.

But bloom they finally do, and spring's bursting upon New England is a wash of hazy green willows and pinkened dogwoods. Thoughts turn to warmer weather and a new crop of spring brides await their special day with eager anticipation.

One of the more romantic settings for a small wedding is the tiny Fishtown Chapel, an original 19th-century building formerly situated several miles west of Mystic, now centrally located on the Seaport grounds. Couples may choose to be married here provided they adhere to one rule: the ceremony must be conducted before dusk as the chapel, true to its era, has no electric lighting!

Mothers of spring brides welcome a renewed array of colorful foods, as asparagus, watercress, and the first early strawberries appear in abundance. The wedding table might also include the ever-popular Cold Salmon Mousse; Spring Blossoms, a decorative (and highly edible!) confection created from puff pastry with a cream cheese and spring herb filling; and the crowning touch of an Apricot Brandy Pound Cake for the bride who wants "a little something different."

March also brings the annual Victorian Yankee seminar to Mystic Seaport, which provides a highly appropriate setting with its wealth of Victorian buildings and attendant craft displays. Highlighting the daylong program, lecturers regale listeners with tales of 19th-century customs, habits, and fashions and their influence on our American forebears.

One area where we can hardly envy our Victorian cousins is in the lack of the modern kitchen. Imagine, if you can, whipping up an Apricot Mousse, circa 1880. The victorian cook, struggling with few measuring utensils and no glass containers, would have had difficulty beating egg whites into stiff peaks without our modern electic mixer; once she had them, she would have been hard pressed to refrigerate them adequately without a visit from the iceman. Even then, it would seemingly have been a risky business.

The Victorian Age may be touted as the romantic era, but we suspect it was perhaps a tad more romantic in the parlour than in the kitchen. Thanks, but we'll opt for less romance and more conveniences any day!

BEVERAGES

AFRITA Cocktail
Yield: I serving

This drink, was created while cruising the Bahamas in a ketch named AFRITA, Arabic for "a female devil." It goes down easily at brunch, or any other time, but be forewarned — the name speaks for itself!

For each serving allow:

I part Nassau Royale (a rum-based liqueur)
2 parts dark rum
3 parts unsweetened grapefruit juice
ice

Blend all ingredients in shaker, or mix and serve over ice.

Caribbean Cruiser
Yield: 2 servings

It's March and still snowing in New England. Mix up a couple of these, sit under a sun lamp and put on a little Calypso music.

4 ounces light rum
2 ounces canned cream of coconut
I cup canned papaya nectar
I teaspoon lime juice
chilled club soda
pineapple spear for garnish (optional)

1. Put first four ingredients in shaker. Mix well.
2. Pour into glasses, add a splash of club soda and pineapple spear.

Celebration Punch
Yield: about 30 4-ouce servings

**Weddings, anniversaries, graduations, christenings . . .
Spring overflows with the celebration of life's passages. Cheers!**

3 750 ml bottles champagne, chilled
½ cup Triple Sec
½ cup brandy
3 pints Italian-style lemon water ice

1. In 5- to 6-quart punch bowl, combine champagne, Triple Sec and brandy.
2. Stir in lemon water ice and serve promptly.

Recommendation: do not double. Replenish as needed.

Mint Juleps

Make a big pitcherful for a Derby Day party or sailing regatta.

1 cup sugar
1¾ cups water
16 fresh mint sprigs, finely chopped
2 quarts bourbon
shaved ice
confectioners' sugar
20 fresh mint sprigs

Must be made ahead.

1. Combine first four ingredients in large glass container, stirring until sugar dissolves. Cover and let stand 4 to 6 hours.
2. Strain mixture into 3-quart pitcher, discarding mint.
3. "Frost" rims of glasses by dipping them in water, then confectioners' sugar. Fill each glass with shaved ice and then with bourbon mixture. Garnish with mint sprig.

Queen Supreme Punch

Yield: about 18 to 72
4-ounce servings

A delicious fruit punch, plain or spiked.

1 cup sugar
1½ quarts water
1 46-ounce can pineapple juice
2 12-ounce cans frozen orange juice concentrate, thawed
1 12-ounce can frozen lemonade concentrate, thawed
5 4¾-ounce jars strained baby-food bananas

4 1-liter bottles gingerale or lemon-lime soda
rum (optional)

Must be made ahead.

1. In a 6-quart container, mix together first six ingredients. When well blended pour mixture into four 1-quart wide-mouthed freezer containers or empty milk cartons. Store in freezer until needed.
2. When ready to use, mix one 1-quart container of punch mixture, slightly thawed, with 1 bottle gingerale or lemon-lime soda, stir to blend and thaw. If desired, add 1 cup rum per quart of mix.

Raspberry Razzmatazz

Yield: 8 servings

Pretty 'n pink.

1 10-ounce package frozen raspberries
1 6-ounce can frozen lemonade concentrate
ice
club soda or gingerale, chilled
sugar to taste

1. Combine raspberries and lemonade concentrate in blender; purée.
2. Strain mixture; divide among 8 tall glasses filled with ice; add gingerale or club soda and sugar to taste.

Royale Punch

Yield: 20 4-ounce servings

Kir Royale, the popular apéritif, is the inspiration for this punch.

Fresh berries, grapes or other fruit
  for ice ring
½ cup crème de cassis (black currant liqueur)
1 750 ml bottle dry white wine, chilled
2 750 ml bottles champagne, chilled

Must be made ahead.

1. Prepare ice: fill a 6-cup ring mold with cold water two-thirds full. Arrange fruit in mold and freeze until firm. Unmold by dipping in warm water. Store in plastic bag in freezer until needed.
2. To serve punch, pour cassis and wine into small punch bowl. Add ice ring and slowly pour in champagne.

Strawberry Punch

Yield: 20 6-ounce servings

Lovely for a bridal shower.

2 quarts ripe fresh strawberries, hulled
1½ cups Cointreau or orange-flavored
  liqueur
3 750 ml bottles very cold dry white wine
1 750 ml bottle very cold white port
1 750 ml bottle chilled sherry
  (dry or sweet to taste)
ice ring made with fresh strawberries
  (optional)

Must be made ahead.

1. In an 8- to 10-quart punch bowl, soak strawberries in liqueur for several hours.
2. Just before serving add all wines to bowl along with ice ring or block of ice.

APPETIZERS

Appetizer Shrimp Balls

Yield: about 4 dozen

An unusual hors d'oeuvre with a taste of the Orient.

1 pound raw shrimp, shelled
  and chopped fine
¼ pound ground pork
1 tablespoon cornstarch
½ teaspoon salt
1 teaspoon minced garlic
1 teaspoon sugar
1 tablespoon soy sauce
1 tablespoon dry sherry
2 tablespoons water

peanut oil for frying
Chinese Duck Sauce and
  Hot Chinese Mustard (optional)

1. Drain any excess liquid from shrimp; mix with pork. Add remaining ingredients and combine well.

2. Shape mixture into ¾- to 1-inch balls. Cover with plastic wrap; chill.

3. Heat 1 tablespoon oil in wok or electric skillet over high heat. When oil smokes, add shrimp balls and cook about 4 minutes, turning frequently. Serve immediately with duck sauce or hot mustard, if desired.

Cajun Quiche

Yield: 8 luncheon servings
16 appetizer servings

A spicy seafood quiche that even real men will eat.

Pastry for 1-crust 10-inch pie
1 6-ounce can crabmeat, drained
1 6- to 7-ounce can shrimp, drained
2 green onions, chopped
1 cup shredded Cajun-style cheese*
4 eggs, lightly beaten
1½ cups heavy cream
½ teaspoon salt
⅛ teaspoon cayenne pepper

*If Cajun-style cheese isn't available, use ½ cup sharp Cheddar cheese, ½ cup Monterey Jack, ¼ teaspoon chili powder and ¼ teaspoon garlic powder.

1. Preheat oven to 425°. Line 10-inch pie plate with pastry; bake for 5 minutes. Cool slightly.

2. Lower oven temperature to 375°. Rinse seafood in cold water; drain well. Place in pie shell, top with onions and sprinkle with shredded cheese.

3. In small bowl, whisk eggs with cream; add salt and cayenne pepper and blend well. Pour over cheese and seafood in pie shell.

4. Bake 30 to 40 minutes, until knife inserted near center comes out clean. Serve hot or at room temperature. Slice thinly for appetizer servings.

Curried Crab Bites

Yield: 48 appetizers

These little bites are deceptively easy.

1 8-ounce can water chestnuts,
 drained and chopped
8 ounces crabmeat or imitation crabmeat
1 cup (4 ounces) shredded Swiss cheese
⅔ cup mayonnaise
3 green onions, sliced
½ teaspoon curry powder
1 teaspoon lemon juice
1 17¼-ounce box frozen puff pastry sheets
 (2 sheets), thawed

1. In a large bowl, mix together all ingredients except pastry. Refrigerate in airtight container until needed, up to 24 hours ahead.
2. Preheat oven to 350°. Unfold pastry and roll out slightly. Using a 1¾-inch diameter cutter, cut 24 circles from each sheet. Place pastry on baking sheets and cover each with a rounded teaspoon of crab mixture. Bake 20 to 25 minutes, until golden and puffed.

Nutty Chicken Strips

Yield: about 2½ dozen appetizers

Whether you make 2½ dozen or 12½ dozen, you'll still run out of these.

3 whole chicken breasts, skinned,
 boned and halved
1 cup biscuit mix
2 teaspoons paprika
¼ teaspoon salt
⅛ teaspoon cayenne pepper
⅓ cup ground pecans
⅓ cup evaporated milk
⅔ cup butter, melted

1. Preheat oven to 425°. Heavily butter two jellyroll pans.
2. Cut chicken breasts into ½ x 3-inch strips with a very sharp knife.
3. Combine next five ingredients; mix well.
4. Dip chicken strips in milk; coat generously with pecan mixture.
5. Arrange half of strips in a single layer in each jellyroll pan. Pour melted butter around and over them.
6. Place one pan in center and one in upper third of oven; bake 12 to 15 minutes, reversing pan positions after 7 minutes. Turn out on serving plate and serve immediately.

Connecticut was the birthplace of America's first cookbook. Amelia Simmons wrote American Cookery (all of forty-six pages!) and had it published in Hartford in 1796.

Spring Blossoms

Yield: about 3 dozen

Flaky puff pastry flowers with herbed cream cheese filling.

1 17¾-ounce box frozen puff pastry sheets
   (2 sheets), thawed
1 8-ounce container soft cream cheese with
   chives spread, at room temperature

Garnishes:
paprika, watercress or parsley sprigs

1. Preheat oven to 375°. Unfold pastry and place on lightly floured surface. Roll lightly to eliminate creases of fold.

2. Using a 2½-inch diameter round cutter with scalloped edge, cut about eighteen circles from each sheet.

3. Gently press pastry circles into ungreased cups of miniature muffin pans. Pastry will resemble a flower. Fill each lined cup with about ½ teaspoon cream cheese.

4. Bake 15 to 20 minutes or until filling puffs a little and blossom is lightly browned. Cool slightly, remove from pan onto wire rack and top each with a sprinkle of paprika or a sprig of watercress or parsley. Serve warm.

Chicken Oriental

Yield: 6 dozen

Skewered cubes of marinated chicken wrapped with snow peas.

⅓ cup soy sauce
½ teaspoon fresh minced ginger root
   or ⅛ teaspoon ground ginger
2 whole chicken breasts, skinned and boned
1 13¾-ounce can chicken broth
36 fresh snow peas, blanched,
   strings removed

Tahini Dipping Sauce:

1 cup plain yogurt
2 tablespoons tahini*
2 tablespoons soy sauce
½ teaspoon ground ginger

Must be made ahead.

*Available in oriental or food specialty shops.

1. Combine soy sauce and ginger in shallow dish; add chicken breasts, turning to coat. Cover and marinate in refrigerator at least 4 hours or overnight.

2. Bring chicken broth, chicken and marinade to boil in large saucepan; reduce heat and simmer 15 minutes. Remove from heat; cool.

3. Separate blanched pea pods into halves. Cut chicken into 1-inch cubes. Wrap a snow pea half around each cube of chicken and secure with wooden pick. Cover and chill until ready to serve. Serve with Tahini Dipping Sauce, which is made by combining all ingredients and refrigerating for several hours.

Sausalito Crab Dip

Yield: about 3 cups

May be served hot or cold.

1½ cups sour cream
1 tablespoon lemon juice
⅛ teaspoon Tabasco sauce
1 package Knorr's Leek Soup mix
1 6-ounce package frozen crabmeat, thawed
   and drained or 6 ounces imitation crabmeat
1 14-ounce can artichoke hearts, drained
   and chopped
½ cup freshly grated Parmesan cheese
1 tablespoon fresh dill
   or 1 teaspoon dried dill
crackers or round loaf of bread

1. Combine all ingredients; stir until
   well blended.
2. Cover and refrigerate at least 2 hours
   or overnight.
3. Serve at room temperature with crackers,
   or serve warm in hollowed out round loaf
   of bread, reserving cubes from center to
   use for dipping.

**Leftover dip makes a delicious sandwich filling for
sourdough rolls or pita pockets.**

Cheese Wafers

Yield: 4 dozen

**Best to make these a few days before serving:
the flavor improves with age.**

½ pound (2 sticks) butter, softened
1 pound grated sharp Cheddar cheese
1 teaspoon cayenne pepper
1 teaspoon salt
2 cups flour
1 cup chopped pecans

Must be made ahead.

1. In mixing bowl, combine all ingredients.
   Dough will be sticky.
2. Form into 2 long rolls; wrap in waxed paper.
   Chill or freeze.
3. When ready to serve, preheat oven to 350°.
   Cut rolls into thin slices and place on
   cookie sheets.
4. Bake just until faintly brown, about
   8 minutes. Cool on wire rack. Store in
   airtight container.

Spring Blossoms

Cold Salmon Mousse

Yield: 1½ quart mold

**This recipe comes from the East Bay Lodge on Cape Cod.
It's delicious as a first course or as an hors d'oeuvre with crackers.**

2 cups cooked, flaked salmon
2 scallions, chopped
¼ cup chopped fresh dill
  or 1 tablespoon dried dill
¼ cup fresh lemon juice
2½ cups chicken broth
2 cups sour cream
2 envelopes unflavored gelatin
watercress, for garnish

Must be made ahead.

1. Oil a 1½-quart mold.
2. In blender or food processor, combine salmon, scallion, dill, lemon juice and 2 cups chicken broth; purée until very smooth.
3. Pour purée into large bowl; stir in sour cream.
4. In small saucepan, soften gelatin in remaining ½ cup chicken broth. Place saucepan over low heat and stir until gelatin is completely dissolved.
5. Add gelatin mixture to the salmon-sour cream mixture and blend thoroughly.
6. Pour mixture into mold; chill until set, about 2 hours.
7. To unmold, dip mold briefly in warm water to loosen mousse. Cover mold with platter and invert. Garnish with watercress and serve with crackers, if desired.

Americans were slow to warm to refrigeration, although New England's Jacob Perkins was issued the first patent for a mechanical refrigeration system as early as 1834; it was, however, not to gain universal acceptance for nearly the next one hundred years, and the iceman still cameth door-to-door on into the 20th century.

SOUPS

Asparagus Almond Soup

Yield: 6 servings

A creamy chilled soup thickened with almonds.

1½ pounds fresh asparagus,
  washed and trimmed
1½ quarts chicken broth
½ cup blanched almonds, finely ground
½ teaspoon salt
¼ teaspoon white pepper

Must be made ahead.

1. Simmer asparagus in chicken broth in large covered saucepan for 10 to 12 minutes, or until tender.
2. Remove asparagus from broth with tongs. Cut tips and reserve for garnish.
3. Place asparagus and broth in container of food processor; process until smooth.
4. Return mixture to saucepan; add ground almonds and seasoning; simmer for one minute.
5. Strain soup; chill thoroughly. Garnish each serving with reserved asparagus tips.

English Spring Garden Soup

Yield: 2½ quarts

Puréed essence of spring!

1 cup finely chopped scallions
1 10-ounce package frozen peas, thawed
1 head coarsely cut lettuce
1 10-ounce package frozen spinach, thawed
½ cup chopped parsley
1 teaspoon dried tarragon
3 tablespoons butter
½ teaspoon salt
⅛ teaspoon pepper
2 quarts hot water
3 egg yolks
½ cup heavy cream

1. In large pot or kettle, sauté first five ingredients in butter for 2 minutes; add salt, pepper and hot water. Cover and simmer until vegetables are just tender, stirring occasionally.
2. Strain and RESERVE LIQUID. Purée vegetables using food processor or blender.
3. Return vegetable purée to kettle; add three-fourths of reserved liquid, setting remainder aside to be added at serving time. Heat soup to boil; reduce heat.
4. Beat egg yolks and mix with remaining liquid and cream in small saucepan. Stir while cooking over low heat, but do not allow to boil. When thickened, add to soup, mixing well. Correct seasonings and serve at once.

Chicken Gumbo

A meal in itself and enough for a crowd.

Yield: about 14 cups

4 slices bacon, diced
3½- to 4-pound chicken, cut up
1 quart water
2 celery ribs with leaves, cut up
1 carrot, quartered
1 onion, quartered
2 bay leaves
1 teaspoon salt
⅓ cup vegetable oil
½ cup flour
3 10-ounce packages frozen okra, sliced
1 cup chopped onion
1 cup chopped green pepper
½ cup chopped celery
2 16-ounce cans tomatoes, coarsely chopped
1 10-ounce package frozen
  whole kernel corn
¼ cup chopped parsley
2 garlic cloves, chopped
2 teaspoons Tabasco sauce
1 teaspoon basil
½ teaspoon thyme
1 pound shrimp, shelled and deveined

1. In Dutch oven cook bacon until crisp; remove with slotted spoon and drain. Brown chicken in drippings.

2. Add water, celery, carrot, onion, bay leaves and salt. Bring to a boil over high heat, reduce heat and simmer uncovered for 35 minutes.

3. Remove chicken from broth; cool. Remove meat from bones; cut into cubes. Strain broth and skim off fat.

4. Meanwhile, make a roux: in a saucepan over low heat, heat oil and stir in flour until smooth. Cook, stirring often, until roux is a medium golden brown, about 30 minutes.

5. Pour strained chicken broth back into Dutch oven and stir in roux. Add chicken, bacon and remaining ingredients except shrimp. Cover and simmer over low heat, stirring occasionally, about 1½ hours.

6. Add shrimp; simmer about 10 minutes longer. Correct seasonings. Serve with rice, if desired.

Ham and Vegetable Soup

Yield: 6 to 8 servings

Hearty goodness from leftover hambone.

3 tablespoons butter
½ cup chopped onion (1 medium)
1 cup julienne carrots (2 to 3)
1 cup sliced celery (2 ribs)
3 cups water
3 cups chicken broth
1 hambone
6 sprigs parsley
1 bay leaf
2 cups diced potatoes
  (about 2 medium)
1½ cups julienne cooked ham
½ bunch watercress, cut up (2 cups)
salt and freshly ground pepper to taste

1. Melt butter in kettle and sauté onion, carrots and celery until tender. Add water, broth, hambone, parsley and bay leaf. Bring to a boil, lower heat, cover, and simmer 30 minutes.

2. Add potatoes and ham to kettle. Cook 15 minutes more, or until potatoes are tender.

3. Remove bay leaf, parsley and hambone. Skim off any fat.

4. Add watercress; cook about 2 minutes. Season with salt and pepper to taste.

Portuguese Kale Soup

Yield: 8 to 10 servings

**Spring in New England can still mean cold weather.
Ward it off Portuguese-style with this "Caldo Verde."**

1 46-ounce can chicken broth
2 cups water
1 medium onion, sliced
1 large potato, peeled and sliced
1¼ teaspoons salt, or to taste
⅛ teaspoon black pepper
¼ cup uncooked rice
1 quart measurer packed with
  shredded fresh kale (about 4½ cups)
½ pound Portuguese linguica sausage
  (or substitute Polish or Spanish
  smoked sausage)
1 tablespoon extra-virgin olive oil

1. Place broth, water, onion, potato, salt and pepper in large pot. Cover and cook over medium heat until vegetables are tender, about 20 minutes.

2. Mash potato slightly into liquid or place cooked vegetables with some of the broth in food processor and "pulse" until soup base is smoother but still slightly lumpy. Return to pot with rest of broth.

3. Add rice to pot, cover and cook until tender, 20 to 25 minutes.

4. Bring soup to boil. Add shredded kale and sausage. Boil, uncovered, 3 to 5 minutes. Add oil; correct seasonings.

BREADS

Easter Bread Napoli

An Italian Easter tradition.

Yield: 2 loaves

7 cups flour, divided
½ cup sugar
½ teaspoon salt
2 packages active dry yeast
½ cup milk
½ cup water
⅔ cup margarine
4 eggs, at room temperature
1 teaspoon anise extract
grated rind of 1 lemon
1 teaspoon anise seed
1 egg, beaten

1. In large bowl, mix 1 cup flour, sugar, salt and yeast.
2. In large saucepan, combine milk, water and margarine; heat over low flame until warm. Margarine does not need to melt. Gradually add to dry ingredients; beat 2 minutes.
3. Add eggs, flavorings and 1 cup flour; beat at high speed for 2 minutes. Continue adding flour to make soft dough, using about 5½ to 6 cups flour in all.
4. Knead dough until smooth and elastic. Cover and let rise in warm, draft-free place for about one hour. Punch down; divide in half and place in two 8-inch pans. Cover and let rise about 1 hour. Brush with beaten egg to glaze.
5. Bake at 375° in preheated oven for 25 to 30 minutes. Decorate with Easter ornaments, if desired.

Butterhorns

The aroma of these sweet rolls baking on Saturday mornings has awakened five generations.

Yield: about 6 dozen rolls

1 cup boiling water
½ cup sugar
¾ cup shortening or margarine
2 ounces cake yeast (Red Star brand)
1 cup lukewarm milk
2 eggs, beaten
6 cups flour
1 tablespoon salt
melted butter
cinnamon-sugar mixture
confectioners' sugar frosting

Must be made ahead. Rolls freeze well.

1. Combine water, sugar and shortening in large bowl. When mixture is lukewarm, add yeast and dissolve.
2. Add milk and eggs, stirring by hand NOT mixer.
3. Add flour and salt, beating with spoon until dough is smooth and satiny.
4. Cover dough with waxed paper; refrigerate overnight.
5. Preheat oven to 350°.
6. Divide dough into thirds; place one-third on

floured board. Roll out with floured rolling pin into thin circle. Spread with melted butter; sprinkle with cinnamon sugar. Cut into pie-shaped wedges and roll each from the wide edge toward the point. Place pointed side down on greased cookie sheet. Repeat with remaining dough.

7. Bake 15 or 20 minutes until light golden brown. When cool, frost with confectioners' sugar frosting, if desired.

Portuguese Sweet Bread

Yield: 2 loaves

New England's fishing industries owe much to the Portuguese fishermen, many of whom settled near Mystic Seaport in Stonington Village. This wonderful bread, often served at Easter, is one of their contributions to our regional cuisine.

2 envelopes active dry yeast
¼ cup warm water (110°)
1 cup milk
½ cup (1 stick) butter
1 cup sugar
1 teaspoon salt
2 cups flour
3 eggs, well beaten
4 cups or more flour
1 egg, well beaten

1. In a small bowl, sprinkle yeast over warm water to soften. Meanwhile, scald milk; remove from heat and stir in butter, sugar and salt, stirring until butter is melted. Let mixture cool to luke warm.

2. Beat 2 cups flour into milk mixture until smooth. Add 3 eggs and softened yeast, mixing well. Add about 4 more cups flour, or enough to make a soft dough.

3. Knead dough on floured board until smooth and shiny, kneading in additional flour as needed. Shape dough into ball; place in large, buttered bowl. Cover lightly and let rise in warm, draft-free place until doubled in size.

4. Cut dough in half. Pat each half into a well-buttered pie tin; cover each with dish towel and let rise in warm, draft-free place until doubled in size again.

5. Brush top of dough with beaten egg. Bake at 350° in preheated oven for about 25 minutes, or until nicely browned.

Refrigerator Yeast Biscuits

Yield: 2 dozen

Make the dough in the food processor and refrigerate or freeze until ready to use.

1 package active dry yeast
¼ cup warm water (110°)
5 cups flour
¼ cup sugar
1 tablespoon baking powder
1 teaspoon baking soda
1 teaspoon salt
1 cup shortening
2 cups buttermilk

Unbaked biscuits may be frozen on ungreased baking sheets, covered, until firm. Transfer frozen biscuits to plastic bags. To bake, place frozen biscuits on lightly greased baking sheet, let stand 30 minutes and bake at 450° for 12 to 15 minutes.

1. Dissolve yeast in warm water; set aside.
2. In food processor fitted with steel blade, place flour and next 4 ingredients and pulse once to mix.
3. Add shortening; process until mixture resembles coarse meal. Add yeast mixture and buttermilk, processing until dry ingredients are moistened.
4. Pour into lightly greased bowl, cover and refrigerate until needed.
5. Turn dough out onto floured surface; knead lightly 4 to 5 times. Role dough to ½-inch thickness; cut with 2-inch biscuit cutter. Place on lightly greased baking sheets. Bake at 450° for 12 to 15 minutes.

Sourdough Bread

Yield: 2 loaves

Spring, symbolic of fresh starts, seems the ideal time to make sourdough starter for baking the famous pungent bread. Although the bread is usually associated with San Francisco, there is reason to believe that the starter may have been brought to the California harbor aboard a clipper ship from New England that had sailed 'round the Horn!

Sourdough Starter
2 cups warm water (110°)
1 package active dry yeast
2 cups flour

additional flour for "feeding"

Must be made ahead.

Starter Preparation:

1. In 2-quart glass or plastic container, sprinkle yeast over water; stir with wooden spoon to dissolve.
2. Add flour; beat until smooth with rotary or electric mixer.
3. Cover loosely with cheesecloth, set aside out of drafts and let stand at room temperature 4 to 5 days, stirring 2 to 3 times a day. **Mixture will bubble and have yeasty aroma. Pour off 1½ cups to use in recipe.**
4. After removing 1½ cups starter, it is necessary to "feed" the remainder by adding 2 cups of warm water and 2 cups flour. Let

Sourdough White Bread

1 cup warm water (110°)
1 package active dry yeast
2 tablespoons sugar
2 teaspoons salt
1½ cups Sourdough Starter,
   at room temperature
3½ to 4 cups regular or unbleached flour
shortening
cornmeal
1 egg, slightly beaten

Variation: Sourdough French Bread

Proceed as above through Step 3. Shape
dough into two long loaves; put on
greased cookie sheets sprinkled with
cornmeal. Bake on middle shelf in
preheated 400° oven, with pan of hot
water on bottom shelf, 20 to 25 minutes.

stand, loosely covered, in warm place for
5 hours, or until mixture bubbles; cover and
store in refrigerator. Starter improves with
age but must be used regularly. Always
bring starter to room temperature about
2 hours before using.

1. Rinse large mixing bowl with hot water.
   In it place warm water and sprinkle with
   yeast. Stir in next three ingredients;
   add flour and mix thoroughly with hands or
   wooden spoon. Dough will be soft.

2. Cover bowl with plastic wrap; set in warm,
   draft-free place for 1 hour, or until doubled
   in bulk.

3. Turn out on heavily floured surface; sprinkle
   generously with flour and knead, adding
   more flour if sticky. Knead at least
   10 minutes.

4. Grease cookie sheet or two 1½-quart round
   casseroles with shortening and sprinkle with
   cornmeal. Shape dough into two round
   loaves. Make diagonal slashes across top
   with sharp knife. Cover; let rise 40 minutes
   or until doubled in bulk.

5. Brush with egg; bake at 400° in preheated
   oven for 30 to 35 minutes.

Poppy Cheese Bread

Yield: 2 8½ x 4½-inch loaves

**This quick bread is a nice accompaniment to Ham and
Vegetable Soup (see index).**

3¾ cups biscuit mix
2 cups (8 ounces) shredded
   sharp Cheddar cheese
3 tablespoons poppy seeds
⅛ teaspoon cayenne pepper
1¼ cups milk
1 egg, beaten

May be frozen.

1. Preheat oven to 350°. Grease two
   8½- x 4½-inch loaf pans.

2. Combine biscuit mix, cheese, poppy
   seeds and cayenne; stir well.

3. Combine milk and egg; add to cheese
   mixture and stir about 2 minutes.

4. Divide batter equally between the two pans.
   Smooth top. Bake for 55 to 60 minutes.
   Remove from pan, cool slightly and
   serve warm.

Strawberry Muffins

Yield: about 1 dozen

A lovely springtime addition to breakfast, luncheon or teatime.

½ cup (1 stick) butter, softened
1 cup sugar
2 eggs
2 cups flour
2 teaspoons baking powder
¼ teaspoon salt
⅔ cups milk
1 teaspoon grated lemon rind
1 cup fresh strawberries, chopped
1 tablespoon cinnamon sugar

1. Preheat oven to 375°. Grease or line muffin pans.
2. Cream butter in large bowl; gradually add sugar and eggs, creaming until light and fluffy.
3. Sift together flour, baking powder and salt. Add to creamed mixture alternately with milk, beginning and ending with dry ingredients.
4. Stir in lemon rind and fold in berries.
5. Spoon batter into muffin pans, filling each two-thirds full. Sprinkle sugar lightly over top of batter. Bake 15 to 18 minutes.

Whole Wheat Banana Loaf

Yield: one 8½ x 4½-inch loaf

Wonderful for breakfast or as a healthy snack for children; great for picnics, too.

1 cup whole wheat (graham) flour
¼ cup wheat germ
1 teaspoon baking soda
¾ teaspoon salt
1¼ cups mashed ripe bananas
  (about 4 medium)
¼ cup plain yogurt
½ cup (1 stick) butter or margarine
½ cup sugar
1 egg
½ cup raisins

The whole wheat flour should be almost as fine as white four; coarser stone-ground flour will not work in this recipe. The raisins are essential in order to absorb moisture and prevent a "sad" line at the bottom of the bread.

1. Preheat oven to 350°. Grease an 8½ x 4½ x 2¾-inch loaf pan.
2. Stir together the flour, wheat germ, baking soda and salt. In another small bowl combine bananas and yogurt.
3. In a medium bowl cream together butter and sugar; beat in egg. Gently add flour mixture alternately with banana mixture. Stir just until smooth. Stir in raisins.
4. Turn into loaf pan and bake 55 to 60 minutes, or until toothpick inserted in center comes out clean. Loosen edges and turn out onto wire rack. Turn right side up and cool completely before slicing.

Baked Almond French Toast

Yield: 8 servings

This easy oven-baked method is deliciously efficient!

½ cup (1 stick) butter, melted
6 large eggs, beaten
½ cup milk
¼ cup liquid brown sugar
⅛ teaspoon almond extract
dash salt
1 loaf French or Italian bread,
　cut into ¾-inch slices
Almond Syrup (below)

1. Preheat oven to 450°. Divide ¼ cup butter evenly between two jellyroll pans, spreading to cover bottom. Set aside.
2. Combine remaining butter with next five ingredients in large mixing bowl; mix well.
3. Dip bread slices, one at a time, into egg mixture, coating well. Arrange on jellyroll pans. Bake for 15 to 20 minutes, turning once after 8 minutes. Serve with Almond Syrup.

Almond Syrup

½ cup sliced almonds
2 tablespoons butter
1½ cups liquid brown sugar
½ teaspoon almond extract

Syrup:

1. In small saucepan, sauté almonds in butter until golden.
2. Stir in sugar and almond extract. Serve warm.

Almond Syrup is delicious on baked apples or poached pears.

Variation: Baked Pecan French Toast

Prepare as above substituting rum flavoring for almond extract and pecans for almonds in syrup.

Celery Bread

Yield: 8 servings

An alternative to hot garlic bread.

1 loaf unsliced white bread
½ cup (1 stick) butter, softened
½ teaspoon celery seed
dash cayenne pepper
¼ teaspoon paprika
poppy seeds

1. Preheat oven to 400°.
2. Trim off top and side crusts of bread, leaving only bottom crust intact. Cut though loaf to near bottom, lengthwise along the center and crosswise at 2-inch intervals, forming eight sections.
3. Combine butter with next three ingredients; spread mixture generously over all cut surfaces but not bottom. Sprinkle top with poppy seeds.
4. Bake for 15 to 18 minutes until lightly browned.

Crab and Gruyère Stuffed French Bread   Yield: 4 to 6 servings

Serve either as a hot luncheon sandwich or cut into thinner slices as an appetizer.

1 16-inch loaf French bread
12 ounces (about 3 cups) shredded
  Gruyère cheese
1 pound flaked cooked crabmeat
  or imitation crabmeat
¼ cup mayonnaise
2 tablespoons sour cream
⅓ cup pimento stuffed olives, sliced
2 green onions, chopped

Filling also makes a fine grilled sandwich or, if cut into 1-inch squares, galley-style hors d'oeuvres

1. Preheat oven to 350°.
2. Cut bread in half lengthwise and remove all but outer ½-inch of bread from each section. Sprinkle each half with cheese. Place on ungreased baking sheet.
3. Combine remaining ingredients in small bowl. Spoon crab mixture over cheese on bread.
4. Bake until cheese bubbles, about 20 minutes. Cut each piece in half crosswise.

Deviled Ham Brunch Casserole   Yield: 6 servings

6 slices bread, crusts trimmed
1 4½-ounce can deviled ham
6 ounces mild Cheddar cheese, shredded
1½ cups milk
3 eggs, lightly beaten
½ teaspoon salt
2 green onions, minced
½ teaspoon celery seed
½ teaspoon dry mustard

1. Preheat oven to 350°. Grease a 1-quart soufflé dish.
2. Spread bread with deviled ham. Cut into quarters. In prepared dish, layer bread and shredded cheese, forming three layers.
3. Combine remaining ingredients in 4-cup glass measuring cup, mixing well. Pour over cheese and bread.
4. Place dish in pan of warm water and bake about 1¼ hours, until golden and set.

In the late 1860's, the proper Beacon Hill hostess served a winter breakfast that might have included liver pudding, stewed pigeon, deviled gizzard, and pork cheese. Corn flakes, anyone?

Mushroom-Watercress Sandwiches   Yield: 4 sandwiches

12 ounces fresh white mushrooms
   or spring morels
6 tablespoons unsalted butter
2 teaspoons dry white wine
salt and pepper to taste
1 loaf fresh Italian bread, or other
   crisp crust fresh bread
watercress

1. Clean mushrooms; slice thickly.
2. Heat butter in large cast-iron skillet over medium-high heat; add mushrooms and sauté quickly.
3. When mushrooms are cooked but still crisp, remove from heat and add wine, salt and pepper.
4. Warm Italian bread and slice lengthwise; heap mushrooms on bottom half, cover with watercress and top half of loaf. Slice into four sections. Serve with pot of Irish tea, if desired.

My Irish immigrant mother looked forward to the fruits of my mushroom foraging. The freshly picked white buttons would be sliced and quickly cooked up with a goodly portion of sweet butter, after which Mother and I would pile them high on crisp pieces of Italian bread. With a hot cup of tea and, if I were lucky, a story about life in the "auld sod," Mother and I would travel back to Newry. The smell of mushrooms cooking in butter vividly recaptures those fond remembrances still. — S.K.B., East Haddam, CT

MAIN DISHES

Roast Saddle of Spring Lamb
Yield: 8 to 10 servings

Simple but delicious! A boned, butterflied leg of lamb may also be prepared in this manner, but will require additional cooking time.

1 teaspoon salt
½ teaspoon freshly ground pepper
2 or 3 garlic cloves, minced
½ cup chopped fresh mint
½ cup chopped fresh basil
1 boneless saddle of lamb, about 5 pounds, trimmed and tied
Red currant jelly (Captain's Choice)

1. Combine salt, pepper, garlic and herbs in a small bowl. Using fingers, stuff mixture into openings in lamb and rub over surface. Let stand at least 1 hour at room temperature or up to 3 hours.

2. Preheat oven to 500°. Place lamb, fat side up, on rack in roasting pan. Roast 15 minutes. Reduce temperature to 375°; roast 40 minutes more for rare, 45 minutes more for medium-rare. Let stand 10 minutes before slicing. Serve with jelly.

Lamb Chops with Mint Pesto
Yield: 4 servings

This unusual pesto is a wonderful accompaniment to broiled chops.

Mint Pesto

2 garlic cloves, chopped
½ teaspoon salt
2 cups packed fresh mint leaves
¼ cup fresh parsley leaves
½ teaspoon dried basil
¼ cup pine nuts or walnuts
¼ cup grated Parmesan cheese
½ to ¾ cup olive oil

8 lamb rib chops
2 garlic cloves, split
olive oil
salt and pepper

Pesto preparation:

1. In bowl of food processor, combine all ingredients except oil; process 5 to 8 seconds.

2. With processor running, slowly add oil until mixture is smooth and of desired consistency. Serve at room temperature. Store any unused pesto in refrigerator in airtight container.

Chop preparation:

1. Preheat broiler according to manufacturer's instructions.

2. Rub chops with garlic and oil; place on rack in broiler pan. Broil 3 to 4 inches from heat for 5 to 7 minutes per side or to desired degree of doneness. Sprinkle with salt and pepper. Serve with mint pesto.

Spring Lamb Ragout

Yield: 4 to 6 servings

Chunks of tender meat simmered in broth and wine mingled with young, tender vegetables.

2 tablespoons flour
salt and freshly ground pepper
2 pounds shoulder lamb chops, cut into
   1- to 2-inch pieces
3 tablespoons olive oil, divided
1 medium onion, chopped
2 garlic cloves, minced
½ cup dry white wine
½ cup chicken broth
½ teaspoon rosemary
½ teaspoon grated lemon rind
12 small whole new potatoes, peeled
1 10-ounce package frozen
   whole baby carrots
1 10-ounce package frozen
   deluxe sugar snap peas
½ cup frozen tender tiny peas
½ cup chopped scallions
2 tablespoons chopped parsley

1. Season flour with salt and pepper and place in plastic bag; add lamb and shake to lightly coat.

2. In Dutch oven, heat 2 tablespoons oil over medium high heat; brown lamb in two batches, remove from pan and set aside.

3. Lower heat; sauté onion and garlic until soft, not brown. Return lamb to pot along with any accumulated juices; add wine, broth, rosemary and lemon rind.

4. In another skillet, heat 1 tablespoon oil; toss potatoes, cooking until golden. Add to lamb in pot. Season with salt and pepper, cover and cook slowly for 55 minutes or until potatoes are tender. Add more chicken broth if necessary.

5. Add carrots; cook 5 minutes. Add snap peas and tiny peas; cook 8 to 10 minutes longer, or until all vegetables are tender. Taste for seasonings. Toss in scallions and parsley; serve.

Veal Oscar

Yield: 4 servings

For a very special, very elegant spring dinner.

¾ pound fresh asparagus or 1 10-ounce
  package frozen asparagus spears
1 6-ounce package frozen crabmeat, thawed
  and drained, OR 1 6-ounce can crabmeat,
  rinsed in cold water and drained
8 veal scallops (about 1½ pounds)
3 tablespoons flour
dash salt and pepper
3 tablespoons butter, divided
Bernaise Sauce (below)

1. Cook asparagus until crisp-tender, about 6 to 8 minutes (or according to package directions); drain. Place on platter with crabmeat, cover with foil and keep warm in 200° oven.

2. Place veal between sheets of waxed paper and pound with meat mallet until scallops are ⅛-inch thick.

3. Mix flour with salt and pepper in shallow dish. Dredge veal in mixture to coat lightly.

4. In large skillet, melt 2 tablespoons butter over medium heat. Cook half of veal, turning occasionally, 2 to 3 minutes until cooked through and browned. Remove to platter and keep warm in oven.

5. Melt remaining 1 tablespoon butter in skillet. Sauté remaining veal.

6. To serve, place two veal scallops on each plate. Top with crabmeat, then asparagus. Spoon Bernaise Sauce over all. Pass extra sauce.

Bernaise Sauce

3 tablespoons red wine vinegar
3 tablespoons dry white wine
1 tablespoon finely chopped onion
½ teaspoon tarragon
⅛ teaspoon salt
⅛ teaspoon white pepper
1 tablespoon cold water
½ cup (1 stick) butter, melted
3 egg yolks

Bernaise Sauce

1. In medium saucepan, combine first six ingredients; bring to boil and boil 2 to 3 minutes until reduced by half, leaving about 3 to 4 tablespoons. Strain into blender or food processor.

2. Add water to blender. Meanwhile, melt butter in small saucepan until hot and bubbly.

3. Add egg yolks to blender and process 30 seconds. Slowly add butter in thin stream while machine is running. Keep warm by placing in pan of hot water. DO NOT place over high heat.

Blanquette of Veal

A delicately flavored French classic.

Yield: 6 servings

2 pounds boneless veal,
  cut into 1½-inch cubes
water
3½ cups chicken broth
1 onion, peeled and studded
  with 6 whole cloves
1 carrot, quartered
2 ribs celery, quartered
1 teaspoon salt
1 bay leaf
¾ teaspoon thyme
½ 16-ounce bag frozen small whole onions
8 ounces small fresh mushrooms,
  wiped and trimmed
2 tablespoons lemon juice
3 egg yolks
2 tablespoons cornstarch
¼ cup heavy cream

1. Place veal in large saucepan and cover with 2 inches of water. Bring to a boil; turn down heat and simmer 2 minutes.
2. Pour off liquid and replace with chicken broth; add onion, carrot, celery, salt, bay leaf and thyme. Cover and simmer 1½ hours.
3. Meanwhile, cook small onions according to package directions; set aside. Toss mushrooms with lemon juice; set aside.
4. When veal is tender, remove large onion, carrot, celery and bay leaf. Reserve carrot and finely chop; set aside.
5. In small bowl combine egg yolks and cornstarch; beat until smooth. Add cream.
6. Remove 1 cup cooking liquid and stir into egg yolk mixtue. Add onions, mushrooms and chopped carrot to veal. Stir in egg mixture. Bring to a boil over low to medium heat, stirring constantly. Remove at once and serve hot.

Ham Loaf

A good addition to a brunch or a picnic.

Yield: 6 servings

1¼ pounds ground smoked ham
¾ pound ground pork
2 eggs
½ cup milk
1 cup cracker crumbs
  (saltines with unsalted tops)
ground cloves

Basting Sauce:

1 teaspoon dry mustard
½ cup brown sugar
½ cup water
⅓ cup vinegar

1. Preheat oven to 350°. Grease 2-quart baking dish or loaf pan.
2. Mix first five ingredients together; shape and place in baking dish. Sprinkle with cloves.
3. Mix together all sauce ingredients and pour over loaf.
4. Bake for 1½ hours, uncovered, basting frequently with sauce in pan.
5. Let stand 10 minutes before slicing. Serve warm or at room temperature.

Ham en Croute with Sauce Verte Yield: 6 to 8 servings

For Easter, a festive pastry-wrapped entreé.

1 3- to 4-pound fully cooked
 lean boneless ham

1 tablespoon butter
½ cup chopped mushrooms
2 scallions, chopped
3 tablespoons finely chopped parsley
3 tablespoons finely chopped watercress
1 tablespoon Dijon mustard
pastry for 2-crust pie
1 egg beaten with 1 teaspoon water
watercress for garnish

1. Preheat oven to 350°.
2. Unwrap ham; pat dry. Trim any excess fat. Set aside.
3. Melt butter in small skillet and sauté mushrooms and scallions. Remove from heat and stir in parsley, watercress and mustard.
4. Roll out half of pastry into circle; place ham in center and bring pastry up around sides of ham. Pat mushroom mixture onto ham; cover top with other half of pastry rolled into a round. Use egg wash to "glue" top pastry to bottom along sides; trim excess pastry. Cut pastry flowers from pastry trimmings and "glue" to top in pretty design with egg wash. Brush egg over top and sides.
5. Place ham carefully on rack in baking pan. Bake 1 hour until golden brown.
6. Allow ham to stand 10 minutes before slicing. Garnish with watercress. Serve warm or at room temperature with Sauce Verte, if desired.

Sauce Verte:

1 bunch watercress
2 cups parsley, tightly packed
1 cup mayonnaise
1 cup sour cream
1 tablespoon lemon juice
white pepper to taste

Sauce Verte:

Combine all ingredients in blender or food processor; process until smooth.

Sausage-Artichoke Pie in Phyllo Crust

Yield: 8 servings

**A wonderful way to warm an early spring day.
Good for brunch, too.**

8 sheets phyllo pastry
1 medium onion, finely chopped
1 carrot, finely chopped
1 rib celery, finely chopped
¼ cup (½ stick) butter
½ pound spiced pork bulk sausage
1 14-ounce can artichoke hearts, drained
  and thinly sliced
1 cup whole-milk ricotta cheese
½ cup Parmesan cheese, freshly grated
2 eggs, lightly beaten
1 tablespoon chopped fresh parsley
salt and pepper, to taste
½ cup (1 stick) unsalted butter, melted

1. Preheat oven to 350°. Allow phyllo dough to come to room temperature, keeping leaves covered with damp towel to prevent drying out.

2. Sauté next three ingredients in butter until tender, about 5 minutes; add sausage, crumble and cook until browned, about 10 minutes. Remove from heat and cool.

3. Place mixture in large bowl; combine with all remaining ingredients except unsalted melted butter.

4. Line 9-inch springform pan with four leaves of phyllo dough, brushing each leaf with melted butter as it is placed in pan. (Leaves will overlap edges of pan.) Fill crust with sausage-artichoke mixture; fold overlapping leaves over top of filling.

5. Cut four 9-inch circles from four remaining phyllo leaves. Layer on top of pie, brushing each circle with butter as it is placed. Pour any remaining butter over the top. With scissors, cut through circles of dough to delineate eight wedges so that finished pie will cut more easily.

6. Place pie on cookie sheet and bake 45 minutes, or until top crust is crisp and golden.

The Civil War hastened the spread of processed foods across America, as canned goods were made available for the first time in quantity to Union armies. Little more than a century later Americans continued to bolster this industry with the purchase of twenty-six billion canned and preserved foods.

27

Rosemary Roast Chicken and Vegetables

Yield: 4 to 6 servings

A one-pot dinner guaranteed to become a family favorite.

1 5-pound oven-roaster chicken
¼ cup (½ stick) butter, melted
¾ teaspoon salt
¼ teaspoon black pepper
1 teaspoon minced garlic
2 teaspoons dried rosemary leaves, crumbled
paprika
1 10-ounce package frozen baby carrots
1 16-ounce package frozen
  small whole onions
1 10-ounce package frozen
  whole green beans
1 pound small new potatoes, cooked

1. Preheat oven to 425°. Rinse chicken and pat dry with paper towels. Brush outside of bird with butter.

2. Combine salt, pepper and garlic. Rub bird inside and out thoroughly with mixture.

3. Tie chicken legs together with string; fold wing tips under bird. Sprinkle all over with 1 teaspoon rosemary and paprika; place in roasting pan. Roast 20 minutes, brushing once or twice with butter.

4. Reduce heat to 375°. Roast 35 minutes more. Add carrots, onions and beans to pan, sprinkle with paprika and 1 teaspoon rosemary; shake pan gently to coat vegetables with pan drippings. Roast 20 minutes more, basting chicken once or twice. Add potatoes and brush with drippings. Continue roasting about 15 to 20 minutes more, or until juices run clear when chicken thighs are pierced with fork.

Chicken Piccata

Yield: 6 servings

This classic dish has many variations, but none better than this one.

8 chicken breast halves, skinned,
  boned and flattened
½ cup flour
salt and freshly ground pepper
4 eggs, beaten
2 tablespoons freshly grated Parmesan cheese
½ cup (1 stick) unsalted butter
1 tablespoon capers
1 lemon, cut in wedges

Variation: Veal Piccata

Prepare as above using veal scallops.

1. Dredge chicken in flour seasoned with salt and pepper. Combine eggs and cheese; dip chicken into egg mixture.

2. In large skillet, heat butter until golden and foamy. Sauté chicken until crisp and brown, cooking about 4 to 5 minutes per side. Remove to warm platter.

3. Add capers to butter; heat through. Spoon caper-butter over chicken. Garnish with lemon wedges; serve immediately.

Chicken Asparagus Bundles

Yield: 6 servings

A delightful springtime creation.

6 boneless chicken breast halves
1 8-ounce container soft cream cheese
   with chives and onions
18 fresh asparagus stalks,
   steamed until crisp-tender
butter
paprika

Variation (Appetizer):
After cooking, cool bundles. Slice each bundle into four or five thin slices horizontally. Serve as a first course on plate covered with lettuce and garnished with two steamed, chilled, whole asparagus spears. Serves 8 as first course.

1. Preheat oven to 400°.
2. Flatten breast halves to even thickness with mallet. Trim asparagus stems to about 4 inches.
3. Spread each breast half with about 2 tablespoons cream cheese; place 3 asparagus spears in center and wrap chicken around asparagus forming a roll.
4. Place rolls, seam side down, in a buttered baking dish. Put a small pat of butter on top of each. Bake for 45 minutes. Baste with pan drippings after 30 minutes.
5. To serve, spoon any melted cheese in pan over rolls; sprinkle with paprika.

Chicken Sauté with Artichoke Hearts

Yield: 8 servings

Contributed by a working woman who entertains a lot, this recipe is fast, easy yet sophisticated.

4 boneless, skinless chicken breast halves,
   flattened
salt and freshly ground pepper
2 tablespoons unsalted butter
2 tablespoons extra-virgin olive oil
3 or 4 garlic cloves, chopped
12 ounces fresh mushrooms, quartered
1 large onion, coarsely chopped
½ cup white wine
2 tablespoons lemon juice
¼ cup chopped fresh parsley
¼ teaspoon EACH oregano, thyme and basil
dash soy sauce
2 6-ounce jars marinated artichoke hearts
   undrained
1 7-ounce jar roasted peppers,
   drained and cut in strips
ripe olives (optional)

1. Season chicken with salt and pepper and sauté in butter and oil in large skillet; add garlic, mushrooms and onion and cook until onion is tender.
2. Pour wine over all; add lemon juice, herbs and dash of soy sauce. Add undrained artichoke hearts and drained roasted peppers. Cover and simmer for 10 to 15 minutes until chicken is cooked through.
3. Add ripe olives just before serving. Serve over cooked fresh fettuccine or linguine, if desired.

Crab-Stuffed Chicken Breasts

Yield: 6 servings

Succulent stuffed chicken with a lemony cheese sauce.

6 chicken breasts, skinned, boned and flattened
salt and pepper
1 medium onion, chopped
2 ribs celery, chopped
5 tablespoons butter, divided
5 tablespoons dry white wine, divided
1 6- or 7-ounce can crabmeat, rinsed and drained
½ cup herb-seasoned stuffing mix
¼ cup flour mixed with ½ teaspoon paprika
1 1¼-ounce packet Hollandaise Sauce mix
¾ cup milk
½ cup (about 2 ounces) shredded Swiss cheese

1. Season chicken breasts with salt and pepper.
2. Sauté onion and celery in 3 tablespoons butter in skillet until tender. Remove from heat; add 3 tablespoons wine, crabmeat and stuffing mix; toss together.
3. Divide stuffing mixture among chicken breasts; roll up, secure with wooden picks and coat with flour mixture.
4. Place floured, rolled breasts in 13 x 9-inch baking dish. Drizzle with 2 tablespoons melted butter. Bake in 375° oven for 1 hour. Remove wooden picks and transfer chicken to serving platter.
5. Meanwhile, blend Hollandaise Sauce mix with milk; cook until thickened. Add 2 tablespoons wine and Swiss cheese; stir until cheese melts.
6. To serve, pour sauce over chicken and pass any remaining sauce separately.

Chicken Breasts in Watercress Cream

Yield: 4 to 6 servings

A scrumptious springtime sauté.

3 whole chicken breasts, boned, halved, skinned and flattened
flour, seasoned with salt and pepper
3 tablespoons unsalted butter
½ bunch watercress, finely chopped
2 sprigs fresh tarragon or 2 teaspoons dried tarragon
1 cup heavy cream
salt and pepper, to taste
juice of 1 lemon

Variation: Veal Scallops in Watercress Cream
Substitute 1½ pounds thin veal scallops for chicken. Proceed as above.

1. Dredge chicken breasts in seasoned flour.
2. Heat butter in large skillet; sauté chicken until golden brown. Remove from skillet and place in shallow baking dish. Reserve drippings in skillet.
3. In small bowl mix watercress, tarragon, cream, salt and pepper, and lemon juice. Add to drippings in skillet; bring to simmer, stirring up any browned bits in pan. Just before cream mixture boils, remove from heat and pour over chicken breasts.
4. Bake chicken and sauce in 350° oven for 10 to 15 minutes. Serve with rice, if desired.

Chicken and Ham Lasagna

Yield: 6 to 8 servings

A taste of springtime tucked between layers — asparagus!

8 ounces lasagna noodles
¼ cup (½ stick) butter
1 tablespoon minced onion
1 garlic clove, minced
⅓ cup flour
2 cups chicken broth
1 cup milk or light cream
1 cup freshly grated Parmesan cheese, divided
salt and ground white pepper to taste
dash nutmeg
½ pound fresh mushrooms, sliced
 and sautéed in butter
1 10-ounce package frozen cut asparagus,
 thawed and drained
2 cups cubed cooked chicken
1½ cups shredded Gruyère or Swiss cheese
6 ounces thinly sliced, deli-style cooked ham

1. Cook noodles according to package directions; drain off most of cooking water; replace part with cold water to stop cooking and set aside until needed.

2. In saucepan melt butter; sauté onion and garlic, then blend in flour and cook until light golden. Gradually stir in broth and milk; cook and stir until bubbly.

3. Remove from heat. Stir in ½ cup Parmesan cheese, salt, pepper and nutmeg.

4. In greased 13 x 9 x 2-inch baking dish layer three or four drained noodles to cover bottom. On top of noodles layer mushrooms, asparagus, chicken, Gruyère and about one-third of cream sauce. Top with ham, another layer of noodles and remaining cream sauce. Sprinkle with remaining Parmesan cheese.

5. Bake in 350° oven for about 35 minutes or until heated through. Let stand 10 minutes before cutting.

Lemonade Sole

Yield: 4 servings

An unlikely ingredient produces a superb result.

1 pound fillet of sole, flounder
 or other mild white fish
1 tablespoon butter, melted
3 tablespoons lemonade concentrate, thawed
2 tablespoons chopped fresh parsley
salt to taste
⅛ teaspoon white pepper
½ teaspoon tarragon
2 tablespoons finely chopped green onion
½ cup sour cream or mayonnaise
3 tablespoons Parmesan cheese
paprika
white pepper

1. Preheat oven to 350°. Using pastry brush, grease baking dish or au gratin dish with melted butter.

2. Place fillets in dish; brush with butter, then spoon lemonade concentrate evenly over fish. Cook 8 to 10 minutes, watching carefully, until fish flakes easily.

3. Meanwhile, combine next seven ingredients. Preheat broiler.

4. Spread sour cream mixture over fillets; place under broiler until golden brown. Sprinkle with paprika and pepper. Good served with tiny pearl onions, fresh bread and white wine.

Shad Roe Meunière

Yield: 6 servings

Shad roe is a delicacy with a short-lived season. Try this classic lemon-butter sauce on fresh tuna steaks when roe season is over.

3 pair shad roe
1 cup milk
1 teaspoon salt
flour
6 tablespoons (¾ stick) butter
2 tablespoons vegetable oil
salt and pepper to taste

1 cup (2 sticks) butter
2 tablespoons lemon juice
3 tablespoons chopped fresh parsley
6 lemon quarters

Variation: Tuna Steaks Meunière

Prepare as above using tuna steaks.

1. In a shallow pie plate mix milk and salt; dip roe in mixture, turning to moisten both sides. Drain roe; dredge in flour.
2. In a large skillet over moderate heat, sauté roe in butter and oil for 6 to 7 minutes on each side, or until golden brown. Transfer to heated platter. Season with salt and pepper.
3. Meanwhile, melt 1 cup butter in a large skillet and cook until golden brown, being careful not to burn. Remove from heat and whisk in lemon juice.
4. Pour butter through fine sieve over roe. Sprinkle with parsley and garnish with lemon.

Fish in the Constitution

Yield: 4 servings

The name of this delectable fish recipe derives from the parchment paper in which it is cooked and served.

4 15-inch squares parchment paper
white wine
8 pieces of sole, 2 to 2½ pounds total
2 10-ounce bags fresh spinach
2 12-ounce boxes fresh mushrooms
1 pound MILD Cheddar cheese
bread crumbs
paprika
butter
salt and pepper

1. In shallow dish, marinate fish in white wine while proceeding with preparations.
2. Wash spinach, remove stems and towel dry. Wash and slice mushrooms. Grate cheese.
3. Divide the ingredients evenly among the four sheets of parchment, layering in the following manner: all the spinach, one-third of cheese, half of fish fillets, salt and pepper, one-third of cheese, half of the mushrooms, bread crumbs, remainder of fish, salt and pepper, remainder of cheese, remainder of mushrooms, paprika and dots of butter.
4. Preheat oven to 375°. Wrap up parchment paper so package is entirely enclosed. Melt some butter to brush outside of package so that it does not burn. Cook packages on lightly greased jellyroll pan for 25 minutes.

5. Serve each on dinner plate with parchment package opened and sides rolled back. If desired, accompany with Pecan Rice Mélange (see index), and a salad of sliced tomatoes or Herbed Cherry Tomatoes (see index).

Scallops Primavera

Yield: 6 servings

Oriental seasonings and crisp fresh veggies combine to make this a guaranteed favorite.

1 pound sea or bay scallops
1 cup uncooked converted long grain rice
1 tablespoon oyster sauce
2 tablespoons soy sauce
1½ teaspoons minced fresh ginger, divided
¼ teaspoon sugar

2 tablespoons butter
2 to 3 tablespoons peanut oil
1 garlic clove, minced
2 cups broccoli florets
1 small red pepper, cut into thin strips
½ cup thinly sliced carrots
¼ pound fresh pea pods, strings removed
½ cup sliced scallions
½ pint cherry tomatoes, halved
½ pound asparagus spears, trimmed
  and cut in thirds

1 tablespoon lemon juice
2 teaspoons Dijon mustard
½ teaspoon paprika
¼ teaspoon dill
¼ teaspoon pepper

1. Rinse scallops in cold water and pat dry. If using sea scallops, cut them in half; set scallops aside.

2. Prepare rice according to package directions, but omit salt. When rice is cooked, stir in oyster sauce, soy sauce, ½ teaspoon ginger and sugar. Cover and keep warm.

3. In wok or large skillet, heat butter and 2 tablespoons oil over high heat. Add garlic and remaining 1 teaspoon ginger; sauté 15 seconds. Add broccoli, red pepper and carrots; stir-fry 3 minutes.

4. Add pea pods and scallions; stir-fry 1 minute.

5. Add tomatoes and asparagus, stir-fry 1 minute or until heated through. With slotted spoon, remove vegetables from wok; set aside.

6. Add half of scallops to wok; cook over medium heat 2 to 3 minutes until lightly brown. Remove from wok with slotted spoon.

7. If necessary, add 1 tablespoon peanut oil to wok. Add remaining scallops and sauté 2 to 3 minutes.

8. Stir together lemon juice and remaining seasonings. Return vegetables and first batch of scallops to wok. Stir in lemon juice mixture; heat through. Serve over rice.

VEGETABLES

Bunny-Egg Asparagus

Yield: 8 servings

The name may be silly, but it's a delicious way to use up the Easter eggs!

2 pounds fresh whole asparagus, trimmed
3 tablespoons butter
3 tablespoons flour
1 cup milk
¼ teaspoon salt
⅛ teaspoon white pepper
6 hard-boiled eggs, peeled and sliced
½ pound mushrooms, sliced and sautéed
2 tablespoons fine, dry bread crumbs
paprika

1. Cook asparagus in a small amount of salted water until crisp-tender. Drain, reserving 1 cup cooking liquid.

2. Melt butter in heavy saucepan over low heat. Add flour, stirring until smooth; cook 1 minute, stirring constantly. Gradually add reserved cooking liquid and milk; cook over medium heat until thick and bubbly, stirring constantly. Season with salt and pepper.

3. Preheat oven to 325°; grease a 10 x 6 x 2-inch baking dish. Spread ¼ cup sauce in dish. Layer half each of asparagus, sliced eggs, sautéed mushrooms and sauce. Repeat layers; sprinkle with bread crumbs and paprika. Bake for 20 to 25 minutes, or until hot and bubbly.

Asparagus with Orange Butter Sauce

Yield: 8 servings

What could be more suggestive of spring than asparagus and orange?

½ cup (1 stick) butter
grated rind of one orange
juice of one orange
2 pounds fresh asparagus, trimmed
peeled orange slices for garnish (optional)

1. Combine butter, orange rind and juice in a small saucepan. Bring to boil, reduce heat and simmer, stirring occasionally until mixture is reduced by half and slightly thickened. Set aside and keep warm.

2. In a large skillet in a small amount of salted boiling water, cook asparagus 6 to 8 minutes, or until crisp-tender. Drain.

3. Arrange asparagus in a serving dish. Pour orange sauce over asparagus. Garnish with orange slices, if desired.

Louisa's Carrot Puff

Yield: 6 servings

Guaranteed to please the WHOLE family, even the youngest vegetable resister!

1 cup milk
6 to 8 medium carrots, scraped
   and cut into chunks
¼ cup (½ stick) butter, melted
3 eggs
½ to ¾ cup sugar (sweeten to taste)
2 heaping tablespoons flour
1 teaspoon baking powder
1 teaspoon cinnamon

Carrots will retain some of their crunchiness after cooking. Puff is not a smooth purée.

1. Place raw carrots in blender or food processor container and purée, adding a little of the 1 cup milk if necessary to facilitate chopping.
2. Add remaining ingredients to carrots in blender or processor; blend until smooth.
3. Preheat oven to 350°. Pour carrot mixture into greased 2½-quart casserole. Bake 45 minutes or until center looks set.

Maple Glazed Carrots

Yield: 6 servings

You may have glazed carrots with sugar or honey, but Vermonters glaze theirs with you-know-what!

18 to 24 baby carrots, peeled
½ teaspoon salt, or to taste
¼ cup maple syrup
¼ cup (½ stick) butter
1 teaspoon dry mustard
2 tablespoons chopped fresh parsley

1. Place carrots in saucepan with about 1 inch boiling, salted water. Cover and reduce heat, cooking about 10 minutes or until tender but slightly crisp.
2. Remove carrots from pan with a slotted spoon. Reduce cooking liquid by boiling down to about ½ cup.
3. Add syrup, butter and mustard. Cook over moderate heat until mixture has consistency of heavy syrup.
4. Return carrots to pan and cook, shaking pan often, until carrots are well glazed. Sprinkle with parsley before serving.

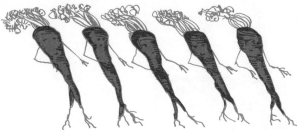

Celery au Gratin

Yield: 6 to 8 servings

An often forgotten vegetable deserves another chance.

5 cups sliced celery, 1-inch thick
2 cups water
salt to taste
¼ cup (½ stick) butter
¼ cup flour
2 cups milk
½ teaspoon salt
½ teaspoon pepper
pinch ground nutmeg
¼ cup shredded Swiss cheese
¼ cup grated Parmesan cheese, divided
paprika

1. In saucepan, bring celery to a boil in salted water. Reduce heat, cover and simmer 5 minutes or until crisp-tender. Drain well.

2. In heavy saucepan, make white sauce. Melt butter and stir in flour; cook 1 minute, stirring constantly. Gradually add milk and cook over medium heat, stirring constantly until thickened. Add seasonings, Swiss cheese and 2 tablespoons Parmesan, along with drained celery.

3. Spoon mixture into lightly greased 1½-quart casserole. Sprinkle with remaining Parmesan and paprika. Broil 4 inches from heat until golden brown.

Marinated Sugar Snap Peas

Yield: 6 servings

Add the lemon juice just prior to serving in order to avoid discoloring the peas.

2 8-ounce packages frozen
   sugar snap peas
salt to taste
½ small red onion, thinly sliced
1 large garlic clove, minced
pinch of sugar
⅓ cup olive oil
freshly ground pepper
juice of one lemon

Must be made ahead.

1. Heat large pot of water to rolling boil; salt lightly. Add peas and cook exactly 1 minute, until crisp-tender.

2. Drain in colander, immediately rinsing under cold running water. Drain well; check for strings and transfer to bowl.

3. Add onion, garlic, sugar, olive oil and pepper to taste. Toss gently. Refrigerate, covered, at least 30 minutes.

4. To serve, let warm to room temperature and add lemon juice. Toss gently to mix.

Lemon Rice

Yield: about 8 cups

Something a little different to go with seafood dishes.

⅓ cup butter
½ cup chopped onion
2 cups long grain converted rice
2 8-ounce bottles clam juice
¼ cup lemon juice
1½ teaspoons salt
water
3 2 x 1-inch pieces lemon peel,
   cut into fine slivers

1. In saucepan melt butter over medium heat. Add onion and sauté until translucent, about 5 minutes. Add rice; sauté just until golden.
2. Combine clam juice, lemon juice and enough water to equal 3 cups liquid. Add to rice with salt. Bring to boil; lower heat, cover and simmer about 25 minutes. Toss in lemon peel before serving.

Orange Rice

Yield: 6 servings

A delicious side dish that also makes a good base for a cold meat salad.

¼ cup (½ stick) butter
2 ribs celery, diced
2 tablespoons minced onion
½ cup water
2 tablespoons grated orange rind
1 cup orange juice
1 teaspoon salt
1 pinch dried thyme
1 cup uncooked converted long grain rice

1. Melt butter in saucepan; cook celery and onion until tender but not brown.
2. Add water, orange rind, juice, salt and thyme; bring to boil.
3. Add rice, reduce heat, cover and cook 25 minutes.

Sugar-Browned New Potatoes

Yield: 6 servings

These golden potatoes look as good as they taste.

¼ cup (½ stick) butter
⅓ cup sugar
18 new potatoes, pared and cooked
½ teaspoon salt, or to taste

1. Heat butter in a large skillet; stir in sugar. Cook, stirring constantly, until sugar is lightly browned. (Mixture may look strange at this point — it's okay.)
2. Add potatoes and cook slowly, turning potatoes occasionally until they are golden brown on all sides.
3. Sprinkle with salt and serve.

Baked Zucchini with Ham

Yield: 4 servings

This delicious vegetable dish also makes a good brunch or luncheon addition.

4 medium zucchini, trimmed and
   halved lengthwise
¼ pound cooked ham, finely diced
4 slices cooked bacon, crumbled
2 tablespoons chopped parsley
2 tablespoons minced onion
freshly ground black pepper
¼ cup (½ stick) butter, melted
2 tablespoons heavy cream
¼ cup freshly grated Parmesan cheese

1. Boil zucchini in salted water to cover for about 2 minutes. Drain squash and arrange, cut side up, in large buttered baking dish.

2. Preheat oven to 325°. In bowl combine ham, bacon, parsley and onion; sprinkle over zucchini. Season with pepper to taste.

3. Drizzle melted butter over zucchini and bake for 25 minutes. Sprinkle with cream and Parmesan; bake 10 minutes more, or until top is lightly browned and bubbly. Serve warm.

Nineteenth-century Europeans rightly saw us as meat eaters. In the 1830's, the average American ate 178 pounds of pork, ham, and beef annually.

SALADS

Asparagus in Raspberry Vinaigrette
Yield: 6 servings

The epitome of springtime!

1½ pounds fresh asparagus, trimmed
⅓ cup olive oil
½ cup raspberry vinegar (see below)
¾ teaspoon salt
¾ teaspoon freshly ground pepper
¼ cup fresh raspberries, or
   unsweetened frozen, thawed
Boston lettuce

Must be made ahead.

1. Cook asparagus in large pot of boiling water until crisp-tender. (Check frequently by piercing stalks with fork.) Drain and immediately immerse in ice cold water.
2. Mix remaining ingredients, except lettuce, in jar with tight-fitting lid; shake well.
3. Drain asparagus and place in shallow serving dish with rim. Pour vinaigrette over asparagus, cover with plastic wrap and chill at least one hour before serving. Serve on bed of Boston lettuce.

Raspberry Vinegar
Yield: 6 cups (3 pints)

Makes a lovely Christmas gift, too.

3 cups fresh raspberries or 1 12-ounce
   package frozen unsweetened raspberries
4 cups cider vinegar
2 cups dry red wine
3 16-ounce clean bottles

Must be made ahead.

Variation: Blueberry Vinegar

Substitute fresh frozen blueberries for raspberries. Add two 2-inch sticks of cinnamon to each pint bottle along with reserved blueberries. Store and use as above. (Wonderful on asparagus!)

1. Thaw raspberries, if frozen, or thoroughly rinse and drain fresh berries.
2. Combine all but ⅓ cup of raspberries with vinegar and wine in a large bowl. Cover; let stand overnight.
3. In stainless steel or enamel saucepan heat vinegar mixture to boiling. Boil, uncovered, for 3 minutes. Strain, discarding solids.
4. Place 2 tablespoons of reserved berries in each of 3 16-ounce bottles. Pour hot vinegar mixture into each bottle; cover tightly. Store in cool dark place 2 to 4 weeks before using. Store in refrigerator up to 6 months. Use on salads or to marinate meats.

Joyous Spring Salad with Raspberry Vinegar   Yield: 4 servings

1 head Boston lettuce
1 bunch watercress
4 ripe pears, sliced
2 ounces crumbled blue cheese
¼ cup raspberry vinegar (see previous page)
⅔ cup olive oil
salt and freshly ground pepper, to taste

1. Tear lettuce into bite-size pieces.
   Toss with watercress, pears and cheese
   in a large salad bowl.
2. Combine vinegar and oil. Pour over salad.
   Sprinkle with salt and pepper.

Strawberry Watercress Salad with Rosy Dressing   Yield: 8 servings

Truly a delight to the eye and the palate.

2 heads Boston or Bibb lettuce
1 small bunch watercress
2 green onions, sliced
1 pint fresh stawberries (ripe but still firm),
   thickly sliced

Rosy Dressing:

3 tablespoons salad oil
2 tablespoons raspberry vinegar
   (see previous page)
1 teaspoon sugar
salt and pepper to taste
1 teaspoon poppy seeds
pinch dried mint

1. Wash and dry lettuce and watercress and
   combine in salad bowl.
2. Place onions and strawberries on top of
   greens and drizzle with Rosy Dressing.
   Present at table before tossing gently.

Dressing:

Place all ingredients in jar with tightly fitting
lid. Cover and shake well. Refrigerate any
unused dressing.

Chicory, Bacon and Pecan Salad   Yield: 6 servings

A slightly piquant, hot dressing distinguishes this salad.

1 head Boston or Bibb lettuce, torn
1 head chicory
½ cup chopped red onion
⅔ cup toasted pecan halves
6 slices bacon
1½ teaspoons firmly packed brown sugar
¼ cup sherry vinegar
¼ teaspoon salt
freshly ground pepper

1. Combine greens, onion and pecans in salad bowl; toss gently.

2. Cook bacon in large skillet over medium heat until crisp. Drain on paper towels.

3. Pour off all but ¼ cup fat from skillet; return to low heat, add brown sugar and stir until dissolved. Blend in vinegar and salt; stir until dissolved.

4. Pour hot dressing over salad. Top with crumbled bacon. Season with freshly ground pepper and toss gently.

Two Pears and Spinach Salad   Yield: 6 servings

Light and attractive.

4 cups torn spinach, washed and dried
½ cup thinly sliced green onion
2 avocados, sliced ("alligator pears")
2 fresh pears, sliced
4 slices bacon, cooked and crumbled
Lime-Parsley Dressing (below)

1. Combine spinach and onions in bowl. Arrange pear and avocado slices on top; sprinkle with crumbled bacon.

2. Toss with Lime-Parsley Dressing.

Lime-Parsley Dressing:

¼ cup white grape juice
¼ cup white wine vinegar
¼ cup olive oil
1 tablespoon chopped fresh parsley
¼ teaspoon grated lime rind
1 tablespoon lime juice
¼ teaspoon salt

Dressing:
Combine all ingredients in a jar, cover tightly and shake vigorously until well blended.

Spring Vegetable Antipasto Salad

Yield: 8 servings

A platterful of choices in a spectrum of delicate green hues.

Creamy Anchovy Dressing:

⅔ cup heavy cream
1½ cups mayonnaise
1 2-ounce can flat anchovies, drained
½ cup chopped green onion
½ cup chopped parsley
2 tablespoons chopped chives

Must be made ahead.

2 ripe avocados
2 tablespoons lemon juice
1 pound fresh asparagus spears, cooked crisp-tender and chilled
1 pound pea pods, cooked crisp-tender and chilled
2 6-ounce jars marinated artichoke hearts, drained
Boston lettuce

Variation:

For an attractive holiday platter add a touch of red cherry tomatoes or tiny whole beets.

Dressing preparation:

1. Combine all ingredients in blender or food processor; purée until smooth.
2. Refrigerate at least 1 hour to blend flavors.

Platter preparation:

1. Halve avocados; peel and pit. Cut into chunks into a medium bowl; toss with lemon juice.
2. Line a large shallow platter with lettuce. Arrange asparagus spears, avocado chunks, pea pods, and artichokes on top.
3. Pour salad dressing into serving bowl and pass, or drizzle dressing over arranged salad.

Asparagus Mold

Yield: 6 to 8 servings

A welcome addition to an Easter buffet.

1 tablespoon unflavored gelatin
¼ cup cold water
1 14-ounce can chopped green asparagus
½ cup mayonnaise
½ cup cream, whipped
½ teaspoon salt
dash pepper
2 tablespoons lemon juice
1 cup blanched almonds, chopped

Must be made ahead.

1. Soften gelatin in water; set aside.
2. Drain asparagus, reserving liquid; add enough water to reserved liquid to measure 1 cup. Heat liquid and pour over softened gelatin. Refrigerate until partially set.
3. Fold in mayonnaise, whipped cream, salt and pepper, and lemon juice. Fold in asparagus and almonds; pour mixture into 4- to 6-cup mold. Chill until firm. Unmold to serve accompanied by extra mayonnaise mixed with a little lemon juice, if desired.

Blushing Grapefruit

Yield: 4 servings

A favorite for brunch.

1 1-pound can grapefruit sections
1 envelope unflavored gelatin
½ cup cold water
3 tablespoons sugar
1¾ cups California blush wine
2 or 3 drops red food coloring

Must be made ahead.

1. Drain grapefruit sections.
2. Soften gelatin in cold water; add sugar. Dissolve in top of double boiler over hot water or microwave for 5 to 10 seconds.
3. Stir wine into gelatin mixture. Add a few drops of red food coloring. Chill until consistency of egg whites.
4. Stir grapefruit sections into gelatin mixture. Divide mixture among four wine glasses. Chill until set.

Cold Spinach Soufflé

Yield: 6 servings

Some cool pizazz for warmer days.

1 3-ounce package lemon gelatin
¾ cup boiling water
1½ tablespoons vinegar
½ cup mayonnaise
¼ teaspoon salt
dash pepper
1 cup chopped fresh spinach
1 tablespoon minced onion
⅓ cup chopped celery
¾ cup creamed cottage cheese

Must be made ahead.

1. Dissolve gelatin in boiling water; add vinegar, mayonnaise, salt and pepper, blending with rotary beater or whisk.
2. Pour into freezer trays; chill until firm one inch around sides, but still soft in center.
3. Return to bowl; beat again until fluffy. Add remaining ingredients
4. Pour into 4-cup lightly oiled mold; chill until firm. Unmold to serve.

DESSERTS

Apricot Mousse
Ethereal!

6 ounces dried apricots
2 cups boiling water
¼ cup apricot brandy
granulated sugar to taste
1 envelope unflavored gelatin
¼ cup water
2 tablespoons lemon juice
1 cup heavy cream
5 egg whites, at room temperature

Must be made ahead.

Yield: 6 servings

1. Place apricots in saucepan with tightly fitting lid. Pour boiling water over them; cover and let stand several hours or overnight.

2. Simmer apricots gently until tender. Drain. Purée in blender or food processor with apricot brandy until smooth. Add sugar to taste while mixture is still warm (about 2 to 4 tablespoons).

3. Soften gelatin by sprinkling it over ¼ cup water. Dissolve over low heat (or microwave for 5 to 10 seconds) and mix thoroughly with apricot purée. Stir in lemon juice. Taste for sweetness, adding more sugar if desired. Chill until thickened.

4. Whip cream just until thick and soft peaks form. Fold into chilled purée. Refrigerate while proceeding to next step.

5. Using clean mixing bowl and beaters, beat egg whites until stiff peaks form. Fold beaten egg whites into apricot mixture until well incorporated. Spoon into 1-quart soufflé dish, mounding in center.

6. Cover and refrigerate until firm, at least 4 hours, or overnight. Garnish with candied violets and fresh mint leaves, if desired.

Josie's Coconut Layer Cake

Yield: 9-inch layer cake

A cherished recipe from a cherished mother-in-law.

2 cups cake flour, sifted before measuring
1⅓ cups sugar
½ cup shortening
⅔ cup milk
4 egg yolks or 2 whole eggs and 2 yolks
3 teaspoons baking powder
1 teaspoon salt
½ teaspoon lemon extract

1. Preheat oven to 375°. Grease and flour two 9-inch round cake pans.
2. Into large bowl, measure all ingredients; with mixer at low speed, beat until well mixed, constantly scraping bowl with rubber spatula.
3. Beat at medium speed 5 minutes, occasionally scraping bowl.
4. Pour batter into prepared pans and bake 25 to 30 minutes or until tester inserted in center comes out clean.
5. Cool layers in pans on wire rack 10 minutes; remove from pans and cool completely before frosting with White Coconut Icing.

White Coconut Icing:

½ cup sugar
¼ cup light corn syrup
2 tablespoons water
2 egg whites
⅛ teaspoon cream of tartar
½ teaspoon vanilla extract
2 cups flaked coconut

Icing preparation:

1. Combine sugar, corn syrup and water in a small saucepan; cover. Heat to boiling; uncover; boil gently, without stirring, until mixture registers 242° on a candy thermometer, or until a small amount of hot syrup falls, threadlike, from spoon.
2. While syrup cooks, beat egg whites with cream of tartar in large bowl with electric mixer until stiff peaks form.
3. Pour hot syrup onto egg whites in a thin stream, beating all the time at high speed until frosting is stiff and glossy. Beat in vanilla and stir in 1 cup of coconut.
4. Frost between cake layers, top and sides of cake. Press remaining coconut onto sides and top of cake while icing is still moist.

Apricot Brandy Pound Cake

Yield: 12 to 16 servings

This family recipe has been used to celebrate baptisms and First Communions and is on file for weddings!

1 cup (2 sticks) butter (no substitute)
3 cups sugar
6 eggs
3 cups flour
¼ teaspoon baking soda
½ teaspoon salt
1 cup sour cream
½ teaspoon rum flavoring
1 teaspoon orange extract
½ teaspoon almond extract
½ teaspoon lemon extract
1 teaspoon vanilla extract
½ cup apricot brandy

This cake freezes well.

1. Preheat oven to 325°. Grease and flour a 9- or 10-inch tube pan.
2. In large bowl of electric mixer, cream butter and sugar thoroughly. Add eggs one at a time, beating well after each addition.
3. Sift together flour, soda and salt three times. Combine sour cream, flavorings and brandy. Add dry ingredients alternately with sour cream mixture, beginning and ending with the flour. Pour into prepared pan; bake for 60 to 70 minutes or until cake tests done. Cool 15 to 20 minutes on wire rack before removing from pan.

Creamy Italian Cheesecake

Yield: 16 servings

Delicately flavored and delightful. Often served at Easter time.

3 8-ounce packages cream cheese, softened
2 pounds ricotta cheese
1 pint sour cream
5 eggs
1½ cups sugar
1½ teaspoons vanilla extract
1 teaspoon grated orange rind
5 heaping tablespoons cornstarch

Must be made ahead.

1. Preheat oven to 350°. Grease and flour a 10-inch springform pan.
2. Using large bowl and electric mixer, cream cheeses and sour cream; add eggs, one at a time, and combine well. Beat in remaining ingredients. Mixture will be thin. Pour into prepared pan.
3. Bake 60 to 75 minutes or until tester inserted near center indicates cake is firm. Cover with foil during last half hour if top becomes too brown.
4. Turn off oven; leave cake in oven with door open for 1 hour. Remove from oven and cool on wire rack for 45 minutes; remove sides of springform pan. Refrigerate cheesecake overnight.
5. To serve, sprinkle top with confectioners' sugar. If desired, accompany with a liqueur glass of Amaretto or Sambucca!

Flirtatious Charlotte

Yield: 8 to 10 servings

She appears to be an elegant lady, but she's really rather naughty!

5 squares (5 ounces) semisweet chocolate
2 tablespoons dark rum
1 envelope unflavored gelatin
5 tablespoons unsalted butter, softened
⅓ cup plus 2 tablespoons sugar
3 eggs, separated
¾ cup heavy cream
2 3-ounce packages lady fingers
¼ cup seedless raspberry preserves
½ cup mini chocolate chips
Crème Anglaise (below)

1. Stir chocolate with rum in heavy saucepan over low heat until chocolate melts. Add gelatin and stir until dissolved and mixture is smooth.

2. Remove saucepan from heat; gradually add butter, stirring constantly. Whisk in ⅓ cup sugar; add egg yolks, one at a time, beating constantly.

3. Set saucepan in basin of ice water; stir until mixture cools. Add cream.

4. In mixer bowl, beat egg whites until frothy; gradually add 2 tablespoons sugar and beat until stiff and sugar is dissolved. Fold egg whites into chocolate mixture.

5. Butter a 1½-quart soufflé dish or other 6-cup mold. Line bottom and sides with lady fingers with browned sides against buttered surface, piecing to cover bottom. Spoon half the chocolate mixture into dish.

6. In small saucepan over low heat, melt raspberry preserves until spreadable. Spoon half of preserves over chocolate and sprinkle with half of mini chips. Spoon in remaining chocolate mixture; spread with remaining preserves and sprinkle with remaining chips. cover with another layer of lady fingers, brown side up.

7. Chill for 6 hours or more. To serve, unmold by dipping the mold briefly in hot water and inverting onto plate. Accompany with Crème Anglaise.

Crème Anglaise:

3 egg yolks
3 tablespoons sugar
½ teaspoon cornstarch
2 cups light cream
1 tablespoon rum or vanilla extract

Must be made ahead.

Crème Anglaise

1. Combine eggs, sugar and cornstarch in top of double boiler.

2. Heat cream in medium saucepan to just below boiling. Stir into egg mixture and place over simmering water.

3. Cook, stirring constantly, until mixture is thickened slightly or just coats back of metal spoon. Stir in rum or vanilla; cool. Chill until ready to use.

Honeymoon Chocolate Pudding-Cake

Yield: 6 to 8 servings

**Acquired over 30 years ago on a honeymoon,
this recipe is actually a brownie baked in its own fudge sauce.**

1 cup flour
2 teaspoons baking powder
1 teaspoon salt
⅔ cup sugar
6 tablespoons cocoa
½ cup milk
2 tablespoons butter, melted
1 teaspoon vanilla extract
½ cup chopped pecans
1 cup brown sugar, packed
1½ cups boiling water

1. Preheat oven to 350°. Lightly grease 9-inch square baking pan.
2. Sift together first four ingredients with 2 tablespoons cocoa. Add milk, butter and vanilla; mix only until smooth. Stir in nuts.
3. Spread batter into baking pan. Combine brown sugar and remaining 4 tablespoons cocoa; sprinkle over top of batter, being careful to cover edges and corners.
4. Pour boiling water over all in pan. DO NOT STIR. Bake about 40 minutes.
5. Serve warm or cool, topped with whipped cream or ice cream, if desired. Coffee ice cream is divine on this!

Maple Bread Pudding

Yield: 6 to 8 servings

**This old-time New England dessert also makes a yummy brunch dish
—it's like French toast in a bowl!**

8 ½-inch thick slices Italian or
   French bread, day old
butter
4 eggs
⅔ cup maple syrup
pinch of salt
¼ teaspoon cinnamon
¼ teaspoon nutmeg
2 cups half-and-half

1. Preheat oven to 375°. Butter well a 7 x 11-inch baking dish.
2. Lightly toast bread on both sides. Place in buttered dish and butter side that faces up.
3. In a bowl lightly beat eggs; add syrup, salt and spices. Gradually stir in half-and-half. Pour mixture over bread.
4. Place baking dish inside a 9 x 13-inch baking pan. Fill pan with hot water about halfway up sides of dish. Bake pudding 30 to 35 minutes or until custard is set. Serve warm.

Maple Mousse Parfait

A rich ice cream-like dessert.

Yield: 8 to 10 servings

6 egg yolks
1 scant cup pure maple syrup
1½ teaspoons gelatin
1 cup milk
1 pint heavy cream, whipped
1 cup chopped nuts

1. In top of double boiler, beat egg yolks until light; stir in maple syrup. Place over hot water and cook, stirring, until thickened to the consistency of mayonnaise. Remove from heat and beat until cool.

2. In a 2-cup glass measure, soften gelatin in milk; microwave 15 to 20 seconds to dissolve, or place cup in pan of hot water and stir gelatin to dissolve.

3. Add gelatin mixture to maple-egg mixture; fold in whipped cream

4. Pour mixture into 8-inch square metallic pan, cover with foil and freeze 1 hour.

5. Remove from freezer; beat until light and smooth and stir in nuts. Spoon into serving dish and keep very cold until needed but DO NOT REFREEZE.

Raspberry-Rhubarb Pie

A delectable duet!

Yield: 8 servings

Pastry for double-crust 9-inch pie
3 cups rhubarb, cut in 1-inch pieces
1½ cups raspberries
2½ tablespoons cornstarch
3 tablespoons Grand Marnier
  or orange liqueur
1 tablespoon lemon juice
½ teaspoon cinnamon
¾ to 1 cup sugar
2 tablespoons unsalted butter

1. Line 9-inch pie pan with pastry.

2. Rinse rhubarb and berries; drain well.

3. In bowl, combine cornstarch, orange liqueur, lemon juice and cinnamon until well blended. Add fruit and sugar; toss to coat. Let stand about 20 minutes, tossing occasionally.

4. Preheat oven to 425°. Pour fruit filling into pastry-lined pan. Dot with butter.

5. Roll remaining pastry about ⅛-inch thick. Cut into ½- to ¾-inch strips and form into a lattice top.

6. Bake pie in middle of oven for 15 minutes. Reduce heat to 350° and bake 45 minutes longer, until filling bubbles and crust is golden brown.

Raspberry Swirl Cheesecake with Whole Berry Sauce

Yield: about 16 servings

Dense, rich cheesecake marbled with luscious raspberry purée.

Crust:

¾ cup imported amaretti cookie crumbs
¾ cup vanilla wafer crumbs
2 tablespoons butter, melted

1 10-ounce package frozen raspberries in syrup, thawed, puréed and sieved
½ cup sugar

Filling:

5 8-ounce packages cream cheese, softened
1 cup sugar
5 eggs
2 egg yolks
3 tablespoons flour
2 tablespoons framboise (raspberry brandy)
½ teaspoon almond extract
1½ teaspoons lemon juice
dash salt
¼ cup heavy cream

Whole Berry Sauce:

1 10-ounce package frozen raspberries in syrup, thawed
½ cup currant jelly
2 teaspoons cornstarch
1 tablespoon cold water

Must be made ahead.

1. Prepare crust: combine all ingredients; press onto bottom of 10-inch springform pan. Refrigerate while preparing filling.

2. In small bowl combine raspberry purée and sugar. Set aside. Preheat oven to 425°.

3. In bowl of food processor combine filling ingredients; process until smooth. Pour into prepared crust.

4. Drop spoonfuls of purée on top of filling; draw knife through both mixtures in swirling motion to create marbling. Let stand 10 minutes.

5. Bake 10 minutes; reduce oven temperature to 250° but DO NOT OPEN DOOR. Bake 2 hours and 5 minutes more. Turn off oven but leave cheesecake in oven 1 hour longer. Remove from oven; run knife around edge of pan to loosen cake. Cool on wire rack 1 hour; cover and refrigerate 4 hours before serving.

6. Remove cake from springform pan. Serve with Whole Berry Sauce, if desired.

Sauce:

1. Drain syrup from berries into saucepan. Reserve berries.

2. Add jelly to syrup; heat to dissolve.

3. Combine cornstarch and water; add to syrup and cook until thick and clear. Gently stir in reserved berries.

Baked Rhubarb

Yield: 4 servings

Select only the young, red shoots before they've had a chance to become woody.

1 cup sugar
½ cup water
½ teaspoon cinnamon
1 pound rhubarb, washed and cut into
  2-inch slices
3 thin slices lemon

Variation:

Reduce sugar to ¾ cup. Crumble Amaretti cookies or Almond Macaroons (see index), over rhubarb before baking. Proceed as in instructions.

1. Preheat oven to 350°.
2. In flameproof baking dish combine sugar, water and cinnamon; cook over low heat, stirring often, until sugar dissolves or about 10 minutes.
3. Add rhubarb and lemon to sugar mixture; cover and bake 30 to 45 minutes, checking for tenderness after half-an-hour.
4. Cool before serving or freezing. Serve with Crème Fraîche (see index), or whipped cream, if desired.

Rhubarb and Wine Bake

Yield: 6 servings

Easy, and its rosy color is so pretty.

4 cups rhubarb, cut into 1-inch slices
1 3-ounce package strawberry gelatin
½ cup sugar
2 cups dry cake mix
  (white or yellow cake)
½ cup dry white wine
¼ cup water
¼ cup (½ stick) butter, melted

If using frozen rhubarb, DO NOT ADD WATER.

1. Preheat oven to 350°.
2. Place rhubarb in a layer in 1½-quart casserole, sprinkle with gelatin and sugar.
3. Sprinkle dry cake mix over rhubarb mixture; pour wine on top, then water. Drizzle melted butter over all.
4. Bake about 50 minutes, or until crusty and golden. Serve warm with vanilla ice cream, if desired.

We had a sweet tooth as far back as 1770, when Christopher Leffingwell established America's first chocolate mill in Norwich, Connecticut.

Swedish Blitz Torte

Heaven isn't always chocolate!

Torte:

½ cup sugar
½ cup (1 stick) butter, softened
3 egg yolks
1 teaspoon baking powder
1 cup cake flour
5 tablespoons milk
1 teaspoon vanilla extract

Meringue:

3 egg whites, at room temperature
¼ teaspoon salt
6 tablespoons sugar
½ cup chopped walnuts

Rich Custard Filling:

½ cup sugar
½ teaspoon salt
⅓ cup flour
1½ cups milk
2 eggs, beaten
1 teaspoon vanilla extract
dash of nutmeg

Variation: Strawberry Meringue Cake

Prepare cake with meringue as above and assemble as for Swedish Blitz Torte substituting 1 cup whipping cream, lightly sweetened and whipped, and fresh sliced strawberries for the custard layer. Top as before with meringue on top.

1. Preheat oven to 350°. Line bottom and sides of two 8-inch round layer pans with waxed paper. To do this easily, lay a piece of waxed paper over one pan. Set second pan on top, pressing paper into bottom pan. Trim edges of paper with scissors and remove top pan. Grease waxed paper.

2. Using electric mixer, beat sugar and butter at low speed; add egg yolks and mix until smooth.

3. Combine baking powder and flour; add to egg mixture alternately with milk. Mix until smooth. Add vanilla.

4. Spread half the batter evenly into each pan. Batter will be stiff and will make a thin layer.

5. Make meringue: with mixer at high speed, beat egg whites with salt until stiff. Add sugar a couple of tablespoons at a time, beating well after each addition to thoroughly dissolve sugar. Spread half of the meringue over each pan of unbaked batter. Sprinkle about ¼ cup chopped nuts over each pan.

6. Bake for 30 to 35 minutes, until lightly browned. Cool completely in pans on wire rack.

7. Meanwhile, prepare Rich Custard Filling: in large saucepan combine first three ingredients; slowly stir in milk. Cook over low heat, stirring until mixture thickens.

8. Stir ⅓ cup of hot mixture carefully into beaten eggs; quickly stir eggs into milk in saucepan and cook until custard begins to boil again. Remove from heat and add vanilla and nutmeg; cool.

9. When cake/meringue has cooled, carefully remove waxed paper. Just before serving assemble torte as follows: put one layer on platter, meringue side DOWN; spread with cooled custard. Top with second layer, meringue side UP.

Strawberry Shortcake

The best shortcake you'll ever eat!

1 quart ripe strawberries, washed,
  hulled and sliced
½ cup sugar, more if berries are tart
2 tablespoons framboise or kirsh (optional)

3 cups flour
4 teaspoons baking powder
½ teaspoon salt
¼ cup sugar
¾ cup (1½ sticks) butter
1 cup milk

Crème Fraîche (see index)
  or sweetened whipped cream

1. Combine sliced strawberries, sugar and liqueur. Stir gently; chill 1 or 2 hours or overnight.
2. Preheat oven to 425°.
3. Sift flour, baking powder, salt, and sugar.
4. Cut in butter until particles are size of a pea.
5. Add milk all at once; stir just enough to moisten particles.
6. On a floured surface knead dough a few times. Roll or press to a ½-inch thickness. Cut with 2½- or 3-inch round biscuit cutter.
7. Bake for 8 to 10 minutes or until light golden brown.
8. Split biscuits; cover bottom of each with ¼ cup berries; cover with other half and an additional ¼ cup berries. Top with Crème Fraîche or sweetened whipped cream just before serving.

Individual Schaum Torte

A scrumptious alternative to shortcake.

9 egg whites, at room temperature
pinch salt
¼ teaspoon baking powder
scant 3 cups sugar
1 tablespoon white vinegar
1 teaspoon vanilla extract
1 quart strawberries, sliced and sweetened
  with ½ cup sugar
Vanilla ice cream or whipped cream

1. Preheat oven to 250°.
2. Combine egg whites, salt and baking powder in large mixer bowl; beat at high speed until stiff peaks form.
3. Slowly add sugar, a little at a time, beating well after each addition. Beat in vinegar and vanilla.
4. Drop 2 to 3 tablespoons on waxed paper lined cooke sheet, mounding upward. Bake 45 minutes.
5. Turn off oven but DO NOT OPEN oven door for 15 minutes. Then open door but do not remove tortes for 15 minutes longer.
6. To serve Schaum Tortes, cut off tops and fill with sliced strawberries and ice cream or whipped cream. Replace top.

Strawberry Bowl Cake

Yield: 12 servings

Light and luscious!

1 6-ounce package strawberry gelatin
2 cups boiling water
2 10-ounce packages frozen strawberries
   in syrup, thawed
1 teaspoon lemon juice
1 12-ounce package jellyroll
1 cup heavy cream, whipped

Strawberry Glaze

reserved strawberry syrup
2 teaspoons cornstarch

Must be made ahead.

1. In large bowl dissolve gelatin in boiling water.
2. Drain strawberries, reserving syrup. Purée strawberries in blender or food processor; add to gelatin with lemon juice. Chill, stirring occasionally, until mixture is as thick as unbeaten egg whites.
3. Meanwhile, cut jellyroll into ¼-inch slices. Line 2-quart rounded mixing bowl with plastic wrap. Arrange jellyroll slices close together to line bowl.
4. Fold whipped cream thoroughly into thickened gelatin mixture. Spoon into jellyroll-lined bowl. Chill until firm, about 3 hours or overnight.
5. Make Strawberry Glaze by combining strawberry syrup and cornstarch over medium heat, stirring constantly until mixture thickens. Cool.
6. Unmold dessert onto serving plate. Garnish with additional whipped cream, if desired and serve with Strawberry Glaze.

Sinful Chocolate-Berry Pie

Yield: one 9-inch pie

The chocolate-lovers' springtime favorite.

30 chocolate wafers, crushed
   to make 1½ cups
⅓ cup butter, melted
½ cup plus 2 tablespoons semisweet
   chocolate chips, divided
1 8-ounce package cream cheese, softened
¼ cup firmly packed brown sugar
½ teaspoon vanilla extract
1 cup whipping cream, whipped
1 pint fresh strawberries, hulled
1 teaspoon shortening

Must be made ahead.

1. Preheat oven to 325°. Combine crumbs and melted butter, mixing well. Press into bottom and sides of lightly greased 9-inch pie plate. Bake for 10 minutes. Cool crust completely.
2. Place ½ cup chocolate chips in top of double boiler; bring water to simmer over low heat and cook until chocolate melts. Set chocolate aside to cool slightly.
3. In bowl of mixer or in processor bowl, beat cream cheese until light and fluffy. Add brown sugar and vanilla, mixing well; add chocolate, mixing completely.

4. Fold whipped cream into cream cheese mixture; spoon filling into prepared crust. Chill at least 8 hours.

5. Set aside 1 large strawberry; slice remaining strawberries into thick vertical slices. Arrange slices over filling, overlapping slightly in concentric rows to form petal effect; place whole berry in center.

6. In small saucepan over low heat, combine remaining chocolate chips and shortening. Cook, stirring occasionally, until chips melt. Drizzle melted chocolate over strawberries.

Berry-Cheese Torte Supreme

A beautiful, lady-like dessert.

Yield: 8 to 10 servings

2 3-ounce packages lady fingers
2 8-ounce packages cream cheese, at room temperature
½ cup sugar
¾ teaspoon vanilla extract
1 teaspoon unflavored gelatin
2 tablespoons cold water
2 cups heavy cream
1 pint fresh strawberries

Must be made ahead.

1. Line bottom and sides of 9-inch springform pan with lady fingers, trimming to fit.

2. Using mixer or food processor, blend cheese and sugar until smooth. Add vanilla.

3. Sprinkle gelatin over water; let stand a minute or two, then place over hot water (or microwave 5 to 10 seconds) to dissolve gelatin. Set aside.

4. Reserving ¼ cup cream, whip remaining 1¾ cups with cheese mixture until soft peaks form. Stir reserved cream into gelatin and immediately pour into whipped mixture; continue beating until mixture begins to stiffen.

5. Pour half of mixture over lady fingers. Place another layer of lady fingers over cheese mixture in pan; cover with remaining cheese mixture. Chill 8 hours or overnight. Shortly before serving, wash, hull and dry berries and place them over entire top of torte. Remove sides of pan just prior to serving.

Transparent Pie

Yield: 8 servings

Could be the culinary rediscovery of the decade!

pastry for single crust 9-inch pie
  (see below)
½ cup (1 stick) butter, at room temperature
1¼ cups sugar
6 egg yolks
½ teaspoon lemon extract
nutmeg
1 cup heavy cream

1. Preheat oven to 250°. Line 8- or 9-inch glass pie plate with pastry, using recipe of preference or the one below.
2. Cream butter and sugar; add yolks, lemon extract and nutmeg, mixing well with wire whisk.
3. Whisk in cream. Pour into prepared pastry shell.
4. Bake 1 hour and 15 minutes at 250°. Raise oven temperature to 350° and bake 15 minute more to caramelize top. Cool completely before serving. This is best made a day ahead and stored at room temperature. Serve garnished on side with fresh whole strawberries, if desired.

Pastry for single crust:

2 cups sifted flour
1 tablespoon sugar
1 teaspoon salt
¾ cup shortening
1 egg yolk
1 teaspoon lemon juice
¼ cup milk

Must be made ahead.

Pie should have light brown crust, caramel brown top and yellow custard insides. Filling will be only ¾ to 1 inch deep.

Pastry:

1. Combine dry ingredients; add shortening and blend with pastry blender.
2. Mix together egg yolk, lemon juice and milk with fork; stir into dry ingredients to make soft dough.
3. Turn dough onto floured pastry cloth, invert bowl and let stand 10 minutes before rolling to fit pan.

This recipe dates back in my grandmother's family to 1830; she brought it with her to Indian Territory (later Oklahoma) when she and my grandfather moved up from Texas in 1902. Grannie made the pie five or six times a year with butter, cream and eggs supplied from our ranch. Now I have this pie on my birthday instead of cake, as does my eldest son. — J.E.H., Omaha, NE

Almond Shortbread Tart

Yield: 12 to 16 servings

A rich, cookie-like tart, good alone or with fresh fruit.

Crust:
2⅔ cups flour
1⅓ cups sugar
1⅓ cups unsalted butter
½ teaspoon salt
1 egg

Filling:
1 cup finely chopped almonds
½ cup sugar
1 teaspoon grated lemon peel
1 egg, slightly beaten
whole toasted almonds

1. Preheat oven to 325°. Grease a 9-inch springform pan.
2. Make crust: combine all crust ingredients in bowl of food processor. Process until dough forms a ball. Wrap in plastic wrap and chill.
3. Meanwhile, make filling: blend all ingredients, except whole nuts, in small bowl of mixer.
4. Divide chilled dough in two equal pieces; spread half in bottom of pan. Spread filling over crust to within ½ inch of sides of pan.
5. Roll remaining dough between two sheets of waxed paper to form a 9-inch circle. Remove top sheet of paper; place dough over filling and remove remaining waxed paper. Press edges together. Garnish with whole almonds.
6. Place a foil-covered baking sheet on oven rack under tart. Bake tart for 55 to 65 minutes or until light golden brown. Cool 15 minutes on wire rack; remove from pan. Cool completely before serving. Cut in thin wedges.

Hazelnut Cheesecake Bars

Yield: 16 to 24 bars

Try using different kinds of nuts in the crust, toasting them to enhance their flavor.

Crust layer:
⅓ cup butter, softened
⅓ cup brown sugar, packed
½ cup chopped toasted nuts*
   (hazelnuts, pecans, walnuts or almonds)
1 cup flour

Cheesecake layer:
1 8-ounce package cream cheese, softened
¼ cup granulated sugar
1 egg
2 tablespoons milk
1 tablespoon lemon juice
½ teaspoon vanilla extract

Recipe may be doubled and baked in a 13 x 9-inch pan.

1. Preheat oven to 350°.

2. Using mixer or food processor, cream together butter and sugar; add flour and nuts (if NOT using food processor, FINELY chop nuts before adding). Mix just until crumb mixture forms.

3. Reserve 1 cup of crumbs for topping. Press remainder into bottom of an 8- or 9-inch square pan. Bake for 12 to 15 minutes.

4. Prepare cheesecake layer: using mixer or food processor, combine all ingredients, mixing until smooth. Spread over baked crust. Sprinkle with reserved crumbs. Bake (at 350°) for 25 minutes.

5. Cool completely and cut into squares. Refrigerate until ready to serve.

*To toast nuts: spread nuts in single layer in baking pan. Toast in hot 400° oven for 8 to 10 minutes, or until lighly browned, stirring occasionally. For hazelnuts, rub warm nuts in a clean towel to remove skins.

Orange Marmalade Bars

Yield: 2 dozen

Vary the type of marmalade used until you find a favorite combination.

Crust:
2¼ cups flour
1 cup sugar
1 cup chopped walnuts
1 cup (2 sticks) butter, softened
1 egg

Filling:
1 11-ounce jar orange marmalade
   (Captain's Choice) Choose from
   Sweet, Bitter, Ginger Marmalade
   or Lemon Marmalade

1. Preheat oven to 350°. Grease bottom and sides of an 8- or 9-inch square baking pan.

2. Using mixer or food processor, prepare crust by combining all ingredients until crumbly. Reserve 1½ cups of mixture.

3. Press remaining crust mixture into bottom of prepared pan. Spread marmalade to within ½ inch of edge of pan. Crumble reserved mixture over preserves.

4. Bake 50 to 55 minutes or until lightly browned. Cool completely before cutting into bars.

Chocolate Layer Bars

Yield: 48 bars

**A decadent chocolate cream cheese layer sandwiched between rich pastry crusts.
A reward for finishing your tax forms!**

Filling:

2 cups (12-ounce package) chocolate chips
1 8-ounce package cream cheese
⅔ cup evaporated milk
1 cup chopped nuts

Pastry:

3 cups flour
1½ cups sugar
1 teaspoon baking powder
½ teaspoon salt
1 cup (2 sticks) butter, softened
2 eggs

1. Heat first three filling ingredients together in a saucepan over low heat until chips melt and mixture is smooth, stirring often. Remove from heat; add nuts. Set aside.
2. With electric mixer or food processor, combine pastry ingredients until coarse crumbs form.
3. Preheat oven to 375°. Press half of crumb mixture into bottom of 13 x 9-inch baking pan. Spread with chocolate filling. Sprinkle rest of crumb mixture evenly over top.
4. Bake 35 to 45 minutes, or until golden brown. Cool; cut into bars. Pig out!

Triple Layer Jam Sticks

Yield: 7 to 8 dozen

A special cookie for that extra-special event.

¾ cup (1½ sticks) butter, softened
2 cups sugar, divided
2 eggs
3 cups sifted cake flour
1 teaspoon vanilla extract
apricot jam (Captain's Choice)
2 egg whites
pinch of salt
1 tablespoon flour
1 cup chopped pecans

1. Preheat oven to 350°. Grease a 15½ x 10-inch jellyroll pan.
2. In mixing bowl or food processor, cream butter and 1 cup sugar until light and fluffy. Beat in eggs; gradually add flour and stir in vanilla.
3. Roll or pat out dough on greased jellyroll pan to a thickness of ¼ inch. Spread evenly with jam. Bake for 6 minutes.
4. In mixer bowl, beat egg whites with salt until frothy. Gradually beat in remaining 1 cup sugar combined with 1 tablespoon flour, beating until stiff peaks form. fold in pecans and spread over jam-covered cookie dough. Chill.
5. Cut dough into sticks approximately 2 x ½-inches. Place sticks on greased cookie sheets. Bake 15 minutes. Cool on wire rack.

FAVORITE SPRING RECIPES

SUMMER

SUMMER

Ah, summer at the Seaport! New Englanders, mindful of their short span of warm weather, pack more activities into this season than any other, and Mystic Seaport bustles with enough festivals, parades, and demonstrations to delight even its youngest visitor.

Good food, as always, plays an important summer role, as fruits, vegetables and various kinds of seafood, scarce in other seasons, become plentiful. Appropriately launching the first round of culinary events, the Seaport's annual Memorial Day weekend Lobster Festival serves up a traditional three-day food fest. Seaport visitors enjoy boiled lobster and corn on the cob under tents while strolling musicians serenade the crowd with timeless sea chanteys and folk tunes.

Your own backyard may lack the strolling musicians, but that's little reason not to prepare some seasonal specialties at home. Fire up your outdoor barbecue and try your hand at Swordfish Steaks with Pesto, Greek Lamb Kabobs with eggplant and fresh mushrooms, or colorful Strawberry Barbecued Chicken. Or take a tip from New Englanders and discover that lobster comes in other flavors besides boiled and broiled: Herbed Grilled Lobster is a treat not to be missed!

Summer abounds with picnic opportunities, and boats are stocked with "pack-and-go" meals and snacks that emphasize ease of preparation, leaving the cook free to participate in the many outdoor opportunities at hand. Those who tie up at the Seaport docks in mid-June will enjoy the Sea Music Festival with its three outdoor stages and continuous performances of sea songs in their natural environment. The 4th of July brings a 19th-century-style celebration revolving around scenes from New England's past, while the end of July marks the popular Antique and Classic Boat Rendezvous, when approximately 50 classic yachts in mint condition parade up and down the river to the appreciative cheering of onlookers.

And did you know that Mystic Seaport has its very own authentic steamboat, the Sabino, built in 1908 to serve the Damariscotta River and later the Maine islands of Casco Bay? Although she makes half-hour trips throughout the day, the Sabino makes a 90-minute excursion each evening, often with live entertainment, down river to Noank and out into Fisher's Island Sound. What better time to pack a cold Walnut Chicken or Shrimp Salad with Pineapple and savor the tranquility of the river, a little Dixieland jazz, and — cross your fingers — a full Mystic moon!

Ah, summer at the Seaport!

BEVERAGES

Fuzz Buster

A frosty toast to fresh peaches!

Yield: 6 to 8 servings

1 6-ounce can frozen limeade concentrate,
  undiluted
¾ cup vodka
2 medium peaches, unpeeled,
  sliced and pitted
¼ cup peachtree schnapps
cracked ice
lime slices (optional)

1. Combine first four ingredients in container of blender; process until smooth.
2. Gradually add ice, processing until mixture reaches desired consistency.
3. Serve in stemmed glasses garnished with lime slice, if desired.

Strawberries 'n Champagne Punch

Yield: 40 to 45 4-ounce servings

The ultimate summer punch.

1 quart strawberries, hulled and sliced
¼ to ½ cup superfine sugar
1 750 ml bottle dry white wine
1 cup Kirsch
4 750 ml bottles champagne, chilled
ice ring with whole strawberries (optional)

Must be made ahead.

1. Place strawberries in a bowl with sugar and white wine. Let stand for 2 to 3 hours to mellow.
2. In punch bowl, place ice ring or large block of ice. Add strawberry mixture, Kirsch and champagne.

Tequila Punch

Yield: 24 servings

Perfect beverage for a Southwestern-style cookout.

2 46-ounce cans grapefruit juice, chilled
4 cups tequila
1 cup fresh lemon juice
2 12-ounce cans ginger ale, chilled
cracked ice

Must be made ahead.

1. Early in the day, combine grapefruit juice, tequila and lemon juice; chill.
2. To serve, pour HALF of mixture over ice in large punch bowl. Slowly pour in 1 can of ginger ale; stir gently to mix.
3. Repeat with remaining ingredients when needed.

Lemonade with Tea Ice

Yield: 4 servings

Lemon with a different twist.

¾ cup freshly-squeezed lemon juice
  (about 4 medium lemons)
½ cup sugar
2 cups cold water
Tea Ice
lemon slices for garnish
mint leaves

Tea Ice:

1½ cups boiling water
4 regular tea bags
½ cup crushed mint leaves

Must be made ahead.

1. Combine lemon juice, sugar and water, stirring until sugar dissolves.
2. To serve, place several Tea Ice cubes in each glass. Pour in lemonade and garnish with lemon slices and mint leaves.

Tea Ice:

1. Pour boiling water over tea bags and mint; cover and let stand 10 minutes.
2. Discard tea bags; strain tea and pour into ice cube trays. Freeze solid. Makes about 2 dozen ice cubes.

Virgin Margarita

Yield: 8 servings

Everything but the tequila!

1 6-ounce can frozen lemonade concentrate, thawed
1 6-ounce can frozen limeade concentrate, thawed
2 egg whites
3 cups water
lemon-lime flavored seltzer water
lime juice
coarse salt
lime slices

Must be made ahead.

1. In bowl combine lemonade and limeade concentrates, egg whites and water. Transfer to freezer container, cover, and freeze 6 hours or overnight, stirring after 2 hours.
2. 30 minutes before serving, remove container from freezer; let stand at room temperature.
3. Dip rims of eight 8-ounce cocktail or margarita glasses into lime juice and then into coarse salt.
4. Spoon ⅔ cup frozen mixture into each rimmed glass; fill with lemon-lime seltzer water. Garnish with lime slice.

White Sangria

A refreshing beverage for porch-sitting.

2 750 ml bottles Sauterne, chilled
1 cup brandy
¼ cup sugar (extra fine, if available)
sliced fruit: 2 oranges, 1 lemon, 1 lime
1 1-liter bottle club soda, chilled

Must be made ahead.

1. In large pitcher, combine all ingredients, except club soda. Chill at least 1 hour.
2. Add ice and club soda to pitcher and serve.

Beach Plum Cordial

Yield: about 1 quart

Late August and September is the time for harvesting this uniquely New England fruit that grows by the sea. The easy preparation of this cordial does not require pitting the fruit.

1 cup beach plums, washed and stemmed
1 cup sugar
1 cup vodka

Must be made ahead.

1. Place ingredients in a clean 1-quart bottle. Shake well.
2. Let stand at room temperature for 3 weeks, gently shaking occasionally.
3. Strain mixture and bottle, or serve!

APPETIZERS

Clams Casino

Yield: 1 dozen clams

**These can be assembled several hours ahead
and refrigerated until ready to broil.**

1½ tablespoons butter
1 Spanish onion, diced
1 green pepper, diced
2 garlic cloves, minced
1 dozen little neck clams, opened,
   empty half shell discarded
3 slices Swiss cheese, cut into 4 squares
4 slices of bacon, cut into 3 pieces
lemon wedges

1. Heat butter in skillet over medium heat; add onion, pepper and garlic and sauté until soft, about 6 minutes.
2. Cover each clam on its shell with about a tablespoon of onion mixture.
3. Top with a square of cheese and piece of bacon. At this point clams may be covered and refrigerated for several hours.
4. Broil until bacon is crisp, watching closely. Serve with lemon wedges.

Mussels with Garlic

Yield: 4 to 6 servings

**Mussels are abundant along the New England coast, free for
the taking. Whether you buy them or gather them yourself,
here is a delicious way to serve them.**

2 tablespoons butter
2 tablespoons olive oil
1 small red pepper, finely chopped
1 small onion, minced
3 garlic cloves, minced
¼ teaspoon crushed red pepper flakes
¼ cup chopped fresh parsley
½ cup dry white wine
¼ teaspoon salt
2 garlic cloves, whole
4 pounds mussels

1. Heat butter and oil in saucepan over medium heat. Add red pepper, onion, garlic and red pepper flakes and cook, stirring often, about 4 minutes or until vegetables are soft. Add wine and salt; cook, stirring occasionally, about 3 minutes. Remove from heat, stir in parsley, cover and keep warm.
2. Scrub mussels, cut away beard and rinse well. Discard any mussels with broken shells and those that do not close when knife point touches inside muscle. Fill a large pot with an inch of water; bring to boil over high heat. Add whole garlic cloves and mussels. Cover; cook 5 to 7 minutes, stirring occasionally, until shells open. Discard any unopened mussels.
3. Place mussels on serving platter. Pour warm sauce over and serve.

Deviled Clams

6 to 8 quahogs, shucked, shells reserved
   or 1 pint preshucked clams
¼ cup (½ stick) butter
1 large onion, minced
¼ cup minced green pepper
1 roasted pepper, minced (from 7-ounce jar)
dash Worcestershire sauce
salt and pepper to taste
1 cup crushed saltine crackers
¼ cup sherry

1. Separate clams from clam liquor; reserve. Mince clams and set aside.

2. Heat butter in small skillet; sauté onion and green pepper until tender. Remove from heat.

3. Add roasted red pepper, seasonings, saltines and sherry, along with clams. Add enough clam liquor to moisten well.

4. Preheat oven to 350°. Butter inside of 6 to 8 quahog shells. Fill buttered shells with mixture. Place in a foil-lined 13 x 9-inch baking pan.

5. Bake for 25 minutes until browned on top. Serve hot, as an appetizer or main dish.

My father, who as a boy sold clams and oysters from a pushcart, always impressed the family with his skill in opening and scooping out the contents of the shells with only a few flicks of the wrist. At home, we bought both clams and oysters in their shells; the shells made excellent serving dishes, and with a minimum of chopping, sautéing and baking, we often had deviled clams for a quick dinner. In today's culture, this may seem like a lot of work, but, for my family, it was "fast food!" — L.K., Mystic, CT

Mexican Meatballs

Serve along with Tequila Punch or Virgin Margaritas (see index for both).

2 cups crumbled corn bread
1 15-ounce jar taco sauce or salsa,
   mild or hot
½ teaspoon salt
1½ pounds lean ground beef
1 8-ounce can tomato sauce
½ cup (2 ounces) shredded
   hot-pepper Monterey Jack cheese

1. Preheat oven to 350°.

2. Combine corn bread crumbs, ½ cup taco sauce and the salt. Add meat; mix well. Shape into 1-inch balls.

3. Place meatballs on rack in broiler pan. Bake, uncovered, for about 20 minutes, or until done. At this point meatballs may be frozen or refrigerated until needed. To reheat, cover with foil and warm in oven.

4. In small saucepan heat together tomato sauce and remaining taco sauce. Place cooked meatballs in chafing dish; cover with sauce and top with shredded cheese. Keep warm over low heat. Serve with wooden picks or scoop up with tortilla chips.

Chastain Shrimp

Yield: 6 to 8 servings

"The most divine shrimp you ever ate."

2½ pounds shrimp
½ cup celery tops
3½ teaspoons salt
¼ cup mixed pickling spice
4 to 5 onions, thinly sliced (use Vidalia,
   if available)
7 or 8 bay leaves

Marinade:

2½ cups vegetable oil
1½ cups white vinegar
2 to 3 teaspoons salt, to taste
5 teaspoons celery seed
¼ teaspoon Tabasco sauce

Must be made ahead.

1. Boil shrimp in water to cover with celery tops, salt and pickling spice; cook just until shrimp turn pink.
2. Cool shrimp; shell and devein. In a container alternate layers of shrimp and sliced onion. Tuck 7 or 8 bay leaves among the layers.
3. Mix together all ingredients for marinade. Pour over shrimp, cover and marinate AT LEAST 24 hours in refrigerator. Drain before serving.

Sabino Shrimp Cocktail

Yield: 10 to 12 servings

Prepared by Chef Don Dawson of The Seamen's Inne for a Dixieland Jazz Cruise aboard the Sabino, this dish put jazz into the evening's menu.

3 pounds cooked shrimp, shelled
   and deveined but with tails on
½ cup extra-virgin olive oil
½ cup vegetable oil
4 scallions, chopped
3 celery ribs, quartered
3 garlic cloves, halved
5 tablespoons grained Dijon mustard
½ cup red wine vinegar
3 tablespoons paprika
¼ to ½ teaspoon Tabasco sauce
   (hotness to taste!)

Must be made ahead.

1. Combine all ingredients, EXCEPT shrimp, in bowl of food processor fitted with steel blade. Process until smooth.
2. Place shrimp in a 13 x 9-inch shallow baking dish and cover with sauce. Refrigerate overnight or 24 hours.
3. Serve with wooden picks and lots of paper napkins!

Poisson Cru (Tahitian Marinated Fish)   Yield: 8 appetizer servings

This dish demonstrates French influence on Tahitian cuisine.
Use the freshest fish possible.

1 pound flounder, sole or other fresh
  white fish
2 large onions, divided
salt and coarsely ground pepper
juice of 3 or 4 large lemons
1 large sweet green pepper
1 cucumber, coarsely chopped
1 14-ounce can UNSWEETENED
  coconut milk*

* available in oriental food shops

Must be made ahead.

1. Skin and bone fish; break flesh into bite-size pieces. Place in shallow baking dish.
2. Coarsely chop one onion and add to fish. Generously season with salt and pepper.
3. Cover fish completely with fresh lemon juice. Cover dish with plastic wrap and refrigerate 6 hours.
4. Remove fish from lemon juice and gently dry with paper towels. Discard onions.
5. Place fish in an attractive glass bowl and combine with coarsely chopped remaining onion, green pepper and cucumber. Cover with coconut milk. Chill thoroughly.
6. Correct seasonings and serve on a bed of Boston lettuce, if desired.

Eggplant Appetizer (Caponata)   Yield: about 2½ cups

Serve with crackers as a spread or with grilled meats as a relish.

1 large unpeeled eggplant, diced
½ cup plus 2 tablespoons olive oil
2½ cups very thinly sliced onion
1 cup chopped celery
1 16-ounce can tomato sauce
¼ cup red wine vinegar
2 tablespoons sugar
2 tablespoons capers, drained
½ teaspoon salt, dash pepper
12 black olives, pitted and slivered

Must be made ahead.

1. Brown eggplant in ½ cup oil until tender; remove from pan and set aside.
2. Add 2 tablespoons oil and sauté onion and celery until tender but not mushy. Return eggplant to pan.
3. Add tomato sauce, bring to a boil, reduce heat and simmer, covered, for 15 minutes.
4. Add vinegar, sugar, capers, salt, pepper and olives; simmer 30 to 45 minutes.
5. Chill overnight before serving. Serve at room temperature.

Norman's Smoked Olives

A very individual recipe.

jar of whole pitted green olives,
  with or without pimento
1 or many thinly sliced garlic cloves
1 tablespoon dill seed (approx.)
1 tablespoon liquid barbecue smoke (approx.)

Add all ingredients to jar of olives. Cover, shake a bit and KEEP FINGERS OUT OF JAR for at least an hour. Enjoy.

When sailing as Second Mate on a research vessel, the Chief Mate and I used to take an occasional and illegal before-dinner martini to unwind from the vagaries of scientific requirements. The olives for this furtive exercise were supplied by the Chief Mate's girlfriend, who had improved upon the natural product with garlic and other spices. The recipe is my version, which seems to elicit rave notices. — N.G.C., Grafton, VA

Pesto Dip with Garden Crudités   Yield: about 2 cups

An ideal hors d'oeuvre for the gardener. Use the freshest vegetables available.

⅔ cup pesto, available pre-made in
  supermarkets or see below
8 ounces cream cheese
¼ cup sour cream or plain yogurt

Vegetables for dipping:

pea pods, zucchini sticks, asparagus, green beans, red radishes, cherry tomatoes, red or green pepper strips, broccoli and other fresh raw veggies.

Pesto:

3 cups fresh basil leaves, packed
3 garlic cloves
½ cup pine nuts or almonds
¾ cup fresh parsley, packed
¾ cup fresh Parmesan cheese
½ cup extra-virgin olive oil
¼ cup melted butter
salt and freshly ground pepper to taste

1. Combine pesto, cheese and sour cream or yogurt in food processor fitted with steel blade. Process until smooth.

2. Transfer dip to bowl, cover and refrigerate a couple of hours to blend flavors.

3. Suggested presentation: line a pretty basket, such as a twig or grapevine basket, with a checkered napkin. Group vegetables of like kind together to produce a look of abundance; arrange groups with an eye toward color, size and texture. Place bowl of dip among vegetables. The result should be a picture of summer's bounty!

Pesto preparation:

1. Combine all ingredients for pesto in container of blender or food processor. Process until smooth.

2. Store, covered, in refrigerator or freeze. Use in dip, on pasta or in minestrone soup. Also good on fresh cooked green beans and other vegetables.

SOUPS

Cream of Carrot and Tomato Soup

Yield: about 3 quarts
(12 servings)

**An ideal soup for late summer when tomatoes
are ripe and juicy. May be served cold on a hot day
or hot when sailing on a brisk day that hints of fall.**

4 cups peeled ripe tomatoes, quartered
2 pounds carrots, trimmed, scraped
   and cut in rounds
6 tablespoons butter, divided
salt and pepper to taste
¼ cup water
3 tablespoons flour
1 13¾-ounce can chicken broth
1 quart half-and-half
Tabasco sauce to taste
1 tablespoon plus snipped fresh dill

1. Put tomatoes in saucepan; cook uncovered, over low heat about 30 minutes.

2. Sauté carrots in 3 tablespoons butter in large skillet for 2 to 3 minutes. Add salt and pepper and water; cover and cook 30 minutes until quite tender.

3. Meanwhile, melt remaining 3 tablespoons of butter in a saucepan and add flour; cook, stirring with wire whisk, for about a minute. Add chicken broth gradually while stirring rapidly with whisk. When mixture is thickened and smooth, cook over low heat, stirring occasionally, for about 30 minutes.

4. Combine tomatoes, carrots and broth. Working in 2 or 3 batches, purée soup in blender or food processor.

5. Return soup to a large pot; bring to boil. Lower heat and add half-and-half. Add Tabasco; correct seasonings. Stir in dill and serve hot, or refrigerate and serve chilled. Garnish with additional fresh dill, if desired.

Noank Gazpacho

Yield: 4 servings

**Unlike the Spanish original,
the vegetables are cooked first, then chilled.**

5 medium-size ripe tomatoes, halved
1 large cucumber, sliced
2 medium green peppers, halved and seeded
1 medium sweet red pepper,
  halved and seeded
1 large Bermuda onion, sliced
1 or 2 garlic cloves
several sprigs of fresh basil
several sprigs of fresh Italian parsley
dash MSG (optional)
salt and pepper to taste
¼ cup olive oil
¼ cup water
2 celery ribs, diced
scallions (optional)

May be served hot.

1. Combine all ingredients except scallions in a large saucepan over medium heat. Cook about 45 minutes, stirring occasionally.
2. Cool. Purée in blender or food processor container. Chill. Serve topped with chopped scallions, if desired.

Chilled Green Pepper Soup

Yield: about 2 quarts

Colorful and refreshing.

8 medium sweet green peppers,
  finely chopped
2 large onions, finely chopped
3 tablespoons butter, divided
1 tablespoon flour
1 cup milk
½ teaspoon salt, or to taste
⅛ teaspoon white pepper
2 13¾-ounce cans chicken broth
1 to 2 cups buttermilk

1 small red pepper, finely chopped

Variation:
Prepare soup with sweet red peppers and garnish with green peppers.

Must be made ahead.

1. In large skillet sauté pepper and onion in 2 tablespoons butter over medium-high heat for 8 to 10 minutes until tender.
2. Melt remaining 1 tablespoon butter in small saucepan; add flour and cook, stirring, 1 minute. Gradually add milk, stirring until sauce is thick and bubbly. Add salt and pepper.
3. Combine white sauce, broth and pepper mixture. Working in two batches, purée soup in food processor or blender. Stir in buttermilk to desired consistency. Chill.
4. To serve, garnish each bowl of soup with chopped red pepper.

Summer Spinach Soup

Yield: 4 servings

A wonderful mix of ingredients. Do include the salmon, if possible.

3 scallions
½ cup cucumber, peeled and seeded
4 sprigs EACH fresh parsley and dill
1 pound fresh spinach
3 cups chicken broth
salt and pepper, to taste
pinch sugar
2 slices smoked salmon (optional)

Must be made ahead.

1. Coarsely chop scallions, cucumber, parsley and dill in food processor, or by hand; set aside.
2. Wash spinach, drain and sprinkle with salt. Place in a saucepan; cook over low heat 4 to 5 minutes, using only water clinging to leaves.
3. Remove from heat and purée undrained spinach in food processor or blender.
4. Add reserved vegetables and chicken broth and blend until all vegetables are finely chopped.
5. Season soup with salt, pepper and pinch of sugar. Chill well.
6. Serve cold, garnishing each serving with thin strips of sliced salmon, if desired.

Fresh Tomato Soup

Yield: 6 servings

A good way to use up tomatoes at the end of gardening season.

2 tablespoons olive oil
2 tablespoons butter
2 medium onions, chopped
2 pounds fresh tomatoes, peeled and quartered
1 6-ounce can tomato paste
2 tablespoons dried basil (or ¼ cup chopped fresh basil)
4 teaspoons dried thyme (or 2 tablespoons fresh thyme)
3 cups chicken broth
1 teaspoon salt, or to taste
ground black pepper

1. Heat oil and butter in large saucepan and sauté onions just until tender.
2. Add tomatoes, tomato paste, basil and thyme, mashing up tomatoes slightly with back of large spoon.
3. Add chicken broth; bring mixture to a boil. Reduce heat and simmer, covered, for 40 minutes. Season to taste with salt and pepper. Serve hot.

BREADS

Garlic-Cheese Spread 'n Bread
Yield: 1 loaf

A different approach to bread when it's too hot to bake.

½ cup (1 stick) butter
3 tablespoons sour cream
½ cup grated Cheddar cheese
1 garlic clove, minced
3 tablespoons grated Parmesan cheese

Try spread on thick-sliced Italian bread and serve with steak or lobster, or on thinly sliced bread as an hors d'oeuvre.

1. Mix together all ingredients until well blended.
2. Spread on bread slices of choice. Broil until bubbly. Serve hot.

South of the Border Bread
Yield: 1 loaf

A filling snack bread or a hearty hors d'oeuvre. Olé!

1 1-pound loaf frozen bread dough, thawed
1 egg, beaten
⅛ to ¼ teaspoon chili powder
¼ pound bacon, fried and crumbled
1 4-ounce can whole green chillies, drained and seeded
4- to 6-ounces shredded sharp Cheddar cheese
poppy seeds

1. Preheat oven to 375°. Grease 13 x 9-inch jelly-roll pan; spread dough with hands to edges.
2. Mix egg with chili powder; spread half of mixture over dough.
3. Cover dough with bacon, then green chilies, spreading flat, and then with cheese.
4. Roll dough lengthwise, stretching at the end to pull over and seal. Place seam-side down, forming a ring and lapping one end inside the other.
5. Glaze with remaining egg wash. Sprinkle with poppy seeds.
6. Bake for 25 minutes. Serve hot or at room temperature.

In the 1850's, it was unheard of to eat oatmeal for breakfast in the summer, as it was "known" to heat the blood.

Glazed Blueberry Muffins, Homestead Farm

Yield: 2 dozen

May be made with fresh or frozen blueberries — a 4-star recipe.

1½ cups sugar
3 cups flour
4 teaspoons baking powder
1 teaspoon salt
2 teaspoons dried orange peel
   (such as Ehler's)
2 eggs, slightly beaten
⅔ cup milk
1 teaspoon vanilla extract
1 teaspoon orange extract
½ cup (1 stick) butter or margarine, melted
2 cups blueberries, thawed and drained
   if frozen

Glaze:

2 tablespoons butter or margarine
¼ cup sugar
1 tablespoon orange juice
½ teaspoon orange extract

Variation:

Lemon juice, lemon extract and lemon peel
may be substituted for the orange.

1. Preheat oven to 350°. Line two muffin pans with paper liners or grease well.

2. In large bowl, sift together sugar, flour, baking powder, salt and dried orange peel.

3. In another bowl, combine eggs, milk, extracts and melted butter.

4. Pour milk mixture all at once into flour mixture; stir just until moistened. Fold in blueberries.

5. Fill muffin cups three-quarters full. Bake 20 to 25 minutes.

6. Meanwhile, prepare glaze: mix together all ingredients in small saucepan; cook over low heat until smooth.

7. When muffins are done, remove from oven and spoon a teaspoon of glaze over each while still hot.

Nectarine Bran Muffins

Yield: 1 dozen

You knew bran was good for you; now you know how to make it taste good, too!

1 cup wheat bran cereal
½ cup orange juice
¾ cup flour
¼ cup whole wheat flour
¼ cup brown sugar, packed
2½ teaspoons baking powder
¼ teaspoon salt
1 egg, beaten
¼ cup vegetable oil
1 large nectarine, chopped (about 1 cup)

Variation: Apple Bran Muffins

In the fall substitute ½ cup apple cider or apple juice for the orange juice and 1 large chopped apple for nectarine.

1. Preheat oven to 400°. Grease or line standard muffin pans.

2. In small bowl combine cereal and orange juice; let stand several minutes for bran to absorb juice.

3. Meanwhile, in large bowl combine flours, sugar, baking powder and salt.

4. Stir egg and oil into bran mixture until well mixed; add to flour mixture along with chopped nectarine. Stir just until dry ingredients are moistened.

5. Spoon batter into prepared muffin pans. Bake for 20 to 25 minutes, or until a wooden toothpick inserted in center comes out clean.

Peach Bread

Yield: 2 loaves

Take this on a weekend cruise for breakfast, lunch or snack.

½ cup (1 stick) butter, softened
1 cup sugar
3 eggs
2¾ cups flour
1½ teaspoons baking powder
½ teaspoon baking soda
1 teaspoon salt
1½ teaspoons ground cinnamon
dash nutmeg
2 cups coarsely chopped fresh peaches
3 tablespoons frozen orange juice
  concentrate, thawed
1 teaspoon vanilla extract

1. Preheat oven to 350°. Grease and flour two 8½ x 4½-inch loaf pans.
2. Cream butter and sugar, beating well. Add eggs, one at a time, beating well after each addition.
3. Combine next six ingredients; add alternately to creamed mixture with peaches, beginning and ending with flour mixture. Stir in orange juice and vanilla.
4. Pour into prepared pans. Bake 50 to 60 minutes or until tester inserted in center comes out clean.
5. Cool in pans 10 minutes; remove and cool completely before slicing.

Peach Coffee Cake

Yield: 8 servings

Wouldn't you like to wake up to this for brunch?

½ cup (1 stick) butter, softened
½ cup plus 2 tablespoons sugar
2 eggs
1 teaspoon vanilla extract
1 cup plus 1 tablespoon flour
1 teaspoon baking powder
½ teaspoon salt
3 medium peaches (about 1 pound)
  peeled and sliced
1 teaspoon cinnamon
dash nutmeg
¼ cup peach preserves
1 tablespoon Cointreau or orange liqueur

1. Preheat oven to 350°. Grease bottom and sides of 8-inch springform pan or an 8-inch square pan.
2. In large mixer bowl, cream butter and ½ cup sugar; add eggs one at a time, beating well after each addition. Add vanilla.
3. In small bowl, combine 1 cup flour, baking powder and salt. Gradually add to creamed mixture; mix well.
4. Spread batter evenly in prepared pan. Arrange peach slices spoke-fashion from center over batter. Combine 2 tablespoons sugar, 1 tablespoon flour, cinnamon and nutmeg. Sprinkle over peaches.
5. Bake 50 to 55 minutes until tester inserted in center comes out clean.
6. Heat peach preserves and liqueur in small saucepan; bring to boil; strain. Brush over hot cake. Remove sides from springform pan; cool cake on wire rack.

MAIN DISHES

Marinated Beef Spirals

Yield: 4 to 6 servings

Dress up a London broil while tenderizing it in a tasty marinade.

2 pounds London broil steak (chuck shoulder)

Marinade:

¾ cup peanut oil
½ cup soy sauce
2 tablespoons vinegar
1½ teaspoons grated fresh ginger root
1 garlic clove, sliced
2 scallions, coarsely chopped

Must be made ahead.

1. Slice beef thinly, across the grain, on the diagonal. Roll strips to form pinwheels and secure with wooden picks. Smaller end pieces can be wrapped one around the other to form larger pinwheels. Place spirals in an oblong glass baking dish.
2. Prepare marinade: place all ingredients in container of blender. Blend until smooth. Pour marinade over spirals being careful to coat each well. Refrigerate and marinate for at least 8 hours.
3. Prepare grill. Cook over hot coals in usual fashion until cooked to desired degree of doneness.

Grilled Eye of Round

Yield: about 4 servings per pound

Simply superb!

1 beef eye of round, any size
Kosher salt
waxed paper

1. Light charcoal briquets in outdoor barbecue. Do not put grill rack on the barbecue.
2. Roll eye of round in Kosher salt until it is well coated on all sides and on ends. Wrap coated meat in 3 layers of waxed paper, twisting the ends tightly to secure them.
3. When the coals in the barbecue are grey, place wrapped meat directly into the hot coals. Roast for 11 minutes on each of the three sides for rare, 12 minutes per side for medium, or 13 minutes per side for well done. The timing must be exact and is the same for any size eye of round.

Marinated Flank Steak

Yield: 4 to 6 servings

Try accompanying steak with a pea pod salad such as the one on page 130 in <u>Christmas Memories Cookbook</u>.

1 2-pound flank steak of beef

Marinade:

¼ cup soy sauce
¼ cup honey
¼ cup vegetable oil
¼ cup fresh lemon juice
2 garlic cloves, minced

Must be made ahead.

1. The night before: wipe steak with paper towels. Lightly score with knife in diamond pattern. Place in nonmetallic baking dish.

2. Mix together all ingredients for marinade; pour over steak taking care to coat entirely. Cover tightly with plastic wrap and refrigerate no less than 24 hours. For ease in transporting to boat or beach, place steak with marinade in a heavy-duty zip-sealed plastic bag. Turn at least once during day.

3. To grill: pour off marinade and cook over hot coals 6 to 7 minutes on first side, 11 to 15 minutes on second side for medium doneness or cook to taste. May also be broiled in oven.

"Beach" Wellington

Yield: 12 servings

Bet you can think of numerous occasions to serve this versatile, portable entrée.

1 pound lean ground beef round
½ pound bulk sausage
1½ cups chopped onion
3 tablespoons butter
salt and ground pepper to taste
2 teaspoons oregano
2 tablespoons minced fresh parsley
1 teaspoon dried basil
½ cup freshly grated Parmesan cheese
½ cup ricotta cheese
1 8-ounce package cream cheese
1 egg, lightly beaten
2 sheets frozen puff pastry, thawed

1. In a large skillet, brown ground beef, drain and place in large mixing bowl. Brown sausage in skillet; drain and add to beef.

2. Sauté onion in butter until tender. Add to meat along with seasonings, cheeses and egg. Mix well. Chill. (May be prepared to this point up to a day ahead.)

3. Preheat oven to 400°. Roll out pastry sheets to form one large rectangle. Place meat mixture in a strip down center of pastry. Fold up ends, then sides of pastry to form a log or roll, dampening edges with water to seal. Place seam side down on cookie sheet. Make diagonal slits partially through top of pastry. Bake 30 to 35 minutes, or until golden brown and puffed.

4. Let stand 30 minutes before serving. Serve with Dill Sauce, if desired.

Dill Sauce:

1 cup plain yogurt
1 cup mayonnaise
1 teaspoon grated onion
2 teaspoons dried dill
dash Tabasco

Sauce preparation: Yield: 2 cups

1. Mix together all ingredients.
2. Chill several hours to blend flavors. Serve with "Beach" Wellington.

Grilled Butterflied Leg of Lamb   Yield: 6 to 8 servings

For an elegant summer cookout!

1 leg of lamb (about 6 pounds) boned and butterflied by butcher
¼ cup red wine vinegar
¾ cup olive oil
2 garlic cloves, minced
½ teaspoon rosemary, crushed
½ teaspoon salt
1 bay leaf, crumbled
¼ teaspoon freshly ground pepper

Must be made ahead.

1. Flatten out meat of boned leg of lamb to make it as uniform as possible for even grilling.
2. Place lamb in shallow baking dish. In small bowl mix together remaining ingredients; pour over lamb. Cover dish with plastic wrap and refrigerate 12 to 24 hours, turning once or twice.
3. About an hour before cooking, remove meat from refrigerator.
4. Prepare grill. When coals are medium-hot, remove meat from marinade and place on grill, fat side up, 5 or 6 inches above coals. Grill 40 to 45 minutes, basting often with marinade, turning occasionally. Test for doneness by cutting a slit in center of lamb: meat should look slightly pink inside and crusty brown outside. Do not overcook; meat will continue cooking for several minutes after it is removed from grill.
5. Carve by cutting thin slices across the grain.

Greek Lamb Kabobs

Yield: 6 to 8 servings

If available, use fresh rosemary and thyme instead of dried.

2 pounds lamb (or beef),
   cut into 1½-inch cubes

Marinade:

1 teaspoon salt
2 cups water
2 cups vinegar
3 bay leaves
2 large onions, sliced
1 tablespoon thyme
   or ½ teaspoon dried thyme
1 tablespoon rosemary or
   ½ teaspoon dried rosemary
1 teaspoon sugar

Vegetables of choice:
   cherry tomatoes, onion wedges,
   green pepper squares, zucchini chunks,
   eggplant cubes, mushrooms

Must be made ahead.

1. Combine all marinade ingredients in saucepan over high heat; bring to boil. Cool to lukewarm.
2. Pour marinade over lamb cubes in glass baking dish. Marinate in refrigerator for 6 to 24 hours, turning occasionally.
3. Thread meat cubes onto skewers with desired vegetables. Cook kabobs over hot coals, brushing occasionally with marinade, until cooked to desired degree of doneness. Good with rice pilaf.

Some cooks choose to cook skewered meat separately from skewered vegetables in order to prevent overcooking of the vegetables. Be sure to brush vegetables with marinade, too.

Barbecued Pork Ribs Napatree

Yield: 4 to 6 servings

Prepare the ribs ahead of time, then grill at the beach or picnic site.

3 pounds country-style pork ribs
¼ cup soy sauce
⅓ cup corn syrup
⅓ cup lemon juice
2 garlic cloves, minced
½ teaspoon dry mustard
¼ teaspoon ground cloves
¼ teaspoon Tabasco sauce
¼ teaspoon salt

Must be made ahead.

1. Cut ribs apart and place in shallow 2-quart non-metallic baking dish.
2. Combine remaining ingredients; pour over ribs. Cover and marinate overnight in refrigerator, turning ribs in marinade at least once.
3. Cook ribs in marinade in microwave at 75% power (medium-high) for 20 minutes.
4. Turn ribs, rotate baking dish and continue microwaving at 75% power (medium-high) for 20 minutes. Discard marinade and fat drippings in pan.
5. At this point ribs may be frozen to grill later or cooked on grill for 10 to 15 minutes per side.

Carolina Bar-B-Que

Yield: 6 to 8 servings

**Southerners treat good barbecue with great reverence
and guard their secret recipes. Two Massachusetts chefs,
with southern connections, share their secrets here.**

1 4- to 8-pound pork roast
  (loin, shoulder, butt or fresh picnic)

Barbecue sauce:

3½ cups cider vinegar
3 cups ketchup
1¾ cups Worcestershire sauce
½ cup honey
4 medium onions, chopped
½ cup brown sugar
1 tablespoon salt
1 tablespoon coarsely ground black pepper
2 tablespoons Tabasco sauce
8 garlic cloves, halved
cayenne pepper to taste

Sauce:　　　　　　　Yield: about 2 quarts

1. Place liquid ingredients in large pot
   and heat slowly almost to boiling. Add onions
   and dry ingredients, stirring constantly until
   well blended.
2. Cover, lower heat and simmer
   45 to 60 minutes, stirring occasionally.

**Sauce may be used as a marinade for
other meats or as a condiment. Freezes well.**

Must be made ahead.

Place pork roast in large bowl and partially
cover with sauce. Cover bowl; marinate in refrigerator overnight, turning roast several times.

Cooking Methods

1. Prepare pork in a water pan smoker.
   Fill water pan with marinade; add water,
   if necessary. For best results use a
   combination of hickory and maple wood
   chips for smoking. Cook pork to an internal
   temperature of 170°. Remove from heat;
   let stand about 20 minutes.
2. If no smoker is available, use kettle grill
   (without water pan). Smoke and cook
   as above.
3. If neither of above methods is available,
   pork may be cooked in a slow oven (300°).
   Baste frequently with sauce to which one
   tablespoon "Liquid Smoke" has been added.
   Allow approximately 45 minutes per pound
   for roast to reach internal temperature
   of 170°.

To serve:

"Chop" or "shred" the roast; mix with several
cups of remaining Barbecue Sauce. Serve Bar-
B-Que as a sandwich on a bun. Delicious with
Calico Coleslaw (see index), french fries and (!)
hushpuppies. Pass extra sauce.

Grilled Game Hens in Blueberry Marinade   Yield: 4 to 8 servings

**Once you've made the delicious Blueberry Vinegar (see index),
you'll want to try these tasty morsels. Count on a whole bird
for hearty appetites, half for the daintier.**

4 Rock Cornish hens
  (about 1 pound each), split
1 pint fresh or frozen blueberries
1 cup Blueberry Vinegar (see index or
  purchased at a gourmet specialty shop)
⅔ cup olive oil
3 small bay leaves
2 teaspoons fresh thyme
  or 1 teaspoon dried thyme
salt and freshly ground black pepper, to taste

Must be made ahead.

**For an elegant picnic, transport marinating birds
in zip-sealed bags packed in a cooler and
grill on boat or beach.**

1. One day before serving, rinse hens, pat dry
and place in shallow baking dish.
2. Combine blueberries and vinegar in
saucepan; heat to boiling and boil 1 minute.
Remove from heat.
3. Stir in remaining ingredients; cool to
room temperature.
4. Pour marinade over hens. Marinate in
refrigerator overnight, turning several times.
5. Prepare grill. When coals are hot, grill hens
a few inches above coals, basting often with
marinade. Birds are cooked when juices from
cut made in thickest part of thighs runs
clear. To insure even cooking, hens may be
microwaved about 10 minutes before
placing on grill. Game hens also may be
roasted in 400° oven for 45 minutes,
basting occasionally with marinade.

Chicken Breasts, Lime and Cantaloupe   Yield: 4 to 6 servings

A light dish without heavy sauces or seasoning.

3 pounds chicken breast halves
1 teaspoon salt
½ teaspoon tarragon
⅛ teaspoon pepper
2 tablespoons peanut oil
1 cup chopped onion
3½ cups chicken broth
juice of 3 limes
1 tablespoon sugar
1 medium cantaloupe, peeled, seeded
  and cut into wedges
1 teaspoon grated lime peel, for garnish

1. Rub chicken with salt, tarragon and pepper.
In Dutch oven over medium heat, heat oil.
Add chicken and brown on all sides. Add
onion and sauté 5 minutes more or until
onions are tender. Add chicken broth. Cover
and cook 35 to 40 minutes or until chicken
is tender.
2. Remove chicken to large platter; keep warm.
Skim off any fat from broth remaining in
Dutch oven. Add lime juice and sugar to
broth; boil rapidly until it is reduced to
1 cup. Add cantaloupe wedges and continue
cooking just until melon is heated through.
3. Arrange cantaloupe around chicken on
platter. Pour sauce over chicken and fruit.
Garnish with grated lime peel.

Stuffed Chicken Breasts Rellenos   Yield: 4 servings

As hot as you like depending on the chilies you use.

4 chicken breast halves,
   skinned and boned
¼ teaspoon salt
2 canned green chilies, halved
   or 4 jalapeño peppers, seeded
4 ounces hot-pepper Monterey Jack cheese,
   cut into 4 strips and 4 slices
½ cup flour
1 egg, beaten
1 tablespoon milk
1 cup soft bread crumbs
vegetable oil
1 16-ounce jar "medium" taco sauce
   (or hotter to taste)
3 tablespoons chopped fresh cilantro
   (coriander)
3 tablespoons chopped green onion
additional chopped cilantro for garnish

1. Pound each chicken breast between sheets of waxed paper, to ¼-inch thickness using a meat mallet or rolling pin. Sprinkle with salt.

2. Place a halved green chile, or seeded jalapeño, and a strip of cheese on each flattened chicken piece. Roll up lengthwise, tucking in edges, and secure with wooden picks.

3. Dredge chicken in flour. Combine egg and milk. Dip chicken in egg mixture and roll in bread crumbs.

4. Preheat oven to 350°. Arrange stuffed breasts in greased baking dish. Bake, covered, for 30 minutes. Uncover and continue baking for 15 minutes more. Combine taco sauce, cilantro and green onion. During last 5 minutes of baking put a slice of cheese and a generous spoonful of taco sauce on each breast.

5. To serve: sprinkle with additional chopped cilantro; pass extra taco sauce.

Strawberry Barbecued Chicken   Yield: 4 servings

How versatile strawberries are!

2 2½-pound broiler-fryers, halved or cut up
1½ teaspoons salt, or to taste
¼ to ½ teaspoon pepper
¼ cup vegetable oil
1½ tablespoons Worcestershire sauce
4 tablespoons lemon juice, divided
1 cup red currant jelly (Captain's Choice)
1 pint strawberries, sliced lengthwise

1. Prepare charcoal grill.

2. Rub chicken pieces with salt and pepper. Combine oil, Worcestershire and 2 tablespoons lemon juice.

3. Place chicken on grill over hot coals, skin side up; grill about 20 minutes, basting occasionally with oil mixture. Turn chicken; cook 20 minutes more, or until done, basting occasionally.

4. Meanwhile, heat jelly to melting point; stir in remaining 2 tablespoons lemon juice, remove from heat and keep warm. Just before serving, gently stir in sliced berries.

5. Pass warm sauce to pour over each portion of chicken.

Cold Walnut Chicken

Yield: 6 to 8 servings

A make-ahead entrée for summer entertaining.

6 whole chicken breasts, boned, skinned
  and halved
2 medium onions, halved
4 garlic cloves, peeled
1¼ teaspoons crushed red pepper flakes
2½ to 3 cups chicken broth
1 teaspoon imported sweet paprika
1½ cups walnuts, toasted at 350°
  for 5 minutes
¼ cup sour cream
1 slice firm white bread, torn
12 walnut halves for garnish
watercress for garnish

Must be made ahead.

1. Place chicken, onion, 2 garlic cloves and red pepper flakes in large pot and cover with broth. Bring to a boil. Cover, reduce heat and simmer until chicken is fork-tender, about 40 minutes.

2. Remove chicken; set aside. Strain broth; skim off fat. Return broth to pot; add paprika. Boil rapidly, uncovered, until liquid is reduced to 1½ cups. Cool to room temperature.

3. Place toasted walnuts in bowl of food processor; process until very fine. Add 2 garlic cloves and sour cream; process until well blended. Add bread; process until mixture forms a paste. With motor running, gradually add cooled broth, scrape sides of bowl and process until smooth.

4. Arrange chicken breasts on large serving platter. Spoon walnut sauce over chicken. Cover tightly with plastic wrap and refrigerate for up to 48 hours.

5. To serve: allow to come to room temperature. Garnish each chicken breast with a walnut half; garnish platter with watercress.

84

GRILLED FISH

Sportsman have known for years that one of the best ways to prepare fresh fish is to grill it. Now grilled fish is growing in popularity and many people find it fun to experiment with different charcoals and wood chips for flavoring, such as mesquite, hickory or cherry wood chips. The following are some general guidelines to consider when grilling.

- Fish steaks are an excellent choice for grilling. To calculate an accurate cooking time, measure the thickness of the fish at the thickest part. A rule of thumb is to allow 10 minutes per inch of fish. If fish is frozen, double this time.

- Dark-fleshed fish is ideal for cooking on the grill because the higher fat content requires less basting. White fish, however, contains little fat and needs to be brushed frequently with an oil, butter or marinade to keep it moist while cooking.

- A hinged wire grill should be used to hold fish steaks. There are also special fish grill baskets for whole fish. Baste the fish and place the wire grill 2 to 3 inches away from heat source. (Place frozen fish 4 to 5 inches away to avoid having the outside of the fish overcook.)

- Once the fish is cooked on top, turn it over and baste again. Test for doneness with a fork inserted into the center to see if the flesh is white. In general, fish is cooked when it loses its translucent appearance and turns white.

- The following fish are best cooked as steaks: bluefish, halibut, salmon, shark, striped bass, swordfish and tuna. Try the following cooked whole: flounder, perch, porgy, trout and weakfish (sea trout).

Grilled Fish Fillets with Summer Herbs

Experiment with herb combinations.

Per serving:

18-inch square heavy-duty foil
¼ pound fresh white fish fillets
1 tablespoon butter, softened
sea salt and lemon pepper, to taste
fresh herbs:
   1 sprig EACH mint, tarragon, thyme
1 teaspoon snipped chives
Alternate herbs:
   lemon balm, anise, licorice basil,
   garlic chives or savory

1. Prepare grill: coals should be medium hot; or preheat oven to 400°.
2. For each serving lay out a square of foil; butter foil with ½ tablespoon butter and place fish on buttered area. Dab top of fish with remaining ½ tablespoon butter.
3. Sprinkle fillet with about ¼ teaspoon each sea salt, lemon pepper and chives. Top with sprigs of tarragon, mint and thyme.
4. Fold foil to enclose fish and crimp edges. Poke 2 steam holes in top.
5. Place packets over coals, or in oven, for 10 minutes for thin fillets, such as sole, or 20 minutes for thicker fillets such as turbot or bluefish.

Grilled Swordfish Steaks with Pesto   Yield: 4 servings

Serve with corn-on-the-cob and sliced beefsteak tomatoes for a summer feast.

4 swordfish steaks (about 3½ ounces each)
salt and freshly ground pepper
oil
1 cup Pesto (see index)
nutmeg
toasted pine nuts

1. Season swordfish steaks with salt and pepper to taste. Place on a lightly oiled grill.
2. Grill 3 to 5 minutes per side, depending on thickness of steaks (keep in mind the 10-minutes-per-inch rule for fish), or until fish flakes easily with fork.
3. Gently transfer steaks to serving plates. Cover with pesto and sprinkle with a dash of nutmeg and toasted pine nuts.

Cape Cod was named in 1602 by the British navigator Bartholomew Gosnold, who found cod, among mackerel, bass, flounder, and haddock, to be the most abundant saltwater fish in Massachusetts Bay.

Sev's Marinated Swordfish

A delectable combination of ingredients enhances the flavor of this summer catch.

4 swordfish steaks (about 4 ounces each)

Marinade:

¼ cup soy sauce
2 garlic cloves, crushed
4 tablespoons tomato sauce
2 tablespoons lemon juice
1 teaspoon dried organo
½ cup orange juice
½ teaspoon ground pepper
¼ cup chopped fresh parsley

Must be made ahead.

1. Mix all marinade ingredients together.
2. Pour over swordfish in shallow glass baking dish. Cover with plastic wrap and marinate for at least 4 hours, turning once or twice.
3. Grill over hot coals about 5 minutes per side (for a total of 10 minute per inch of thickness), basting with marinade occasionally. Serve garnished with orange wedge and parsley, if desired.

Swordfish, Shrimp and Scallops en Brochette

Grilling over mesquite subtly flavors these marinated kabobs.

1 pound swordfish steak, skin removed, cut in 1-inch chunks
½ pound large or jumbo shrimp, shelled and deveined
½ pound sea scallops
juice of 3 limes
½ cup extra-virgin olive oil
½ cup chopped fresh cilantro (coriander)
2 garlic cloves, chopped
salt and freshly ground pepper
2 tablespoons unsalted butter, at room temperature
lime wedges, chopped cilantro for garnish

Must be made ahead.

1. In large bowl or covered plastic container, combine lime juice, oil, cilantro and garlic. Add fish, shrimp and scallops; toss to mix. Cover and marinate at room temperature for about 2 hours, or refrigerate for up to 8 hours.
2. Light charcoal (with a generous amount of mesquite, if available) or preheat broiler. Thread seafood onto 4 long metal skewers, alternating ingredients. Season generously with salt and pepper.
3. Grill over hot coals, about 3 inches from heat, turning until swordfish is cooked through, 5 to 6 minutes.
4. Remove to warm plate. Spread a pat of butter over each skewer; sprinkle with cilantro and serve with lime wedges.

Herbed Grilled Whole Lobsters

Yield: 4 servings

What a way to celebrate the 4th of July!

4 1¼- to 1½-pound live lobsters
½ cup vegetable oil
¼ cup red wine vinegar
½ teaspoon thyme
2 shallots, minced
1 tablespoon fresh parsley, minced
freshly ground black pepper
melted butter, clarified
lime or lemon wedges

1. Split and kill each lobster by placing it, shell side down, on cutting board, inserting a large knife into head and cutting along center through tail, leaving shell intact. Spread lobsters to expose meat.

2. Combine oil, vinegar, thyme, shallots and parsley; brush lobster meat generously with mixture. Season with fresh black pepper to taste.

3. Place lobsters, SHELL SIDE DOWN, on grill over white-hot coals and cook 7 to 8 minutes. Baste again with remaining oil mixture and turn meat side down; cook an additional 7 to 8 minutes, watching lobsters carefully to avoid burning.

4. When done, remove from grill and crack claws with flat side of heavy knife. Serve with drawn butter and lime or lemon wedges.

Grilled Lobster Tails

Yield: 6 servings

For a special occasion.

6 lobster tails, approximately 8 ounces each
¼ cup extra-virgin olive oil
3 garlic cloves, minced
2 tablespoons chopped parsley
2 tablespoons lemon juice
salt and freshly ground black pepper
melted butter, clarified

1. Cut tails in half lengthwise. Remove swimmerettes and sharp edges. Cut 6 pieces of heavy-duty aluminum foil, 12 x 12-inches each. Place each lobster tail on foil.

2. Combine oil, garlic, parsley, lemon juice and salt and pepper. Baste lobster meat with mixture. Bring foil up over lobster; close all edges with double folds.

3. Place packages on grill, shell side down, about 5 inches from hot coals. Cook 20 minutes.

4. Remove lobster tails from foil; place on grill, flesh side down. Cook 2 to 3 minutes longer or until lightly browned. Serve with melted butter.

Sea Bass Vinaigrette

A delicious cold entrée.

Yield: 4 to 6 servings

I whole sea bass (about 4 pounds) cleaned,
  with head intact but gills removed
water
2 large onions, chopped
4 garlic cloves, peeled
salt to taste
I teaspoon whole pepper corns

Vinaigrette:

I cup vinegar
2 cups olive oil

Garnish:

2 hard-boiled eggs, chopped
4 slices bacon, cooked crisp and crumbled
½ cup chopped fresh cilantro (coriander)

Must be made ahead.

1. Place fish in large pot, cover with water and add onions, garlic, salt and peppercorns. Cook over medium heat for 30 minutes or until fish is very tender and flakes easily.

2. Cover and refrigerate overnight in cooking liquid. Early the next day drain off liquid. Prepare vinaigrette by combining vinegar and oil; pour over fish. Refrigerate, basting fish frequently.

3. To serve, present whole fish on platter garnished with chopped egg, bacon and cilantro.

Lobsters were so plentiful in 17th-century New England that storms would wash thousands of them up onto the beaches. In fact, so common were the crustaceans that they were considered food for the needy, who had no means to pay for anything better!

Flounder Roll-ups with Blue Cheese Stuffing

Yield: 6 servings

Everyone always requests this recipe.

½ cup (I stick) butter, divided
¼ cup fresh minced parsley
I medium tomato, chopped
½ cup minced celery
¼ cup firmly packed Blue cheese
3 cups soft bread crumbs
I egg, beaten
½ teaspoon salt
6 flounder fillets,
  about 1½- to 1¾-pounds total
I lemon

1. In a large skillet melt ¼ cup butter. Add parsley, tomato, and celery. Cook about 10 minutes, stirring often. Remove from heat and crumble cheese into mixture. Add bread crumbs, egg and salt, mixing well.

2. Spread mixture on fillets; roll up and fasten with wooden picks. Place in a well-greased 1½-quart oblong baking dish.

3. Melt remaining ¼ cup butter, mix with juice of one lemon. Pour over fish rolls. Bake in preheated 350° oven until fish flakes easily, about 30 minutes.

Lazy Barbecued Shrimp

Yield: 4 servings

This recipe brings back memories of summer vacations at a beach house equipped with a microwave oven.

1½ pounds large shrimp, unpeeled
cayenne pepper
freshly ground black pepper
4 garlic cloves, minced

Sauce:

½ pound (2 sticks) butter
3 tablespoons Worcestershire sauce
juice of 1 lemon
¼ teaspoon Tabasco sauce
salt
plenty of French bread

Shrimp lovers may want to double the recipe and use 3 pounds of shrimp. Micro-cooking time will be about 10 to 12 minutes.

1. Wash and dry shrimp well. Place in a glass baking dish about 9 x 13-inches and sprinkle generously with pepper and minced garlic.

2. In a 4-cup glass measure heat sauce ingredients in microwave at 100% power (high) for 1½ to 2 minutes.

3. Pour sauce over shrimp. Cover with waxed paper. Cook shrimp at 100% power (high) for 7 to 8 minutes, stirring once or twice and heating until all shrimp are pink and tender. Salt to taste.

4. Let stand 3 minutes. Test for doneness. Serve with plenty of French bread for dipping into hot sauce and with plenty of paper napkins!

Coquilles St. Jacques

Very rich and very good.

Yield: 6 servings as first course
    4 servings as entrée

1 pound sea scallops
½ teaspoon thyme
2 bay leaves
1 sprig parsley
12 peppercorns
salt and freshly ground pepper, to taste
½ cup water
½ cup dry white wine
7 tablespoons butter, divided
3 tablespoons flour
2 egg yolks
1 teaspoon lemon juice
⅛ teaspoon cayenne pepper
4 tablespoons Parmesan cheese

1. In a medium saucepan, combine scallops, seasonings, water and wine; bring to a boil. Cover, reduce heat, and simmer exactly 2 minutes. Remove bay leaf, parsley and peppercorns and drain scallops, reserving liquid. Cool scallops in strainer and, if large, cut into ⅛-inch slices.

2. Melt 2 tablespoons butter in saucepan and blend in flour. Stir in 1 cup of reserved liquid and cook over medium heat until mixture is slightly thickened, stirring constantly.

3. Remove sauce from heat; add remaining butter gradually while beating vigorously with wire whisk. Beat in egg yolks, lemon juice and cayenne pepper.

4. Preheat oven to 400°. Using 4 large scallop shells, or ramekins, spoon a little of the sauce into each shell and top with one-

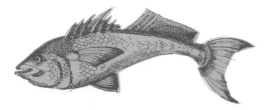

fourth of the scallops. Divide remaining sauce over scallops and sprinkle with Parmesan.

5. Bake scallops 10 minutes until brown and bubbly.

Skipper's Dock Portuguese Stew   Yield: 2 (generous) servings

A popular entrée from the menu of Stonington's favorite waterfront dining spot.

1 medium leek, finely chopped
1 medium onion, finely chopped
3 garlic cloves, crushed
¼ cup olive oil
10 medium tomatoes, peeled, seeded and finely chopped, juice reserved
½ teaspoon saffron
2 bay leaves
2 teaspoons fennel seed
pinch EACH of thyme and basil
salt and pepper, to taste
2½ quarts fish stock or clam juice
2 lobster parts, tail or claw
2 large shrimp, peeled and deveined
8 to 10 bay scallops or sea scallops
6 small cherrystone clams, well scrubbed
12 mussels, well scrubbed, beards removed
several pieces of fresh fish cut into
    1- or 2-inch squares (striped bass, bluefish, swordfish or cod with skin on)
1 pound Portuguese Chorizo sausage
1 loaf day-old French bread
garlic
chopped parsley
olive oil

1. Place leek, onion and garlic in large, heavy saucepan with oil; heat slowly, stirring frequently, until cooked but not brown.

2. Add chopped tomatoes with juice; bring to a boil. Add herbs and seasonings, adjusting for personal taste. Let simmer until tomatoes break down.

3. Add fish stock, fish, shellfish and sausage. Bring to a gentle boil; let simmer until clams open.

4. Meanwhile, slice French bread, rubbing each slice with garlic and sprinkling with parsley and oil; broil until brown; set aside as garnish croutons.

5. Ladle stew into bowls or small service tureens; garnish with croutons.

VEGETABLES

Overnight Baked Beans

**A boon for summertime picnics and reunions,
these beans cook at night in a low oven
so you don't heat up the house on warm days.**

Yield: 6 for Saturday night supper
12 to 14 at a picnic

1 pound navy pea beans, washed
4 tablespoons sugar
4 tablespoons brown sugar
2 tablespoons dark molasses
1 large onion, sliced
1 teaspoon salt
¼ pound short ribs
¼ pound lean salt pork
   (bacon may be substituted)
1 teaspoon dry mustard
parsley flakes (optional)

1. Preheat oven to 200° shortly before 10 p.m.
2. Combine all ingredients in large Dutch oven; cover. (A handful of parsley flakes may be added for "good luck and good taste.")
3. Bake overnight; check beans around 7 a.m. If beans seem runny, raise oven to 350° and bake, uncovered, 45 to 60 minutes longer. If baking beans during the day, plan on 9 to 10 hours baking time. Boston Brown Bread (see index), is the perfect accompaniment, of course!

Corn Grilled in Husks

Connecticut butter 'n sugar corn is the best grown anywhere!

Yield: 6 servings

6 ears corn in husks

Herb Butter:

8 tablespoons butter, softened
2 teaspoons dried oregano
½ teaspoon dried basil
¼ teaspoon dried thyme
1 tablespoon chopped flat-leaf parsley
1 small garlic clove, minced
½ teaspoon freshly ground pepper
¼ teaspoon salt, or to taste

1. Prepare corn by pulling down each husk to the bottom of the ear without detaching; remove silks. Replace husks; secure with twine.
2. Soak ears in cold water to cover at least 30 minutes before grilling.
3. Prepare herb butter by combining all ingredients in small bowl and beating until fluffy.
4. Prepare grill. Drain corn.
5. Grill corn directly on hot coals 20 minutes, turning every 5 minutes until corn is tender and husks are evenly charred.
6. Remove husks; roll corn in herb butter.

Peppers with Almonds

Yield: 12 servings

5 tablespoons olive oil
1 cup slivered almonds
2 pounds red bell peppers, cut into
  ½-inch wide strips
1 pound yellow bell peppers, cut into
  ½-inch wide strips
1 pound green bell peppers, cut into
  ½-inch wide strips
6 tablespoons red wine vinegar
¼ cup sugar
salt
1 to 2 tablespoons warm water

1. In large heavy skillet, heat oil over medium heat. Add almonds and sauté until light brown, about 5 minutes.
2. Add peppers, vinegar, sugar and salt. Mix to coat peppers well. Increase heat to medium-high, cover and cook 10 minutes, stirring occasionally.
3. Uncover and continue cooking until peppers are tender, stirring occasionally and adding water if peppers begin to stick, about 5 minutes. Serve warm or at room temperature.

Grilled Garlic Potato Wedges

Yield: 6 servings

Cook these potatoes over the coals along with the steak.

¼ cup (½ stick) butter, softened
2 garlic cloves, minced
¾ teaspoon salt
⅛ teaspoon pepper
6 medium-size potatoes, scrubbed well and
  each cut into 6 wedges

1. Cream together butter, garlic, salt and pepper.
2. Cut an 18-inch square of heavy-duty foil. In the center of foil layer potato wedges and garlic butter.
3. Seal foil securely. Cook on grill until tender, 25 to 30 minutes. Test for doneness by piercing through foil with skewer.

Herbed Cherry Tomatoes

Yield: 8 servings

Be careful not to let tomatoes become mushy.

2 pints cherry tomatoes
½ cup fresh bread crumbs
½ cup packed minced fresh parsley
3 tablespoons extra-virgin olive oil
2 garlic cloves, minced
1 teaspoon fresh thyme
  or ½ teaspoon dried thyme
¼ teaspoon salt, or to taste
⅛ teaspoon pepper

1. Preheat oven to 425°.
2. Place tomatoes in shallow baking dish. Combine remaining ingredients and spoon over tomatoes; gently toss to coat.
3. Bake 6 to 8 minutes. Do not overcook.

Herbed Fresh Tomato Sauce

Yield: 3½ cups

A quick sauce for pasta.
Microwave preparation makes it ideal for summer.

1 tablespoon extra-virgin olive oil
2 cups sliced fresh mushrooms
¼ cup chopped green onions
2 to 3 garlic cloves, minced
3 large fresh tomatoes, peeled
   and coarsely chopped
1 teaspoon lemon juice
1½ teaspoons dried organo
½ teaspoon dried basil
⅛ teaspoon dried thyme
½ teaspoon salt, or to taste
¼ teaspoon pepper

1. In a 12 x 8 x 2-inch microwave-safe baking dish, combine olive oil, mushrooms, green onions and garlic. Cover and microwave at 100% power (high) for 4 to 5 minutes, stirring once.
2. Stir in remaining ingredients. Microwave at 100% power (high) for 6 to 7 minutes, or until thoroughly heated, stirring twice.
3. Serve over hot cooked pasta.

Pepper-Cheese Zucchini

Yield: 8 to 10 servings

A winner at a 4-H Food Show.

2 pounds zucchini, cubed
½ cup milk
1 pound Monterey Jack cheese, grated
¼ cup chopped fresh parsley
1 4-ounce can green chili peppers, diced
3 tablespoons flour
1 teaspoon salt
4 eggs, beaten
1 teaspoon baking powder
1 tablespoon butter, melted
1 cup fresh bread crumbs

1. Cook squash in a large saucepan in boiling salted water until barely tender, about 3 to 5 minutes; drain well and set aside.
2. Preheat oven to 325°.
3. Combine all remaining ingredients except butter and bread crumbs. Stir in squash.
4. Sprinkle bottom and sides of greased 2-quart baking dish with ½ cup bread crumbs. Pour in squash mixture.
5. Top with remining bread crumbs mixed with butter. Bake 30 to 40 minutes.

In 1858, Ezra Warner of Waterbury, Connecticut, received the first U.S. patent for the can opener, proving once again that necessity is truly the mother of invention!

Oven-fried Zucchini

Yield: 4 to 6 servings

**Something else to do with the season's bounty
for folks who usually won't eat it.**

1 pound fresh zucchini
¼ cup Parmesan cheese
¼ cup flour
½ cup bread crumbs
2 teaspoons salt
½ teaspoon paprika
1 egg, well beaten
vegetable oil

1. Preheat oven to 400°. Thinly coat a 15-inch jellyroll pan with oil.
2. Cut clean zucchini into ¼-inch slices.
3. Combine next five ingredients.
4. Dip zucchini pieces into beaten egg, then into crumb mixture.
5. Place zucchini on baking sheet in single layer. Drizzle a little oil over squash.
6. Bake 20 minutes, turning once halfway through cooking. Serve hot.

Tuscan-style Grilled Vegetables

Yield: 6 servings

A favorite side dish!

Dressing:
2 garlic cloves, minced
½ cup extra-virgin olive oil
¼ cup vegetable oil
¼ cup red wine vinegar
1 tablespoon minced fresh oregano
   or ½ teaspoon dried oregano
1 generous pinch EACH dried basil
   and dried thyme
1 teaspoon sugar
1 teaspoon salt
1 teaspoon coarsely ground black pepper

3 small eggplants
4 small zucchini (about 6 ounces each)
3 small red peppers
3 small yellow peppers
3 small green peppers

Must be made ahead.

1. Combine dressing ingredients in a small bowl; set aside.
2. Cut each eggplant and zucchini in half lengthwise (if larger eggplant is used, cut in fourths). Cut each pepper in half lengthwise; discard seeds.
3. Preheat broiler according to manufacturer's directions. Brush broiler pan with a little dressing. Arrange vegetables, cut-side down, in pan; brush with ⅓ cup dressing. (This may need to be done in two batches, depending on size of broiler and pan.) Broil 7 to 9 inches from source of heat for about 7 minutes. (Or bake at 450°.) Turn and brush with ⅓ cup dressing. Broil 8 to 10 minutes or until fork-tender and beginning to brown.
4. Remove vegetables to an oblong baking dish. combine dressing from pan with remaining dressing and pour over vegetables, coating well. Cover and refrigerate at least 8 hours, stirring occasionally. Bring to room temperature before serving; drain off dressing and arrange on platter.

Baked Ratatouille

Yield: 12 to 15 servings

An excellent choice for a share-a-dish picnic or family reunion.

2 large onions, sliced thinly
1 eggplant (about 1 to 1½ pounds)
  cut into ½-inch cubes
6 medium zucchini, thickly sliced
2 green peppers, seeded and cut into chunks
4 ripe tomatoes, cut into chunks
4 garlic cloves, minced
2 teaspoons salt, or to taste
1 tablespoon fresh basil, chopped
  or 1 teaspoon dried basil
½ cup chopped fresh parsley
¼ cup extra-virgin olive oil

1. In a greased 5- to 6-quart casserole, layer onions, eggplant, zucchini, peppers and tomatoes, sprinkling each layer generously with garlic, salt, basil and parsley.

2. Drizzle olive oil over top layer. Cover and bake at 325° for 3 hours. Baste top occasionally with some of the liquid. If vegetables become soupy, uncover during last hour of cooking.

3. Serve hot or at room temperature. Freezes well.

Crisp Cucumber Pickles

Yield: 12 pints

Fresh and delicious.

7 pounds (about 16 to 18) cucumbers,
  unpeeled, sliced crosswise
2 gallons water
3 cups pickling lime
1½ quarts (6 cups) vinegar
4½ pounds (9 cups) sugar
1 teaspoon ground cinnamon
1 teaspoon celery seed
1 teaspoon allspice
1 teaspoon mace
1 teaspoon ginger

Day One:

1. In a large non-metallic container, combine water and lime. Add cucumbers and let soak for 24 hours.

Day Two:

2. Remove cucumbers from lime water and soak in fresh water for 4 hours, changing water every hour.

3. Put remaining ingredients in a large pan; bring to boil. Pour mixture over cucumbers and let sit for 24 hours, covered.

Third Day:

4. Put cucumbers and syrup in large pot on top of stove; bring to simmer and cook 1 hour.

5. Pack cucumbers in hot jars, cover with syrup, and seal.

Plum and Pear Chutney

Yield: 7 half-pint jars

**This Indian chutney preserves two of summer's fruits.
A nice change from bottled mango chutney.**

1½ cups sugar
1 cup cider vinegar
2 tablespoons minced fresh ginger root
2 teaspoons curry powder
½ teaspoon crushed red pepper flakes
1 teaspoon salt
2 garlic cloves, minced
1 large onion, chopped
1 whole small orange, finely chopped
1 cup raisins
2 pounds firm red plums
  (Santa Rosa or Laroda), quartered
  and pitted to make about 5 cups
2 pounds firm ripe pears, peeled
  and coarsely chopped to make 4 cups

1. In large 5-quart pot combine all ingredients except plums and pears. Bring to a boil.
2. Add plums and pears; boil gently, uncovered, stirring frequently until thickened, about 30 to 40 minutes.
3. Ladle into 7 sterilized half-pint jars, leaving ½-inch head space; close jars with sterilized lids. Process in boiling water for 5 minutes; cool.

Beach Plum Jelly

Yield: about 6 to 8 half-pint jars

A New England delicacy.

4 pounds fully ripe beach plums
3½ cups water
7½ cups sugar
½ bottle Certo

1. Prepare juice: in large pan, crush unpeeled, unpitted beach plums. Add water; bring to a boil and simmer, covered, 30 minutes. Place in cheesecloth or bag and squeeze out juice. Measure 4 cups into large saucepan.
2. Make jelly: add sugar to 4 cups juice in large saucepan; mix well. Place over high heat and bring to boil, stirring constantly. At once stir in Certo, then bring to a full, rolling boil and boil hard 1 minute, stirring constantly.
3. Remove from heat, skim, pour quickly into glass jars with two-part lids and process 5 minutes with boiling water bath method.

SALADS

Fajita Salad

Yield: 6 servings

**Grill extra flank steak one night
and make this Tex-Mex dish the next night.**

Dressing:

½ cup olive oil
¼ cup fresh lemon juice
¼ cup coarsely chopped cilantro (coriander)
4 green onions, coarsely chopped
2 large garlic cloves, minced
½ teaspoon salt, or to taste
¾ teaspoon freshly ground black pepper

1 15½-ounce can pinto beans,
   drained and rinsed
2 avocados, sliced
3 medium tomatoes, seeded and diced
1 pound flank steak or london broil,
   cooked rare to medium-rare and sliced
   thinly across the grain
1 head romaine lettuce, shredded
1 large bunch watercress, coarsely chopped
6 flour tortillas, warmed

1. Place all dressing ingredients in a screw-top jar and shake well.
2. Combine pinto beans and 3 tablespoons dressing in a medium bowl. In another bowl combine avocado and tomatoes with 3 tablespoons dressing. Toss lettuce and watercress with remaining dressing.
3. On each plate place a warm tortilla; top with a layer of greens. Place sliced steak on greens, then beans and top with tomato and avocado.

Coriander Chicken Salad

Yield: 6 servings

An oriental-inspired salad by way of San Francisco.

2 pound chicken breasts, skin left on

Marinade:

2 tablespoons soy sauce
2 tablespoon dry sherry
2 tablespoon vegetable oil
2 tablespoons water
4 tablespoons fresh coriander leaves (cilantro)
1 tablespoon Hoisin sauce
1 tablespoon grated ginger root
1 teaspoon roasted sesame oil
1 teaspoon dry mustard
salt to taste

1. Combine marinade ingredients in glass baking dish large enough to accommodate chicken. Add chicken and turn to coat. Refrigerate in marinade overnight, turning chicken pieces once or twice.
2. Preheat oven to 450°. Reserving marinade, place chicken on rack in foil-lined pan. Bake 15 to 20 minutes on each side or until browned and done. Pour marinade over chicken the last 2 minutes of baking. Cool.
3. Shred chicken finely along grain. Use as much skin as desired, shredding with cleaver.

1 tablespoon dry mustard

½ cup finely chopped peanuts
   or almonds

¼ cup sesame seeds, browned
   in 1 teaspoon roasted sesame oil

2 cups deep-fried rice sticks (optional)

2 cups shredded iceberg lettu...

2 green onions with tops, s...

¼ cup fresh coriander le...

2 tablespoons Ch... ...gar

Must be made ahead.

4. Skim off excess fat from pan drippings.
   Mix dry mustard into drippings in pan. Stir
   chicken thoroughly into drippings. If too
   dry, add a few tablespoons boiling water.

5. Combine nuts, sesame seeds and rice sticks.
   Set aside.

6. Combine and have ready lettuce, green
   onions and coriander leaves.

7. To serve: toss everything together lightly.
   Sprinkle with vinegar. Serve with extra
   vinegar and sesame oil at table.

Composed Chicken Salad with Sweet Summer Dressing

The dressing is delicious with other salads, too.   Yield: 4 to 6 servings

1 head Bibb lettuce
3 cups shredded fresh spinach leaves
3 boneless chicken breasts, cooked
   and cut into 2-inch strips
2 or 3 ripe avocados, peeled and sliced
2 or 3 large ripe fresh tomatoes
6 slices extra-thick bacon, fried and crumbled
½ cup finely chopped scallions
3 hard-boiled eggs, chopped (optional)
alfalfa sprouts

Sweet Summer Dressing:

½ cup sugar
2 tablespoons cider vinegar
2 tablespoons water
1 tablespoon lemon juice
2 tablespoons ketchup
½ cup vegetable oil
pinch of salt
1 teaspoon onion juice or
   2 slices of onion

1. For each serving: cover plate with Bibb
   lettuce leaves. On top of lettuce place ½ cup
   shredded fresh spinach.

2. Arrange strips of chicken in center of plate.
   On one side of chicken arrange sliced
   avocado; on other side place fresh
   tomato wedges.

3. Sprinkle each plate with crumbled bacon,
   scallions, egg and alfalfa sprouts.

4. Drizzle Sweet Summer Dressing over all.

Sweet Summer Dressing:

1. In blender or food processor, mix together
   all ingredients until well blended.

2. Chill. Shake well before using.

Chicken Avocado Salad

Yield: 4 to 6 servings

Created by a chef living aboard a 28-foot sailboat, this salad is as light and glorious as a perfect sail.

1 11-ounce can mandarin oranges
1 3¼-ounce can ripe pitted olives
¼ cup sliced water chestnuts
1½ cups cubed cooked chicken breast
¼ cup finely chopped celery
½ small red onion, thinly sliced and
    separated into rings
1 medium ripe avocado

Dressing:

⅓ cup mayonnaise
⅓ cup sour cream
2 teaspoons tarragon
syrup reserved from mandarin oranges
    (about 3 to 4 tablespoons)

lettuce leaves
salt and freshly ground pepper

1. Drain mandarin oranges and reserve syrup for dressing.
2. Drain olives and water chestnuts, discarding liquid.
3. Combine cubed chicken, celery and onion. Add drained oranges, olives and water chestnuts.
4. Peel and cube avocado. Gently mix into salad.
5. Prepare dressing: mix together mayonnaise, sour cream and tarragon. Thin to desired consistency with mandarin orange syrup, about 3 to 4 tablespoons.
6. Pour dressing over salad mixture; toss gently. Add salt to taste, if desired.
7. Cover and refrigerate until needed. Serve on a bed of lettuce with freshly ground black pepper to taste.

Paella Salad

Yield: 8 to 10 servings

Start with cold Saffron Risotto.

1 recipe Saffron Risotto (see index),
    substituting ½ cup chopped green pepper
    for mushrooms and omitting cheese
2 cups cubed cooked chicken
½ pound shelled cooked shrimp
½ pound sliced Chorizo
1 cup cherry tomatoes, halved
½ cup pitted ripe olives
1 bunch scallions, sliced
2 tablespoons chopped roasted peppers

Dressing:

½ cup olive oil
¼ cup red wine vinegar
1 tablespoon capers, drained
pinch red pepper flakes
salt and pepper to taste

1 dozen steamed mussels (optional)

1. In a large bowl, mix cooked saffron rice with next seven ingredients, tossing lightly to mix.
2. In a jar with tightly-fitting lid, place dressing ingredients. Shake well. Pour over rice mixture in bowl and toss well to coat. May be refrigerated but allow to return to room temperature before serving.
3. Garnish with steamed mussels, if desired.

Spicy Sz

Yield: 4 servings

Chinese Noodles with Shrimp — an unusual blend of flavors.

12 ounces fresh Chinese noodles or
   16 ounces linguine
½ tablespoon peanut oil
½ pound cooked shrimp,
   shelled and deveined
1 cup slivered lean ham
4 green onions, slivered
2 sweet red peppers, seeded and slivered
1 cup leafy ends of fresh cilantro (coriander)

Dressing:

2 tablespoons soy sauce
3 tablespoons red wine vinegar
2 tablespoons finely minced fresh ginger root
1½ tablespoons sugar
2 tablespoons sesame oil
1 teaspoon chili paste with garlic
½ teaspoon salt
½ cup crunchy peanut butter

1. Cook noodles in a large amount of salted boiling water according to package directions; drain and rinse. Cut noodles for ease in serving and toss with peanut oil.
2. Cut cooked shrimp on diagonal into thin slices. Toss with noodles along with remaining salad ingredients. Set aside; do not add dressing until ready to serve.
3. Meanwhile, prepare dressing: combine all dressing ingredients in jar with tight-fitting lid. Shake until well blended. Toss dressing with salad just prior to serving. Serves four as a main dish.

Shrimp Salad with Pineapple

Yield: 6 to 8 servings

If time permits, substitute fresh pineapple chunks for the canned.

1 pound cooked shrimp, shelled and deveined
2 cups cooked, chilled rice
1 8-ounce can pineapple chunks, drained
1 cup cashews
2 medium green peppers, diced

Dressing:

2 tablespoons white wine or
   rice vinegar
5 tablespoons peanut oil
2 tablespoons ketchup
½ teaspoon salt
ground white pepper
½ teaspoon sugar
¼ teaspoon thyme
¾ teaspoon roasted sesame oil

Must be made ahead.

1. Combine salad ingredients in a large bowl. Mix well.
2. In a screw-top jar, combine all dressing ingredients and shake well. Pour over salad in bowl and toss well to coat.
3. Refrigerate at least four hours before serving to allow flavors to mix. For special pizzaz, serve in a hollowed-out fresh pineapple half.

Spinach, Shrimp and Cashew Salad

Yield: 6 to 8 servings

1 10-ounce package fresh spinach
1 head iceberg lettuce
6 to 12 ounces cashew nuts
1 pound boiled shrimp
  (or cooked cubed chicken or lobster)

1. Wash greens, dry thoroughly and toss together in salad bowl. Toss with cashews and shrimp.
2. When ready to serve, add dressing and toss well.

Dressing:

⅓ cup sugar
1 teaspoon salt
1 teaspoon dry mustard
1 teaspoon grated onion
¼ cup vinegar
1 cup vegetable oil
1 teaspoon celery seed

Dressing:

1. In blender, combine sugar, salt and dry mustard. Add onion and vinegar.
2. Pour oil SLOWLY into mixture with blender running; blend at low speed. Be sure each addition of oil is well blended before adding more.
3. Add celery seed. May be prepared ahead but do not toss with salad until ready to serve.

Broccoli Tortellini Salad

Yield: 6 1-cup servings

Ideal for picnics and sailing.

1 7-ounce package cheese tortellini
1 cup fresh broccoli florets, blanched
½ cup finely chopped fresh parsley
½ 7-ounce jar roasted peppers, cut into strips
1 6-ounce jar marinated artichoke hearts, undrained
2 green onions, chopped
¼ cup sliced ripe olives
2½ teaspoons chopped fresh basil
  or ¼ teaspoon dried basil
½ teaspoon dried oregano
2 garlic cloves, minced
½ cup prepared Italian dressing
5 or 6 cherry tomatoes, halved
grated Parmesan cheese

1. Cook tortellini according to package directions. Drain and rinse in cold water. Drain again.
2. In large bowl combine all ingredients except cherry tomatoes and Parmesan cheese. Cover and refrigerate 4 to 6 hours to blend flavors.
3. Just before serving, add cherry tomatoes; sprinkle with cheese.

Must be made ahead.

If preparing a day ahead, do not add broccoli until adding tomatoes.

Variation:

Adding hard salami, summer sausage or tuna will make this a main dish salad.

BASIL

Layered Gazpacho Salad

Yield: 8 servings

Hostesses will appreciate the advance preparation.

2 medium cucumbers
1 teaspoon salt
⅔ cup olive oil
⅓ cup red wine vinegar
2 garlic cloves, minced
1 tablespoon chopped fresh basil
  or 1 teaspoon dried basil
1 teaspoon salt
½ teaspoon freshly ground pepper
½ pound mushrooms, thinly sliced
1 bunch scallions, thinly sliced
½ cup minced fresh parsley
4 tomatoes, cut into wedges
2 green peppers, seeded and thinly sliced
½ pound Provolone cheese, cut into slivers
4 hard-boiled eggs, sliced

Must be made ahead.

1. Peel and thinly slice cucumbers into a bowl; sprinkle with salt and let stand 30 minutes.
2. Meanwhile combine oil, vinegar, garlic, basil, salt and pepper in a large salad bowl. Add mushrooms and scallions.
3. Drain cucumbers, pat dry with paper towels and add to bowl. Mix in parsley.
4. Make a layer of tomato; top with a layer of green pepper slices. Cover bowl and chill salad for about 4 hours.
5. Just before serving add cheese. Toss salad gently; garnish with egg slices.

Crunchy Pea Salad

Yield: 12 servings

Especially delicious with fresh peas from the garden.

1 10-ounce package frozen petite peas, thawed or 1½ cups fresh peas, steamed
¼ cup chopped green onions, including tops
1 cup thinly sliced celery
1 cup chopped macadamia nuts (about a 3½-ounce jar)
¼ cup crisp-cooked bacon, crumbled
1 cup sour cream
¼ cup Special Café Dressing (recipe below)
lettuce

Special Café Dressing:

1 cup red wine vinegar
1 teaspoon freshly ground pepper
⅔ teaspoon lemon juice
1 tablespoon Worcestershire sauce
1 teaspoon Dijon mustard
1 garlic clove, crushed
1 teaspoon sugar
2 cups vegetable oil

1. Combine peas, green onions, celery, nuts and bacon.
2. Mix together sour cream and Special Café Dressing; fold into pea mixture.
3. Cover and chill for at least 2 hours.
4. Serve on a bed of crisp lettuce greens.

Dressing:

In blender or food processor combine all ingredients, adding oil gradually. Process until well blended. Chill until needed.

Dijon Mustard Vinaigrette

Yield: about 1 cup

With the abundance of fresh greens to choose from in the summer, no recipe is really needed for a salad — just a super salad dressing. This is it.

¼ cup rice wine vinegar
¼ cup vegetable oil
½ cup olive oil
¼ cup Dijon mustard
2 tablespoons chopped fresh parsley
salt and freshly ground pepper to taste

Place all ingredients in a jar with a tight-fitting lid and shake until creamy.

Grandma Murphy's Salad Dressing

Yield: about ¾ cup

A sweet-tart dressing especially nice on fresh spinach salad.

6 tablespoons vegetable oil
3 tablespoons sugar
3 tablespoons cider vinegar
salt and pepper

1. In a jar with tightly-fitting lid combine all ingredients and shake well.
2. Store at room temperature to avoid dressing thickening in refrigerator. Use within one week.

Cukes German Style

Yield: 10 to 12 servings

Good at cookouts or picnics.

3 long cucumbers
1 small onion, minced
3 tablespoons olive oil
1 tablespoon vinegar
salt and freshly ground pepper
¼ cup chopped fresh chives
¼ cup chopped fresh parsley

Must be made ahead.

1. Wash cukes. Thinly slice unpeeled cukes and put in ice water for 1 hour. Holding slices in hands; press out liquid between palms.
2. Place cukes in large bowl; add onion, oil, vinegar, salt and pepper and mix well. (If dressing seems insufficient, repeat oil and vinegar in same proportions and correct seasonings.) Mix in chives and parsley, reserving some to sprinkle on top. Refrigerate at least 2 hours before serving.

Boating Slaw

Yield: 6 to 8 servings

**Stays fresh and crisp for nine days
— perfect for an extended sail.**

1 medium cabbage, about 1 pound, shredded
1 large onion, finely chopped
1 medium green pepper, finely chopped
½ cup cider vinegar
½ cup sugar
½ cup vegetable oil
salt to taste
freshly ground black pepper
1 tablespoon celery seed

Must be made ahead.

1. Combine cabbage, onion and green pepper in a large bowl.
2. Heat together vinegar, sugar and salad oil to boiling point. Immediately pour over cabbage mixture.
3. Add salt, ground pepper and celery seed to taste. Allow to cool completely at room temperature.
4. Cover and store in refrigerator or cooler. Chill at least 1 day before serving. Flavor improves with age.

Calico Coleslaw

Yield: 12 to 16 servings

A Sweet 'n Sour Pennsylvania Dutch-style salad.

1 small green sweet pepper, diced
1 small red sweet pepper, diced
1 small yellow sweet pepper, diced
1½ cups diced onion
3 stalks celery, diced
1 large, very green cabbage, shredded
2 cups sugar, divided
2 cups wine vinegar
1 cup vegetable oil
1 tablespoon mustard seeds
1 tablespoon celery seeds
salt and pepper to taste

Must be made ahead.

1. Combine all vegetables in large bowl; mix well. Sprinkle 1¾ cups sugar over vegetables.
2. Combine ¼ cup sugar, vinegar, oil, celery seed and mustard seed in small saucepan; bring to boil. Remove from heat and pour over slaw.
3. Stir coleslaw gently to coat. Refrigerate overnight. Great with barbecued meats.

DESSERTS

Banana Pops

Delight all the little monkeys at your house!

Yield: 6 servings

3 bananas
2 tablespoons orange juice
I 6-ounce package semisweet chocolate chips
I tablespoon shortening
¾ cup finely chopped peanuts or other nuts
  or flaked coconut

Must be made ahead.

1. Peel bananas and cut in half crosswise; brush with orange juice. Insert wooden skewers in cut end, place on waxed paper lined cookie sheets, and freeze until firm.

2. In top of double boiler over hot water, combine chocolate and shortening, stirring occasionally until chocolate melts; blend smooth and cool slightly.

3. Spoon chocolate evenly over frozen bananas; roll in nuts or coconut. Serve at once or wrap in plastic wrap and return to freezer.

Party Ice Cream Mold

Beautiful colors in an ideal warm weather dessert.

Yield: 10 to 12 servings

I quart vanilla ice cream, softened
½ cup frozen pineapple-orange juice
  concentrate, partially thawed
I pint pistachio nut ice cream, softened
I pint raspberry sherbet, softened
toasted coconut

Must be made ahead.

1. Chill 7-cup mold in freezer. Quickly spread vanilla ice cream as evenly as possible with back of spoon or spatula to cover inside of mold making a shell lining about I-inch thick. Return to freezer to harden ice cream.

2. Spread partially thawed juice concentrate in thin layer over ice cream; freeze.

3. Layer pistachio ice cream, then raspberry sherbet, spreading in mold and freezing in same manner as above.

4. Store covered mold in freezer until an hour or so before serving.

5. To unmold, dip mold into warm water and turn onto chilled plate. Garnish top and sides with coconut. Return to freezer to harden.

Frozen Lemon Mousse

Yield: 6 to 8 servings

A cool, light, refreshing dessert for a summer meal.

2 tablespoons unsalted butter
⅓ cup heavy cream
4 large eggs
1 cup sugar
juice of 2 large lemons (about ¾ cup)
freshly grated rind of 2 lemons
4 large egg whites, at room temperature
⅛ teaspoon cream of tartar
¼ cup sugar

Garnish:

lemon peel curls,
	fresh mint leaves (optional)

Must be made ahead.

1. Melt butter with cream in medium, heavy-bottomed saucepan. Remove from heat.
2. In small bowl beat together whole eggs, sugar, lemon juice and rind. Slowly add to warm cream mixture; return to low heat. Stir constantly until mixture thickens noticeably. DO NOT BOIL.
3. Strain thickened mixture; cover with plastic wrap and refrigerate until thoroughly chilled.
4. Beat egg whites with cream of tartar until soft peaks form. Gradually add ¼ cup sugar, beating until dissolved and egg whites are stiff.
5. Stir one-fourth of chilled custard into whites. Gently fold in half of remaining custard until thoroughly mixed. Repeat with remaining custard.
6. Transfer to serving bowl; cover and freeze until needed. Let stand at room temperature 15 minutes before serving. Garnish with curls of lemon peel and mint leaves or sauce with cooled Vermont Blueberry Sauce (see index).

Frozen Mocha Mousse

Yield: 6 servings

No ice cream machine is necessary to produce this rich frozen dessert. Scrumptious!

¾ cup sugar
⅓ cup strong coffee
4 egg yolks
1 square (1 ounce) unsweetened chocolate, melted
1 teaspoon vanilla extract
1½ cups heavy cream
cinnamon
grated chocolate for garnish

Must be made ahead.

1. In saucepan over medium-high heat, cook sugar and coffee together for 5 minutes. Set aside.
2. In large mixer bowl, beat egg yolks until light. Slowly and gradually pour coffee syrup over eggs, mixing thoroughly. Add melted chocolate. Cool; add vanilla.
3. Whip cream until it just begins to hold its shape. Gently but thoroughly fold into coffee mixture.
4. Pour mixture into 8-inch square metal pan; freeze, without stirring, about 4 hours.
5. Spoon into parfait glasses and garnish with cinnamon and grated chocolate.

Piña Colada Soufflé

Yield: 6 servings

If you like the drink, you'll love this chilled dessert.

6 egg yolks
½ cup confectioners' sugar
¼ cup cream of coconut
1 cup crushed pineapple, well-drained
  (about a 20-ounce can)
2 envelopes unflavored gelatin
¼ cup dark rum
4 egg whites, at room temperature
1 cup heavy cream
toasted coconut (optional)

Must be made ahead.

1. Lightly oil the inside of 1-quart soufflé dish.
2. In large bowl of mixer, beat egg yolks and sugar until smooth and fluffy; add cream of coconut and pineapple. Mix well.
3. Sprinkle gelatin over rum in top of double boiler. When gelatin is soft, dissolve over hot water (or soften in glass ramekin and microwave 10 seconds). Cool; add to pineapple mixture.
4. In small mixer bowl, beat egg whites until stiff. In another bowl beat cream until it mounds.
5. Fold cream into pineapple first, then fold in egg whites. Spoon into soufflé dish, mounding in center. Chill several hours. Sprinkle with toasted coconut.

Plum Clafouti

Yield: 6 to 8 servings

A classic country French dessert.

5 or 6 medium, ripe plums,
  pitted and sliced
7 tablespoons sugar, divided
⅛ teaspoon almond extract
2 eggs, separated
1 teaspoon vanilla extract
½ cup milk
½ cup flour
pinch salt
confectioners' sugar

1. Preheat oven to 350°. Butter 1½-quart shallow baking dish.
2. Toss sliced plums with 3 tablespoons sugar (more if plums are tart) and almond extract in small bowl.
3. In large bowl of mixer, beat egg yolks with 2 tablespoons sugar until thick; beat in vanilla. Add milk alternately with flour, beating smooth after each addition.
4. In small mixer bowl, beat egg whites with salt until soft peaks form. Add remaining sugar a tablespoon at a time; beat until stiff but not dry.
5. Stir about one-third of egg whites into batter, then fold in rest.
6. Pour one-third of batter into prepared dish. Spoon on plums with juice. Pour on remaining batter. Bake 35 to 40 minutes, or until firm and golden brown. Sprinkle with confectioners' sugar. Serve warm, with Crème Fraîche, if desired.

Supreme Crème

Yield: 8 to 10 servings

The name says it all!
A wonderful complement to fresh fruit.

4 egg yolks
½ cup sugar
1 teaspoon cornstarch
7 ounces whipping cream, heated
4 ounces rum or liqueur
8 ounces cream cheese,
  at room temperature

Must be made ahead.

1. In heavy saucepan beat egg yolks and sugar with wire whisk until thick. Add cornstarch; slowly stir in hot cream.

2. Place mixture over medium heat and, while stirring with wooden spoon, heat to just below the simmer.

3. Remove from heat; add half of the rum. Cool completely.

4. Whip cream cheese and into it beat the cooled custard; add remaining rum. Cover and refrigerate mixture overnight.

5. To serve: spoon cream into individual serving dishes and cover with the prettiest, freshest whole strawberries or raspberries you can find. Or serve with blueberries, sliced fresh peaches or nectarines.

Crème Fraîche

Yield: about 1 cup

A very versatile topping.

1 cup whipping cream
2 tablespoons cultured buttermilk

1. Have whipping cream and buttermilk at room temperature, 70° to 80°.

2. Pour into small bowl or screw-top jar; stir or shake well. Cover and set aside at room temperature for 12 to 24 hours.

3. Stir gently and refrigerate, several hours or overnight, until ready to serve. Will keep in refrigerator 7 to 10 days.

Vermont Blueberry Sauce

Yield: about 2 cups

A simple but delicious sauce with many uses: on vanilla ice cream, orange sherbet, pound cake or angel food, pancakes or johnnycakes, sliced fresh peaches or nectarines, or Frozen Lemon Mousse (see index).

1½ cups blueberries, fresh or frozen
¼ cup sugar
¾ teaspoon cinnamon
¼ teaspoon nutmeg

1. Combine all ingredients in saucepan over low heat; cook, stirring frequently, for about 10 minutes.

2. Serve warm or cold.

Hummingbird Cake

Yield: 12 to 16 servings

A Bahamian woman sold this cake by the slice from her stand in Freeport. Ingredients were finagled from her and the recipe worked out at home in Connecticut.

3 cups flour
1 teaspoon baking soda
1 teaspoon salt
1 teaspoon cinnamon
2 cups sugar
1½ cups vegetable oil
3 large eggs, lightly beaten
1 8-ounce can crushed pineapple
  with the liquid
2 cups mashed bananas (about 5 bananas)
3½ ounces flaked coconut
1½ teaspoons vanilla extract

1. Preheat oven to 350°. Butter and flour 10-inch tube pan with removable bottom.
2. In large bowl sift together first 4 ingredients; add sugar and combine well.
3. In another bowl combine next 4 ingredients; add to dry ingredients, and stir until just combined.
4. Stir in coconut, and vanilla.
5. Pour into prepared pan. Bake 1 hour 10 minutes to 1 hour 20 minutes or until tester comes out clean.
6. Cool cake on wire rack 15 minutes; remove sides of pan and cool cake completely on tube on rack. Run knife around bottom of pan and tube; invert cake on plate. The Bahamian chef sold her cake unfrosted, but it is also good with Cream Cheese Glaze (see index).

Aunt "Bo's" Chocolate Layer Cake with Fudgy Cocoa Cream Frosting

Yield: 9-inch layer cake

Memories of old-time church picnics and lawn parties conjur up images of chocolate layer cake. Here it is, as good as you remembered.

2 ounces unsweetened chocolate
½ cup boiling water
1 teaspoon vinegar
½ cup milk
½ cup (1 stick) butter, softened
1½ cups sugar
2 eggs, beaten
2 cups flour
1 teaspoon baking soda
1 teaspoon vanilla extract

1. Preheat oven to 350°. Grease and flour two 9-inch layer pans.
2. In small bowl, pour boiling water over chocolate; beat until chocolate is melted and smooth. Set aside.
3. Mix vinegar with milk in another small bowl; set aside.
4. Cream butter and sugar until light and fluffy; beat in eggs.
5. Stir soda into sour milk. Add flour alternately with milk mixture, beginning and ending with

flour. Add vanilla and chocolate mixture; beat well.

6. Divide batter between layer pans. Bake for 25 to 35 minutes. Cool 15 to 20 minutes; remove from pans, cool and frost.

Fudgy Cocoa Cream Frosting:

1 pint heavy cream, well chilled
4 tablespoons cocoa
6 tablespoons confectioners' sugar
1 teaspoon vanilla extract
dash salt

Cake is similar to one knowns as "Philadelphia Red" or "Red Velvet."

Do not keep at room temperature for extended time because of cream.

Fudgy Cocoa Cream Frosting:

1. Chill mixing bowl and beaters before using.

2. Place all ingredients in chilled bowl. Whip as if whipping cream.

3. Frost cake between layers, on side and top. Decorate with chocolate sprinkles or chopped nuts, if desired.

Black and Blue Pie

In her 1861 cookbook, Christianity in the Kitchen, Mrs. Horace Mann implored the cook to beat a particular cake batter vigorously for three hours!

Maine Black-and-Blue Pie

Yield: 6 to 8 servings

Featuring two of summer's treasures — blackberries and blueberries.

pastry for double-crust 9-inch pie
3 cups blueberries
2 cups blackberries
¾ to 1 cup sugar (depending on tartness of blueberries)
3 tablespoons cornstarch
1 teaspoon grated lemon zest
1 egg white beaten with 1 teaspoon water
¼ cup heavy cream

You may wish to place foil on rack below pie to catch any overflow juices.

1. Preheat oven to 425°. Line 9-inch pie plate with pastry.

2. In large bowl combine berries with sugar, cornstarch and lemon zest; toss gently to mix.

3. Spoon filling into pastry shell. Dampen rim of pastry with egg wash. Cover filling with top pastry and cut an 8-inch "X" in center. Fold back points from center and seal triangle points to pastry with egg wash to create a square in center of pie. Crimp edges together.

4. Bake 15 minutes at 425°. Lower oven to 350°; cover pie with foil and bake 30 minutes. Remove pie from oven; carefully spoon heavy cream into center. Return pie to oven and bake 15 minutes more. Cool completely. Serve with whipped cream or Crème Fraîche (see index), if desired.

Choco-Cherry Swirl Pie

Yield: 6 to 8 servings

Worth the effort of pitting the cherries!

Crust:

1⅓ cups crushed chocolate wafer crumbs
3 tablespoons butter, melted

Filling:

1 cup pitted, diced fresh sweet cherries
3 tablespoons rum
1 quart premium vanilla ice cream, softened
1 1-ounce square semisweet chocolate
1 tablespoon milk

Must be made ahead.

1. Preheat oven to 375°. Combine crust ingredients; press into 9-inch pie pan. Bake 8 minutes. Cool.
2. Prepare cherries; combine with rum and fold into softened ice cream.
3. Melt chocolate; stir milk into chocolate.
4. Spread ice cream into crust. Swirl chocolate mixture through ice cream.
5. Freeze until firm.

Fresh Peach Tart

Yield: 6 to 8 servings

A food processor makes this elegant dessert a snap.

Crust:

1¼ cups flour
¼ teaspoon salt
½ cup (1 stick) butter, cut in chunks
2 tablespoons sour cream

4 large ripe peaches, peeled and thinly sliced

Custard:

4 tablespoons sour cream
1 cup sugar
¼ cup flour
¼ teaspoon salt
¼ teaspoon almond extract
¼ teaspoon mace
3 egg yolks

1. Preheat oven to 375°. Make crust: place butter chunks in food processor fitted with steel blade. Pour flour, salt and 2 tablespoons sour cream over butter and process until mixture is crumbly. Press mixture into bottom of a greased 9-inch tart pan with removable bottom. Bake 20 minutes or until lightly golden.
2. Arrange peach slices over crust in concentric circles, overlapping slightly for a petal-like design.
3. Make custard: combine remaining sour cream, sugar, flour, salt, almond extract, mace and egg yolks in processor and process 5 to 10 seconds or until blended. Pour over peaches. Bake 35 to 40 minutes or until firm.
4. Cool on wire rack. When completly cooled, remove sides of tart pan. Serve at room temperature.

Chewy Cheesecake Cookies

Yield: about 2½ dozen

**A sophisticated little cookie, ideal for accompanying
fresh fruit, sorbets, or other light desserts.**

½ cup (1 stick) butter, softened
1 3-ounce package cream cheese, softened
1 cup sugar
1 cup flour
½ cup chopped pecans

May be made in food processor.

1. Preheat oven to 375°.
2. Cream butter and cream cheese in large
   bowl of mixer. Gradually add sugar, beating
   until light and fluffy.
3. Add flour; beat well. Stir in nuts.
4. Shape dough into 1-inch balls; place
   2 inches apart on ungreased cookie sheet.
   Using heel of palm, gently flatten each
   cookie until about 2 inches in diameter.
5. Bake 10 to 12 minutes or until cookies are
   lightly browned around edges. Cool 2 to 3
   minutes on cookie sheet before removing to
   wire rack.

Pecan Cookies

Yield: about 4 dozen

Try these with fresh fruit.

1 cup (2 sticks) unsalted butter, softened
1 cup sugar
1 egg yolk
2 cups flour
1 teaspoon cinnamon

1 egg white, beaten
1 cup chopped pecans

1. Preheat oven to 350°.
2. Cream butter, sugar and egg yolk in large
   bowl. Gradually add flour and cinnamon.
3. Press mixture into 13 x 9-inch baking pan.
   Brush top with egg white; spread with
   chopped nuts.
4. Bake 30 to 40 minutes (less for chewy,
   more for crisp). Cool; cut into bars.

**One early cookbook instructed housewives to preserve
eggs by smearing them with mutton fat and layering
them tightly with their large ends pointing skyward in
a package of bran.**

Oatmeal Lace Cookies

Yield: 5 to 6 dozen

As light and delicate as Queen Anne's Lace.

½ cup (1 stick) butter, softened
½ cup sugar
½ cup dark brown sugar
1 egg, well beaten
scant ½ cup flour
½ teaspoon baking soda
½ teaspoon salt
½ teaspoon vanilla extract
1½ cups oats, regular or one-minute
  but NOT instant

1. In large bowl, cream butter and sugars; add egg and beat until smooth.

2. Mix in next four ingredients in order given; thoroughly stir in oats.

3. Preheat oven to 350°. Cover flat cookie sheets with aluminum foil.

4. Drop small amount of dough, about ½ teaspoonful, about two inches apart on prepared sheets.

5. Bake cookies on middle rack of oven for 8 to 10 minutes, or until cookies spread, are mahogany brown and very thin.

6. Remove from oven and carefully slide cookie-laden foil onto flat surface to cool for 10 minutes.* To remove from foil do not try to lift cookies but, rather, peel back foil. Store in airtight container.

*A cane chair seat makes an ideal cooling rack for foil sheets.

When I was a boy, my family had a cook named Aggie, who made the tastiest, crispest, most lacy cookies imaginable. If I happened to smell a batch baking, I could generally cadge one or two; once boxed, however, they were reserved for special people and not for me. Now, after years of experimentation, I have finally achieved a reliable method of producing the same cookies, and I am sure Aggie couldn't do any better! — R.W., New Canaan, CT

Barbara's Brownies

Yield: 4 dozen

Some chocoholic sailors would never heed the call of the sea without these aboard.

1 12-ounce bag semisweet chocolate chips
3 tablespoons unsalted butter
3 eggs
1 cup sugar
½ teaspoon vanilla extract
1 heaping tablespoon sour cream
  (about 1½ tablespoons)
6 heaping tablespoons flour
  (about ½ cup)
¼ teaspoon baking powder
¼ teaspoon salt
½ cup chopped nuts (optional)

1. Preheat oven to 350°. Grease a 13 x 9 x 2-inch baking pan.

2. In saucepan over low heat, melt chocolate chips and butter, stirring occasionally, until mixture is fudge-like.

3. In mixing bowl, beat eggs, sugar, vanilla and sour cream.

4. Add flour, baking powder and salt to egg mixture. Mix in melted chocolate mixture and nuts.

5. Spread mixture into prepared pan. Bake 25 to 30 minutes. Brownies will pull away from sides of pan slightly when cooked completely. Cool before cutting into squares.

Wolves-in-Sheeps'-Clothing

Yield: 18 cupcakes

Wickedly rich brownies masquerading as innocent cupcakes. Great for picnics!

1 cup (2 sticks) unsalted butter
2 ounces semisweet chocolate
2 ounces unsweetened chocolate
1 to 1½ cups chopped pecans
1 cup unsifted flour
1¾ cups sugar
¼ teaspoon salt
4 eggs, beaten
1 teaspoon vanilla extract

1. Preheat oven to 325°. Grease well or line muffin pans for 1½ dozen cupcakes.

2. Melt butter and chocolate in top of double-boiler over simmering water. Stir remaining ingredients into melted chocolate by hand. Do NOT over-mix or use electric mixer.

3. Fill muffin cups almost full as batter does not rise much. Bake 25 to 30 minutes; do NOT overcook. Cupcakes should be moist.

4. Cool on wire rack. Frosting is totally unnecessary, but sprinkle with confectioners' sugar if you feel compelled to embellish.

FAVORITE SUMMER RECIPES

AUTUMN

AUTUMN

No season is more evocative of New England cuisine than fall, and with good reason — the foods and the season richly complement one another. The brilliance of Cape Cod cranberries echoes the vibrant transformation of the leaves; the firm, crisp crunch of an apple imitates the sparkling clarity of the air.

And what would fall be without chowder, that reassuring layer of autumn insulation against the frigid days to come? Mystic Seaport celebrates this culinary tradition in early October with its Chowderfest, offering a selection of clam chowders prepared by several area civic groups. Visitors are served the hearty fare under tents along the Mystic River, savoring not only the feast but the backdrop of passing boats, historic riverfront homes, and exquisite foliage. And the chowderfest certainly keeps alive the Great New England Chowder Debate: the pros and cons of the creamy-based versus the clear. (Clear broth, you say? You must be from Rhode Island!)

Seagoing craft of every description are what Mystic Seaport is all about, and October fittingly brings the annual Schooner Race, when a variety of the two-masted vessels cast off from the Seaport to spend the day competing in the by-now-chilly waters of Fisher's Island Sound. In fact, the racing season for many New England sailors extends as far into fall as the weather permits (and sometimes when it doesn't). Warm up the nautical diehards in your house with such specialties as Veal and Apple Stew, Pork Chops with Pumpkin Sauce, or a wholesome Harvest Chicken Casserole, guaranteed to please even the hungriest autumn mariner.

The end of November finds kids of all ages frolicking on the Seaport's Village Green as they participate in Children's Field Day, an event designed to introduce today's youngsters to such forgotten pastimes as hoop rolling and stilt walking. You just might want to pack a few Old-Fashioned Hermits into small pockets that day as fortification for some plain old-fashioned exercise and fun!

BEVERAGES

Bloody Marietta

Yield: 4 drinks

A lighter, less spicy version of the classic Bloody Mary for those who prefer wine.

2 cups tomato juice
1½ cups sauterne
¼ cup fresh lemon juice
⅛ teaspoon Tabasco sauce
½ teaspoon Worcestershire sauce
4 slices lemon

1. In 1-quart glass pitcher combine tomato juice, sauterne, lemon juice, Tabasco and Worcestershire sauce. Stir to mix.
2. Pour mixture into four tall glasses filled with ice cubes. Stir well and garnish with lemon slice.

Blue Blazer

Yield: 2 drinks

Although the name conjures up images of a yacht club party, it probably derives from the color of the flaming scotch.

1 tablespoon honey
½ cup boiling water
½ cup Scotch, warmed
2 thin slices of lemon

1. Combine honey and water in a warmed heavy mug.
2. In another warmed mug, ignite the Scotch.
3. Pour the flaming Scotch into the honey and continue pouring the mixture back and forth between mugs until flames go out.
4. Pour drink into warmed wineglasses; garnish with lemon slice.

Champagne with Pears

Yield: 6 servings

The perfect toast for a sparkling fall day.

1 2-pound can Bartlett pear halves in heavy syrup
2 ounces Pear Williams or other pear brandy
1 750 ml bottle champagne, chilled
1 fresh pear, thinly sliced

Must be made ahead.

1. Drain canned pear halves, reserving ½ cup of syrup. Purée pears, reserved syrup and pear brandy in food processor or blender. Refrigerate until well chilled.
2. When ready to serve, add chilled champagne to pear purée; stir until mixture is well mixed. Serve in chilled champagne glasses garnished with thin slice of fresh pear.

Honey Buttered Hot Wine

Yield: 4 servings

Take a thermos of hot wine along for your tailgate picnic.

2 cups Rhine wine
¼ cup Cointreau or Triple Sec
3 tablespoons honey
1 tablespoon sugar
4 teaspoons butter
4 lemon slices
4 cinnamon sticks

1. In medium saucepan, combine wine, liqueur, honey and sugar; heat to boiling.
2. Pour into four mugs. To each mug add 1 teaspoon butter, a lemon slice and cinnamon stick. (Or pour into thermos. Carry butter pats in cooler and lemon slices and cinnamon sticks in separate small plastic bags.) Recipe may be doubled.

Mystic Mulled Cider

Yield: 10 to 12 servings

In Mystic, fall means a trip to a local cider press for the best fresh cider.

2 quarts fresh apple cider
½ cup rum
⅓ cup light brown sugar
juice of 1 lemon
½ teaspoon whole allspice
3-inch piece cinnamon stick
apple brandy (optional)

1. In large saucepan combine all ingredients except brandy. Heat until nearly bubbling but DO NOT allow to boil.
2. Strain mixture into warmed punch bowl.
3. Serve cider in punch cups, adding a tablespoon or apple brandy to each cup, if desired.

Witch's Brew

Yield: 10 cups

This one is for the kids' Halloween party.

1 quart fresh apple cider, chilled
2 cups lemonade, chilled
1 1-liter bottle lemon-lime soft drink, chilled
Monster's Ice Cube

Monster's Ice Cube:

1 or 2 surgical rubber gloves
   or new laytex gloves and rubber band
OR round metal bowl and 1 orange

Just before serving, combine cider, lemonade and soft drink in a large bowl. Float Monster's Ice Cube in brew.

Monster's Ice Cubes: there are two varieties

a. The Floating Hand — fill a rubber glove or two with water; secure glove top with rubber band. Stand glove upright in freezer until frozen solid.
b. The Eyeball — Freeze the orange in water in a metal bowl. It will protrude in a disgusting way.

APPETIZERS

Clams au Gratin
Yield: 8 servings

**An elegant first course served on scallop shells.
The use of fresh herbs is imperative
— no parsley flakes, freeze-dried chives or garlic powder, please!**

12 ounces Monterey Jack cheese, shredded
3 6½-ounce cans chopped clams, drained
2 tablespoons chopped fresh parsley
2 tablespoons chopped fresh chives
2 large garlic cloves, minced
generous dash cayenne pepper
⅛ teaspoon freshly ground black pepper
juice of one-half lemon
4 slices pumpernickel bread, halved
8 lemon wedges

Variation:

For hors d'oeuvres, use toasted party-size
pumpernickel with a heaping teaspoonful of
clam mixture on each; broil.

1. Preheat broiler according to manufacturer's
   directions.
2. Combine all ingredients, except bread and
   lemon wedges, until well mixed.
3. Place a half slice bread on each of 8 scallop
   shells (or 8 small ovenproof plates or
   ramekins). Mound clam mixture on top,
   dividing evenly among shells.
4. Broil until golden brown and bubbly.
   Serve hot with lemon wedge and parsley
   for garnish.

Moules Grillées (Grilled Mussels)
Yield: 6 to 8 servings

**A specialty at Harbor View Restaurant in Stonington,
one of southeastern Connecticut's premier restaurants.**

2 quarts large mussels, scrubbed
  and beards removed
⅔ cup dry white wine
1 pound (4 sticks) unsalted butter
6 garlic cloves, peeled and chopped
2 tablespoons minced parsley
2 tablespoons minced chervil
freshly ground black pepper and salt
1 cup buttered fresh bread crumbs
lemon wedges for garnish

1. In large pot, steam mussels in wine until
   shells open. Remove mussel meat and place
   each on a half shell.
2. Prepare the garlic butter by combining
   butter, garlic, parsley, chervil, salt and a
   generous amount of black pepper.
3. Preheat broiler. Put 1 teaspoon butter on
   each mussel; sprinkle with fresh bread
   crumbs. Place on baking sheet; broil until
   bubbly. Serve with lemon wedges.

**Deeming them unworthy of human consumption,
the Pilgrims fed mussels and clams to their pigs!**

Chinese Pork and Ginger Balls with Plum Good Dipping Sauce

Yield: about 3 dozen meatballs

You may want to double the recipe for meatballs because they disappear quickly.

Meatballs:

1 pound lean ground pork
1 8-ounce can water chestnuts, drained and finely chopped
2 garlic cloves, minced
1 teaspoon finely chopped ginger root
2 tablespoons soy sauce
1 tablespoon sherry
salt to taste

1. Combine all ingredients in bowl; blend thoroughly. Shape into 1-inch meatballs.
2. Heat oven to 425°. Place meatballs on broiler pan and bake 10 to 15 minutes. Serve hot with Plum Good Dipping Sauce

Plum Good Dipping Sauce:

1 cup finely chopped onion
2 tablespoons butter
4 4¾-ounce jars baby food strained plums with tapioca
⅓ cup honey
⅓ cup lemon juice
¼ cup soy sauce
¼ cup water
1 tablespoon finely chopped ginger root

Meatballs, without sauce, freeze well. Reheat, wrapped in foil, in 350° oven for 30 minutes or until heated through.

Plum Good Dipping Sauce Yield: 3½ cups

1. In saucepan, sauté onion in melted butter over medium heat until soft. Add remaining ingredients. Bring mixture to boil; reduce heat and simmer 10 minutes.
2. Serve warm or cover and refrigerate up to two weeks.

Sausage Strata

Yield: 6 to 8 servings

May be made ahead and reheated for brunch or cut into small squares for hors d'oeuvres (about 2 dozen).

6 slices good white bread, crusts trimmed
1 pound bulk sausage, browned and drained
1 cup shredded Swiss cheese
3 eggs, slightly beaten
2 cups light cream
1 teaspoon prepared mustard
½ teaspoon salt
dash pepper
½ teaspoon nutmeg

1. Preheat oven to 350°. Butter bottom of 9 x 13-inch baking dish; line with bread slices.
2. Spread sausage over bread; sprinkle cheese evenly over sausage.
3. Combine remaining ingredients and pour over sausage and cheese.
4. Bake 50 to 60 minutes or until golden brown and set.

Cheese Crispies

Don't laugh — just try them!

1¼ cups (5 ounces) grated
   sharp Cheddar cheese
½ cup (1 stick) cold butter, cut in chunks
¾ cup flour
¼ teaspoon salt
⅛ teaspoon cayenne pepper
1¼ cups crispy rice cereal

Must be made ahead.

Variation:

Do not chill dough but shape into 1-inch balls.
Place an inch apart on baking sheet, flattening
with tines of fork. Bake as above.

1. In bowl of food processor combine all
   ingredients except cereal. Process until
   dough forms a ball.

2. Add cereal and pulse four or five times just
   until cereal is blended. Place dough on
   waxed paper and form into a roll about
   12 x 2-inches. Wrap and chill an hour or
   two until firm (or prepare ahead and chill
   up to 24 hours).

3. Preheat oven to 375°. Slice roll into ¼-inch
   slices; place one inch apart on ungreased
   cookie sheet. Bake 10 minutes. Remove
   from cookie sheet onto wire rack. Serve
   warm (or wrap and freeze up to one month;
   reheat wrapped in foil or microwave).

Fried Mozzarella Italiano

A hearty and unusual appetizer.

1 pound Mozzarella cheese,
   cut into 1-inch cubes
3 eggs, well beaten
½ cup flour
¾ cup Italian-seasoned,
   dry bread crumbs
vegetable oil
Italian Tomato Sauce

1. Dip cheese cubes in egg, roll in flour and
   dip in egg again, then in bread crumbs.
   Place on waxed paper; chill 1 hour.

2. In large saucepan or deep-fat fryer, heat oil
   to 375°. Fry chilled cubes in hot oil; drain
   on paper towels.

3. Serve immediately with Italian Tomato Sauce.

Italian Tomato Sauce:

2 garlic cloves, minced
1 tablespoon olive oil
1 28-ounce can Italian plum tomatoes,
   chopped and undrained
generous pinch of sugar
pinch of salt
1½ teaspoons Italian seasoning
dash of pepper

Sauce preparation:

1. Sauté garlic in oil in heavy skillet; stir in
   remaining ingredients and bring to boil.

2. Reduce heat; simmer uncovered,
   45 minutes or until mixture is thickened,
   stirring occasionally.

Mini Reubens

Yield: about 30 appetizers

1 8-ounce can sauerkraut, rinsed and drained
½ 16-ounce bottle Thousand Island
   salad dressing
8 ounces deli corn beef, chopped fine
8 slices Swiss cheese
1 loaf party-size rye or pumpernickel bread

1. In bowl combine drained sauerkraut with salad dressing. Use more or less dressing for desired consistency, not too runny. Add chopped corn beef; mix well.
2. Cut each slice of cheese into 4 small squares. Lightly toast bread.
3. Place toasted bread on foil-covered baking sheet. Top each piece with tablespoon of kraut mixture; cover with a square of cheese.
4. Place under preheated broiler just until cheese melts. Watch closely. Serve hot.

Hickory Cheese Ball

Yield: about a 1-pound cheese ball

Serve the cheese on apple and pear slices for a touch of fall.

1 8-ounce package cream cheese, softened
1 10-ounce package Long Horn Cheddar
   cheese, grated
½ teaspoon lemon juice
½ teaspoon liquid Hickory Smoke seasoning
1 tablespoon grated onion
1½ cups finely chopped walnuts or cashews

Must be made ahead.

1. Place all ingredients, except nuts, in mixing bowl; combine thoroughly, using hands, if desired.
2. Form mixture into a ball; roll in chopped nuts.
3. Wrap securely in plastic wrap and refrigerate at least 24 hours before serving. Serve with crackers or thin slices of apple and pear.

Oyster Spread

Yield: about 2 cups

The aficionados of this hors d'oeuvre may be limited, but they will be passionate!

1 8-ounce package cream cheese, softened
2 to 3 tablespoons mayonnaise
1 teaspoon Worcestershire sauce
1 tablespoon grated onion
salt, to taste
freshly ground pepper
1 3½-ounce can smoked oysters, chopped
dash Tabasco sauce

Must be made ahead.

1. Combine all ingredients, mixing well. Refrigerate 8 hours or overnight to blend flavors.
2. Serve at room temperature with toasted rye or pumpernickel rounds, crackers or melba toast.

Muhammara (Turkish Nut Dip)

Yield: about 1½ cups

A delicious dip derived from ground nuts and sweet peppers, excellent with crudités. AFIYET OLSUN! (Turkish for "Bon Apetit")

¾ cup broken walnut or hazelnut meats (do not use black walnuts)
1 very small garlic clove
3 thick slices of light or white bread, lightly toasted
2 very ripe, sweet red peppers, cored and seeded
1 small fresh or canned green chili pepper, seeded if too hot (or ground cayenne pepper to taste may be substituted)
juice of 1 lemon
2 to 3 tablespoons olive oil
salt and black pepper, to taste
crudités, toasted pita bread

Must be made ahead.

Although not traditional Middle Eastern fare, MUHAMMARA makes a splendid chilled soup when thinned with yogurt and garnished with parsley or coriander (cilantro).

1. Toast nuts in a moderate oven until fragrant. When cooled, finely chop them with garlic and bread in food processor. Add red peppers, green peppers and lemon juice; process to a thick paste.

2. With processor running, add olive oil until consistency is similar to pesto.

3. Season to taste with salt, pepper and additional lemon juice. Chill at least 2 hours. Serve with toasted pita, celery and other crudités. (Especially attractive served in a blue bowl.)

Nineteenth-century New England cooking was greatly enhanced by exotic ingredients brought home by merchant ships. As a trader in oriental carpets, I've come to know the Levantine coasts where American clippers once docked to take on spices, dried fruit, and nuts. Culinary curiosity has led me into scores of Middle Eastern kitchens; the recipe for this delicious hors d'oeuvre, a specialty of southeastern Turkey and northern Syria, is one of my most cherished "finds." — H.C., Groton Long Point, CT

SOUPS

CHOWDER

New Englanders approach chowder as a culinary free-for-all with little agreement on even the basic ingredients. It used to be that Bostonians liked it cream-style, Rhode Islanders made it with a broth base, and nearer New York folks added tomatoes, Manhattan-style. The variations are as endless as the arguments as to which recipe is THE traditional one. Every September the Great Chowder Cook-Off is held in Newport and every October Mystic Seaport holds its annual Chowder Fest. The debate goes on . . .

"The BEST Clam Chowder in New England"   Yield: 10 servings

Turner Fisheries Bar and Restaurant's recipe was Boston's chowder champ
for 3 years before winning the coveted regional title of "Best"
at the Great Chowder Cook-Off in Newport in 1987.
Chef Norman Wade credits the right balance of clams
and wholesome ingredients.

6 quahogs
10 cherrystones
1 cup water, divided
¼ cup (½ stick) butter, clarified
1 garlic clove, minced
1 medium onion, chopped and blanched
1 rib celery, chopped and blanched
¼ teaspoon thyme
½ teaspoon white pepper
1 small bay leaf
¼ cup flour
1 quart clam juice
1 large potato, diced and blanched
1 pint heavy cream
salt and pepper to taste

If fresh clams are not available, substitute
12 to 14 ounces canned or frozen clams and use
an additional cup of bottled clam juice.

1. Wash clams thoroughly. Place quahogs in pot with ½ cup water; cover tightly and steam until clams open. Repeat this process with cherrystones. Remove clams from shell, chop coarsely and reserve broth in separate container.

2. In same pot add clarified butter and garlic; sauté 2 to 3 minutes. Add onions, celery and seasonings and sauté until onions are translucent.

3. Stir in flour to make roux; cook over low heat, stirring constantly, for 5 minutes. Do not brown.

4. Slowly add the reserved and bottled clam juice and stir constantly to avoid lumps. Simmer for 10 minutes. The soup will be very thick at this point so be careful it does not burn.

5. Add potatoes and cook until tender. Stir in cream and clams and heat to just below boiling point. DO NOT BOIL. Season to taste.

Mike's Clam Chowder Base

Yield: 3 gallons chowder

A creamy chowder base which may be frozen in 1-quart containers. Add evaporated milk to serve. Excellent for a crowd.

Roux:

1 pound salt pork, ground
1 very large onion, finely chopped
approximately 4 cups flour

Potatoes:

5 very large potatoes, scrubbed, peeled
  and diced into small cubes
water

Clams and Base:

8 cups cooked, chopped clams
3½ quarts (13 to 14 cups) clam juice
celery salt, salt and pepper to taste

evaporated milk (no substitutes)

MIKE'S CLAM CHOWDER BASE

When we were first married and in the restaurant business, my husband once purchased an enormous electric mixer from a defunct Boston hotel. So large was this mixer that it sported a four-speed transmission, a dough hook hefty enough to snag a whale, and a 90-quart bowl! While it may have saved Mike a lot of time in the restaurant, it surely contributed to his greatest flaw at home: his chowder is wonderful, but he simply doesn't know how to make it for a group smaller than 40! — S.M., Mystic, CT

Roux preparation:

1. In large, heavy skillet over moderately low heat, cook salt pork and onions until salt pork is completely melted and onions are soft.

2. Add enough flour (approximately 4 cups) to skillet to "tighten" the roux. The measurement is not exact, but you will need enough flour to absorb all of the grease and produce a mixture the consistency of mashed potatoes. Add flour SLOWLY, stirring constantly. Remove from heat; set aside.

Potato preparation:

1. Wash potato cubes well in cold water.

2. To blanch: fill large kettle with enough water to cover potatoes but do NOT add them yet. Bring water to boil; THEN add potatoes. When water returns to second boil, remove pan from heat at once. Drain potatoes; set aside.

Clam Base preparation:

1. In large kettle, bring clam juice and clams to boil; add roux, stirring constantly to form thick base. Remove from heat.

2. Season to taste with celery salt, salt and pepper.

3. Add potatoes.

4. Cool. You should have approximately 6 quarts (1½ gallons) base. If desired, divide into plastic containers and freeze.

To serve:

1. Thaw base, if frozen, and combine equal amounts of base and evaporated milk; that is, one quart of evaporated milk to each quart of base.

2. Heat slowly, preferably in top of double boiler, until potato cubes are tender. DO NOT BOIL. Adjust seasonings. Serve hot with chowder crackers.

Watch Hill Award-Winning Clam Chowder

Yield: 6 servings

This recipe from the Watch Hill Inn (R.I.) won Second Place in the 1987 Great Chowder Cook-Off. We thank Dana Valery Catalano, proprietor, for sharing it with us.

2 ounces (about 3 strips) diced bacon
4 ounces diced Spanish onion
2 ounces diced celery
2½ cups clam juice
1 pound chopped clams
½ pound diced (red) new potatoes
1 teaspoon black pepper
½ teaspoon thyme
1 pint heavy cream

1. In large pot, cook bacon until golden brown; add onion and celery and sauté until soft and transparent.
2. Add clam juice, clams, potatoes and seasonings; cook until potatoes are tender.
3. Slowly stir in cream, heat through but DO NOT BOIL. Serve hot.

Noank Quahog Chowder

Yield: a pot full!

A clear broth chowder, locally referred to as "Noank" chowder, very popular in southeastern Connecticut and Rhode Island.

2 to 4 ounces salt pork, diced
2 medium onions, sliced
6 to 8 Idaho baking potatoes, peeled and very thinly sliced (⅛ to ¹⁄₁₆-inch thick)
1 quart quahogs and juice
water
salt and pepper, to taste

Must be made ahead.

1. Start chowder at least 24 to 36 hours before serving (cook Friday morning to serve Saturday night). Try out salt pork in bottom of large soup pot or kettle until fat is released; add onions and stir until translucent.
2. Potatoes should be sliced, not diced. "Clam flavor can't permeate cubes and you'll taste potatoey lumps." Add potatoes to pot along with juice drained from quahogs and enough water to cover by an inch or two. Cook until potatoes are tender.
3. Meanwhile, chop clams. "You want recognizable clam pieces, but chowder's not for chewing." When potatoes are tender, add chopped clams to pot. Simmer 10 to 15 minutes; cool and refrigerate at once, 24 to 36 hours.
4. To serve, reheat chowder just to boiling point. "This is a strong chowder, so, if you wish, you can add a little warm milk to your second bowl, but this is rather heretical."

Scallop Chowder

Chowder's not just for clams.

Yield: 4 to 6 servings

1 ½ pounds sea scallops or bay scallops
4 scallions, finely chopped
4 tablespoons unsalted butter
6 tablespoons dry sherry
4 teaspoons Worcestershire sauce
1 ¼ teaspoons Old Bay Seasoning*
2 tablespoons flour
1 pint half-and-half
chopped parsley, paprika for garnish

*available at most fish markets

1. Rinse scallops and pat dry. Cut sea scallops in ½-inch pieces.
2. In large skillet over medium heat, sauté scallions in 1 tablespoon butter. Add scallops and stir continuously in pan until opaque, 2 to 4 minutes; do not overcook. Remove skillet from heat; add 2 tablespoons sherry, 3 teaspoons Worcestershire sauce and ¼ teaspoon Old Bay Seasoning. Stir and set aside.
3. In large saucepan, melt 3 tablespoons butter. Using wire whisk, gradually add flour. Cook and stir until mixture is golden; gradually add half-and-half, 4 tablespoons sherry, 1 teaspoon Worcestershire sauce and 1 teaspoon Old Bay Seasoning. Blend well. The result should be a thin, fragrant sauce.
4. Just before serving, add scallops with juices from skillet to half-and-half mixture. Heat over medium heat, stirring constantly until steamy; do not boil.
5. Serve in warm bowls; garnish with chopped parsley and paprika, if desired.

Baked Fish Chowder

Put it in the oven and forget about it for an hour.

Yield: 6 to 8 servings

2 pounds haddock, pollack or similar white
    fish fillets
¼ cup (½ stick) butter
salt and pepper
3 or 4 potatoes, peeled and sliced
3 onions, sliced
2 or 3 tablespoons chopped celery leaves
2 garlic cloves, minced
1 to 2 teaspoons dried dill, to taste
¾ cup vermouth or white wine
2 cups boiling water
4 cups half-and-half (or milk)

1. Preheat oven to 375°. Butter large casserole.
2. Place fish in bottom of casserole; dot with half the butter and sprinkle with salt and pepper.
3. Layer potatoes and onions over fish; dot with remaining butter and sprinkle with seasonings: celery leaves, garlic, dill, salt and pepper.
4. Add vermouth, then pour boiling water over all. Cover and bake 1 hour.
5. Scald half-and-half and add just before serving, stirring to break up fish. Serve with Pilot crackers, if desired. Any leftovers may be gently heated on top of stove in heavy saucepan. Chowder freezes well.

Texas "Chowder"

**An original recipe by an imaginary Mexican
cook on a cattle drive across the Llano Estacado and brought to Mystic
where it immediately won the First Bi-annual Chili Cook-Off.**

Yield: enough for 6 people
or 2 Texans

Carne:

3 garlic cloves, chopped
2 medium to large onions, chopped
1 large bay leaf
1 jalepeño pepper, finely chopped
corn oil
1 to 1½ pounds ground meat (pork or beef)
¾ teaspoon salt
¾ teaspoon thyme
½ teaspoon sage
½ teaspoon cayenne pepper
½ teaspoon (scant) black pepper
2 teaspoons cumin
1 to 2 good shakes of Tabasco sauce
2 to 3 tablespoons chili powder

Chili Sauce:

1 6-ounce can tomato paste
6 ounces water
2 16-ounce cans pork and beans
(pork pieces removed)
1 teaspoon sugar
salt, thyme, sage, cayenne, black pepper,
cumin, Tabasco, onion and chili powder
in same amounts as in carne above
1 tablespoon masa (finely ground cornmeal),
if available

Best made ahead.

**This chili is prepared in two parts in one pot:
the carne, or meat, and the chili, or sauce.
The carne portion may be used as a filling for
tacos, enchiladas, etc.**

Carne preparation:

1. Sauté garlic, one onion, bay leaf and
jalepeño pepper in enough oil to do the job,
until onions just begin to turn brown at
the edges.

2. Add ground meat and next seven seasonings; cook until meat is well done. Stir in
chili powder and cook briefly. Carne should
be dark brown.

Chili preparation:

1. Reduce heat and add tomato paste, one can
water, beans, sugar and the other onion to
the carne. Then repeat the seven seasonings
and chili powder in the same amounts as
previously. Add masa, if available.

2. Let chili simmer for a couple of hours, then
allow it to rest overnight, if possible.

3. To serve; toss a few slices of Longhorn
Cheddar cheese or Monterey Jack and plain
saltines in bowl of hot chili. Accompany with
lemonade, iced tea, or domestic or imported
beer, Margaritas or tequila shots with salt
and lime. Finish with peppermint ice cream
to soothe the stomach and refresh what is
left of the mouth.

**This recipe makes a mild to medium chili, usually reserved for
those Texans not yet weaned or recovering from stomach
transplant surgery. For Real Chili (HOT) add one or more jalepeños
and more cayenne. For milder chili, cut back on spices in this order:
Tabasco, black pepper, jalepeño, and the cherished cayenne last.**

Creamy Harvest Soup

Yield: 6 servings

A delectable cream soup.

3 tablespoons butter
2 large leeks, washed and chopped
2 celery stalks, chopped
1 large carrot, scrubbed and chopped
stems from 1 bunch parsley
3 garlic cloves, minced
1½ teaspoons dried thyme, crumbled
1 46-ounce can chicken broth
1 teaspoon salt, or to taste
3 large carrots, scrubbed
¼ pound green beans, trimmed
1 large red bell pepper
1 medium zucchini
2 medium tomatoes, seeded
3 ears of corn, husked
⅓ cup heavy cream
freshly ground black pepper
⅓ cup mixed finely chopped fresh herbs
  (basil, parsley and thyme)

1. Melt butter in large heavy saucepan over medium-low heat. Stir in next six ingredients. Cover and cook, stirring occasionally, about 20 minutes.
2. Add broth and salt; bring to boil; reduce heat, cover partially and simmer until vegetables are tender, about 30 minutes. Strain and return soup to pan.
3. Dice carrots, green beans, red pepper, zucchini and tomatoes into ½-inch pieces. Scrape corn off cob into bowl.
4. Bring soup to boil; add carrots and boil 5 minutes. Add green beans and bell pepper; boil 5 minutes. Add zucchini; boil 5 minutes. Add tomatoes and corn; simmer. Stir in cream and ground pepper. Taste and adjust seasonings. Continue cooking until soup is heated through, about 5 minutes more. Sprinkle each serving generously with chopped herbs.

Spiced Squash Soup

Yield: 8 servings

This spicy soup originated in Granada, the "Nutmeg Island."

2 slices bacon, minced
1 onion, chopped
1 13¾-ounce can beef broth
1 broth can of water
4 cups peeled, cubed winter squash
  (Hubbard, butternut, acorn or pumpkin)
1 tablespoon Worcestershire sauce
⅛ teaspoon Tabasco sauce or to taste
freshly grated nutmeg

1. In heavy soup kettle over low heat sauté bacon until almost crisp
2. Add chopped onion and cook until tender. Add beef broth, water and cubed squash. Simmer 30 to 45 minutes or until squash is very tender.
3. In blender or food processor, purée squash and broth. Return to kettle; add seasonings and more water as needed to reach desired soup consistency.
4. Serve hot with gratings of nutmeg on top.

BREADS

Whole Wheat Molasses Bread

Yield: 2 loaves

2 cups milk
¼ cup (½ stick) butter
1 egg
½ cup molasses
½ teaspoon salt
2 packages active dry yeast
3½ to 4 cups white flour
3 cups whole wheat flour

1. In saucepan heat milk and butter until lukewarm (110°). Pour mixture into large bowl and add egg, molasses, salt, yeast and 2 cups white flour; beat 2 minutes in mixer with dough hook.

2. Add 3 cups whole wheat flour and mix; gradually stir in remaining 1½ to 2 cups white flour.

3. Knead dough 7 to 10 minutes with dough hook or by hand. Place in greased bowl; turn dough to grease top. Cover and let rise in warm, draft-free place for 1½ hours or until doubled in bulk.

4. Punch down dough and form into loaves. Place loaves in buttered pans, cover and let rise 1 hour.

5. Preheat oven to 375°. Bake loaves about 35 minutes. Remove from pans and cool loaves on sides.

Squash Rolls

Yield: 1½ dozen rolls

A wonderful bread with Thanksgiving dinner.

1 cup warm water (110°)
¾ cup sugar
2 packages active dry yeast
3 tablespoons oil
2 teaspoons salt
1 cup puréed cooked squash (acorn or butternut or use 2 4¼-ounce jars strained baby food squash)
½ cup non-fat dry milk powder
5 cups flour

1. Combine warm water and sugar in large bowl of mixer. Add yeast; let stand 5 minutes.

2. Add next four ingredients; beat at low speed with mixer. Gradually beat in 2 cups flour. Add remaining flour. Knead gently.

3. Cover and let rise in draft-free place until doubled in bulk. Punch down. Roll dough to 1-inch thickness. With oiled hands shape into small balls 1½-inches in diameter.

4. Place rolls in 8 x 10-inch baking pan just touching one another. Cover and let rise until doubled.

5. Bake at 400° for 20 minutes.

Bran Bread

Yield: 1 loaf

A brown molasses quick bread, slightly different from the traditional steamed Boston brown bread.

1½ cups flour
3 teaspoons baking powder
½ cup sugar
½ teaspoon salt
½ cup raisins (optional)
1 cup milk
3 tablespoons molasses
1½ cup bran buds
1 egg, beaten
¼ cup vegetable oil

1. Preheat oven to 350°. Grease a 9-inch loaf pan.
2. Sift together first four ingredients; add raisins.
3. In another bowl add milk to molasses; stir in bran buds. Add egg and oil to bran mixture and mix thoroughly.
4. Combine bran mixture with dry ingredients. Stir just until mixed and moistened.
5. Pour into prepared loaf pan. Bake for about 1 hour.
6. Cool in pan about 5 minutes; remove and continue cooling on wire rack. Serve with sweet butter, if desired.

At our family gatherings, it was always my mother who brought the brown bread. We doubled or tripled the recipe, depending on how many aunts, uncles and cousins were to be there. Of course, there was always some churned butter to go with this bread. During the Depression, most everyone had a cow, and my father insisted that a Jersey cow gave the best butter. — Mrs. D.W.O., Arlington, VA

133

Bake Shop English Muffins

Yield: about 15 muffins

This popular item in the Seaport Stores' Bake Shop is surprisingly easy to make at home. We bet once you've tried 'em you'll want to bake them often.

6 cups sifted flour, divided
⅓ cup non-fat dry milk powder
1½ tablespoons sugar
1 teaspoon salt
2 packages active dry yeast
2⅓ cups warm water (110°)
½ cup (1 stick) butter, melted
shortening
cornmeal
4-inch muffin rings*

*Available at some gourmet specialty shops or by order from the Mystic Seaport Museum Stores

1. Sift together 3 cups flour, powdered milk, sugar, salt and yeast into large mixing bowl. Stir in warm water and mix well. Cover bowl and let rise in a warm, draft-free place for 1½ hours until doubled in bulk.

2. Grease baking sheets with shortening and sprinkle with cornmeal. Lightly coat insides of muffin rings with shortening.

3. Slowly stir melted butter and remaining 3 cups flour into dough until all is well blended. Dough will be sticky.

4. Coat hands with shortening. Pinch off about 3 ounces of dough (slighly smaller than a tennis ball) and place in center of muffin ring on prepared baking sheet; attach dough to sides of ring by gently pushing with fingers. Sprinkle lighly with cornmeal. Proceed until all dough is used. Cover baking sheets with plastic wrap and let rise in warm, draft-free place until muffins are doubled in size.

5. Preheat oven to 350°. Gently remove plastic wrap and bake muffins about 15 minutes or until light brown.

6. Remove from baking sheet to wire rack with spatula. When cool, remove muffin rings. Muffins freeze well.

Home cookery retained a by-guess-and-by-golly nature until 1800, when James Lamb of Middletown, Connecticut, invented the first stove with even heat distribution.

Ginger Marmalade Biscuits

Yield: 1½ dozen

These biscuits are really special made with ginger marmalade but sweet or bitter orange marmalade may be used.

2 cups flour
4 teaspoons baking powder
½ teaspoon salt
¼ cup plus 1 tablespoon shortening
1 egg, slightly beaten
⅓ cup milk
⅓ cup ginger marmalade (Captain's Choice)

1. Preheat oven to 425°.
2. Combine first three ingredients; mix well. Using pastry blender or food processor, cut in shortening until mixture resembles coarse meal.
3. Combine remaining ingredients in a small bowl. Add to flour mixture, stirring by hand until moistened. Turn dough onto floured surface; knead lightly, 8 to 10 times, adding a little flour if dough is too sticky.
4. Roll dough to ¾-inch thickness; cut with 2-inch round, floured cutter. Place on ungreased baking sheet. Bake 8 to 10 minutes or until golden brown.

Three-Grain Pear Muffins

Yield: 1 dozen

What a yummy way to sneak "health food" into kids!

1 to 2 medium pears, chopped
   (about 1½ cups)
½ cup milk
⅓ cup vegetable oil
1 egg
¾ cup flour
¾ cup cornmeal
½ cup whole wheat flour
½ cup regular oats
⅓ cup sugar
¼ cup golden raisins
2 teaspoons baking powder
½ teaspoon salt
pinch nutmeg

1. Preheat oven to 375°. Grease well or line one muffin pan.
2. In medium bowl combine first four ingredients; stir well. In another bowl combine remaining ingredients. Add liquids to dry ingredients and stir just until blended.
3. Spoon batter into prepared muffin cups. Bake 25 to 35 minutes, or until brown and wooden toothpick inserted in center comes out clean. Cool on wire rack. Serve warm, if desired.

Apple Muffins

Yield: 2 dozen

These sweet morsels are good for breakfast or snacks.

3½ cups flour
3 cups peeled, cored shredded baking apples
  (about 3 apples)
2 cups sugar
1 teaspoon baking soda
1 teaspoon cinnamon
¼ teaspoon nutmeg
⅔ cup vegetable oil
⅔ cup milk
½ cup chopped pecans

1. Preheat oven to 350°. Grease two standard muffin pans.
2. Mix together first six ingredients in a large bowl. In smaller bowl combine remaining ingredients and add to first mixture, stirring gently, just until moistened.
3. Fill muffin cups one-half to two-thirds full; bake 25 to 30 minutes. Serve warm or cool on wire rack.

Apple Flip Coffee Cake

Yield: 8 to 10 servings

Easy enough to make Sunday morning and let rise while you read the newspapers.

2 tablespoons butter, melted
½ cup sugar
1 teaspoon cinnamon
1 large apple, thinly sliced
1 tablespoon raisins

1 package active dry yeast
¾ cup warm water (110°)
¼ cup sugar
1 teaspoon salt
2½ cups flour
1 egg
¼ cup (½ stick) butter, melted

1. Cover the bottom of a 9-inch square baking pan with butter. Combine sugar and cinnamon and sprinkle over bottom of pan. Arrange apple slices in rows over sugar and sprinkle with raisins.
2. Dissolve yeast in water in large bowl; add ¼ cup sugar, salt and 1 cup flour, beating a couple of minutes. Blend in egg, butter and remaining flour.
3. Drop dough by spoonfuls over apples in pan. Cover and let rise in warm, draft-free spot for 1 hour.
4. Preheat oven to 375°. Bake for 25 to 35 minutes, until lightly browned. Remove from oven and immediately invert onto serving plate. Serve warm.

JOHNNYCAKES

Native Americans probably taught the Pilgrims at Plymouth how to make a type of griddle cake from stone-ground cornmeal which the Indians called "jonakin." New Englanders still make this regional specialty 350 years later — johnnycakes! And the unequivocal ingredient in any variation is still stone-ground cornmeal.

Vermont Johnnycake

Yield: Yield: 8 servings

Thick baked cornbread served in wedges and topped with maple syrup.

1⅓ cups flour
1 cup stone-ground yellow cornmeal
¼ cup sugar
3 teaspoons baking powder
1 teaspoon baking soda
½ teaspoon salt
1 cup milk
¼ cup (½ stick) melted butter or shortening
1 egg, lightly beaten

1. Preheat oven to 400°. Grease well a 9-inch layer cake pan.
2. Combine all dry ingredients in medium bowl. Combine milk, butter and egg in large measuring cup.
3. Make a well in center of dry ingredients; pour in liquid ingredients and stir just to moisten. Pour into prepared pan.
4. Bake 20 to 25 minutes or until nicely browned and springy to touch. Serve hot with lots of syrup.

Rhode Island Johnnycakes

Yield: about 12 4-inch cakes

**Made with white cornmeal and cooked on a hot griddle.
Some Rhode Island cooks would omit the sugar, others the eggs.**

3 eggs
2 cups stone-ground white cornmeal
2 teaspoons baking powder
2 tablespoons flour
1 teaspoon salt
2 tablespoons sugar (optional)
1 tablespoon melted butter or shortening
milk (1 to 2 cups)

1. In medium bowl, beat eggs well. Add remaining ingredients, stirring in enough milk to make thin batter.
2. Pour batter onto hot griddle (use ¼ cup measure to dip batter). Cook until brown on one side; flip and brown on other side. Serve with butter and maple syrup.

Variation:
Break completely with tradition! Try serving johnnycakes topped with smoked salmon and Crème Fraîche (see index) or sour cream; sprinkle with plenty of fresh snipped dill.

Rhode Island Spoon Bread

Yield: 6 servings

**A Southern specialty adapted by a Rhode Islander
using the state's famous stone-ground white cornmeal.**

⅔ cup stone-ground white cornmeal
2 cups light cream or milk
2 tablespoons butter
1 teaspoon salt
2 teaspoons sugar
½ teaspoon baking powder
2 eggs, separated

1. Mix together first five ingredients in saucepan. Stir and cook over low heat until thickened to the consistency of thin oatmeal.

2. Remove from heat; cool to lukewarm.

3. Preheat oven to 350°. Grease a 1½-quart casserole.

4. Stir baking powder into cooled cornmeal mixture. Beat egg yolks slightly and add.

5. Beat egg whites until stiff; fold into batter.

6. Pour into prepared baking dish. Bake about 45 minutes, until top is lightly browned. Serve immediately, spooned right from casserole, with butter. (Consistency will be like custard.)

Baked Wine and Cheese Omelet

Yield: 8 to 10 servings

**A rich and filling egg strata,
a little different and better than most.**

½ loaf of Italian bread, cut into small cubes
3 tablespoons butter, melted
8 ounces shredded Swiss cheese
4 ounces shredded Monterey Jack cheese
4 slices Genoa salami, chopped
8 eggs
1¾ cups milk
¼ cup dry white wine
2 large green onions, chopped
2 tablespoons sharp prepared mustard
¼ teaspoon pepper
dash cayenne pepper
¾ cup sour cream
⅓ cup Parmesan cheese

Must be made ahead.

1. Grease a 13 x 9-inch baking dish. Spread bread cubes over bottom and drizzle with butter. Sprinkle with shredded cheeses and salami.

2. Beat together eggs, milk, wine, onions, mustard and peppers until foamy. Pour over cheese and bread.

3. Cover dish with foil. Refrigerate 24 hours or overnight.

4. Remove dish from refrigerator 30 minutes before cooking. Preheat oven to 325°. Bake for 1 hour; uncover and spread with sour cream and sprinkle with Parmesan. Bake uncovered 10 minutes to brown sour cream.

MAIN DISHES

Steak Black Jack

Yield: 2 to 4 servings

A favorite of patrons at Mystic's Captain Daniel Packer Inne.

2 14-ounce sirloin strip steaks
1 ounce crushed black peppercorns
2 tablespoons oil
12 fresh mushrooms, quartered
3 ounces Jack Daniels bourbon whiskey

1. Pound crushed peppercorns into one side of sirloin steaks.
2. Place steaks, on peppercorn side, in a skillet with oil over high heat; sauté for 2 minutes.
3. Add mushrooms to skillet; reduce heat to medium and cook for 2 minutes.
4. Turn steaks; sauté for 4 minutes.
5. Drain off fat in skillet; add Jack Daniels and ignite. Burn off alcohol and serve immediately.

Pot Roast Carbonnade

Yield: 6 to 8 servings

The classic method of cooking beef stew in beer is used here to prepare pot roast.

3 to 4 pounds beef chuck, rump
  or round roast
2 tablespoons oil
1 12-ounce can beer
1 cup beef broth
1 1.9-ounce package French onion soup
  and recipe mix
1 teaspoon black peppercorns, crushed
¼ cup cider vinegar
1 tablespoon brown sugar
2 tablespoons EACH flour and butter
  (optional)

1. Preheat oven to 325°. Dry meat with paper towels. In Dutch oven, brown meat on all sides in hot oil. Add beer, broth, soup mix and peppercorns. Cover and bake for 1½ to 2 hours.
2. Remove meat from pot, slice and keep warm on serving platter. Heat liquid on top of stove on high heat until slightly reduced; add vinegar and brown sugar.
3. If desired, at this point sauce may be thickened by making a roux of flour and butter; slowly add sauce, stirring constantly until thickened.
4. Adjust seasonings. Pour some sauce over meat and serve the rest separately.

Deviled Short Ribs

Yield: 4 servings

**Serve up these on Halloween night
along with an apple cider "Witches Brew," (see index).**

2 tablespoons dry hot mustard
2 to 3 teaspoons salt, or to taste
¼ teaspoon ground pepper
½ teaspoon chili powder
2 tablespoons lemon juice
4 tablespoons olive oil
2 garlic cloves, chopped
2 small onions, cut in wedges
3 pounds short ribs of beef

Must be made ahead.

1. Combine all ingredients, except the ribs, and mix thoroughly. Marinate the ribs in the mixture, in non-metallic ovenproof baking dish, at least 8 hours, preferably overnight.

2. Place ribs, along with marinade, in preheated 425° oven for 15 minutes, or until brown. Cover dish, reduce heat to 350° and continue baking for 1 to 1½ hours, or until ribs are tender. Serve with curly noodles ("monsters' hair"), if desired.

Beef Stew with Fruit

Yield: 10 to 12 servings

A thick, rich stew flavored with autumn spices.

4 pounds beef stew meat, cut in
    1-inch cubes
1 cup flour
3 tablespoons vegetable oil
1 teaspoon salt
1 teaspoon pepper
½ teaspoon cinnamon
½ teaspoon ginger
6 carrots, thinly sliced
2 medium turnips, finely diced
1 13¾-ounce can beef broth
1 cup red wine
1 cup dried apricots
1 cup prunes

May be made up to two days ahead.

1. Place meat cubes in heavy-duty plastic bag with flour; shake to coat well.

2. Heat oil in large Dutch oven; brown meat, in two batches. Return all meat to pot.

3. Season meat with salt, pepper and spices. Add vegetables, broth and wine; bring to boil, lower heat, cover and simmer for 1 hour. Stir occasionally to prevent sticking.

4. Add fruit and more broth or water if stew becomes too thick. Cover and cook an additional hour, stirring occasionally and adding liquid as needed.

Mama Cerullo's Meatballs and Sauce

Yield: about 2 quarts sauce
about 4 dozen meatballs

Mama and her son, the chef, have collaborated in writing down this recipe for an authentic Italian meat sauce.

Sauce:

2 to 4 tablespoons olive oil
1/8 teaspoon red pepper flakes
dozen or more raisins
dozen or more pine nuts
1/4 teaspoon MSG (optional)
1 garlic clove the size of a nickel,
  crushed and halved
1 tablespoon fresh parsley
salt and freshly ground black pepper to taste
1/2 pound ground chuck*
1/2 pound ground or chopped pork*
  or crumbled Italian sausage
Parmesan cheese
32 ounces Italian plum tomatoes
sugar
12 ounces tomato paste
water, as needed

Hints from Mom: It's the sautéing of the flavorings in the oil and the browning process of the meat that are the secrets.

*For serving sauce without meatballs, double the amount of meat in the sauce recipe.

Meatballs:

6 or 7 slices Hollywood Light bread, crumbled
water (about 1/3 cup)
1 1/2 teaspoons salt
pinch red pepper flakes
1/2 teaspoon minced garlic
black pepper to taste
dozen pine nuts, finely chopped
2 tablespoons chopped fresh parsley
3 or 4 eggs
1 1/2 pounds ground chuck
additional pine nuts
raisins

Mom doubles this recipe, but then, she has ten children!

Sauce preparation:

1. Cover bottom of large, preferably non-aluminum, saucepan with oil; add next seven ingredients. Sauté over medium-low heat for 5 to 8 minutes, tipping pan as necessary to coat all ingredients with oil.

2. Add meat and cook, stirring frequently, until browned and just beginning to stick to bottom of pan. Do not allow to burn. Sprinkle with grated cheese.

3. Add tomatoes and 1 teaspoon sugar. Taste for seasonings. Lower heat and simmer about 30 minutes. Stir once or twice with wooden spoon.

4. Add tomato paste and at least 1 teaspoon more sugar; adjust salt and cook an additional 30 minutes.

5. Add meatballs (preparation below) with pan scrapings. If sauce is thick, add 1 to 2 cups water as needed. Otherwise meatballs will absorb most of sauce during cooking. Cook about an hour. Skim fat before serving.

Meatball preparation:

1. Preheat oven to 350°. Coat inside of baking dish or jellyroll pan with oil.

2. Moisten bread crumbs until mushy but firm. (Too much water will cause meatballs to fall apart.) Squeeze bread while adding water.

3. Add all dry ingredients; stir thoroughly. Add eggs; mix well. Add meat and mix with hands until all ingredients are evenly distributed.

4. Shape meatballs to desired size, golf ball size or smaller. Place in rows in baking dish. Drop a dozen or so pine nuts and raisins among the meatballs. Bake 30 to 40 minutes.

5. Add meatballs to sauce with any scrapings and the pine nuts and raisins.

Veal and Apple Stew

Yield: 8 servings

A delicious, plate-scraping trio — veal, apples and cream.

3 pounds veal stew meat, cut in 1-inch cubes
salt and freshly ground pepper
3 tablespoons butter
2 large onions, very thinly sliced
generous pinch cinnamon
pinch thyme
2 teaspoons ground sage
¼ cup dry vermouth
¼ cup chicken broth
2 medium tart apples,
  peeled and coarsely shredded
2 tablespoons apple jelly
1 cup heavy cream
1½ tablespoons lemon juice

1. Generously season veal with salt and pepper. Heat butter in large heavy kettle or Dutch oven until it foams and begins to brown. Add veal, tossing to coat each piece well.

2. Spread onion slices over meat; sprinkle with cinnamon, thyme and sage. Add wine and broth, cover, and simmer for 1½ to 2 hours or until veal is very tender. Stir gently to blend.

3. With slotted spoon remove meat and onions to bowl; cover with foil. Add apples to pot and cook over high heat, stirring frequently, until apples are tender and liquid is reduced to a thick sauce, about 3 to 4 minutes.

4. Stir in jelly and cream; cook over high heat until mixture blends. Lower heat; return meat and onions to pot along with lemon juice. Stir thoroughly, adjust seasonings and serve. Good with hot buttered noodles and fresh spinach salad.

Bobotie

Yield: 4 to 6 servings

An unusual baked curry dish.

1 or 2 thick slices of bread
1 cup milk
1 pound lean ground lamb or beef
1 tablespoon butter
1 onion, chopped
1 apple, chopped
½ cup raisins
¼ to ½ cup (a handful) chopped almonds
2 teaspoons vinegar
2 teaspoons lemon juice
1 tablespoon curry powder
½ teaspoon salt
½ teaspoon mixed herbs
ground black pepper
2 eggs

1. Soak bread slices in milk; squeeze out excess milk, reserving both milk and bread.

2. Brown meat in large skillet, adding a little oil if necessary; remove from skillet with slotted spoon and drain on paper towels.

3. Melt butter in skillet and cook onion until soft; remove from heat.

4. Combine onion, meat, bread and remaining ingredients except reserved milk and eggs. Mix well, breaking up bread while stirring all together. Spread mixture into buttered ovenproof dish, pressing down gently.

5. Preheat oven to 350°. Whisk milk and eggs together; pour over meat mixture. Bake 30 to 40 minutes. May be served hot or at room temperature.

Lamb Chops with Roquefort Sauce

Yield: 4 servings

Blue cheese lovers take note! This sauce could be used with beef, too.

1½ tablespoons olive oil
1½ tablespoons butter
2 garlic cloves, divided
1 large sweet red pepper, cut in ¼-inch strips
4 lamb shoulder chops
⅓ cup chicken broth
⅓ cup white wine
oregano
salt and pepper
1 cup light cream
4 ounces Roquefort cheese, crumbled

1. In large skillet heat oil and butter. Add one minced garlic clove and red pepper. Cook stirring occasionally, until pepper is tender, about 3 minutes. Remove with slotted spoon, cover with foil and keep warm.

2. Add chops to skillet with remaining garlic, adding more oil if necessary; cook until chops are browned on both sides.

3. Add broth, wine, a generous sprinkle of oregano, salt to taste and pepper. Bring to boil, cover, reduce heat to low and simmer 15 minutes until chops are tender.

4. Remove chops to heated platter; keep warm. Reduce liquid in skillet over high heat to about ¾ cup. Add cream; cook until thickened slightly. Blend in cheese, whisking until cheese melts and sauce is smooth.

5. Spoon sauce over chops; top with sautéed pepper strips.

Pork Chops with Pumpkin Sauce

Yield: 8 servings

Bewitching results from Jack-o-Lantern leftovers!

8 boneless pork loin chops, pounded thin
   (about 1½ pounds)
garlic salt
white pepper
1 tablespoon butter
¾ to 1 cup light cream
¾ cup mashed cooked pumpkin
dash ground nutmeg
toasted broken pecans

**Variation: Chicken Breasts
with Pumpkin Sauce**
Substitute skinned, boned chicken breast halves for pork chops. Cook about 5 minutes per side.

1. Trim chops of any excess fat. Season with garlic salt and white pepper to taste.

2. In a large skillet heat butter; add chops and cook over moderate heat for 8 to 10 minutes or until nicely browned on one side. Turn and continue browning for another 8 to 10 minutes. Chops should cook 20 to 25 minutes in all. Remove to heated platter and keep warm.

3. Add ¾ cup cream to skillet, scraping browned bits from bottom and sides of pan. Add pumpkin, another dash of garlic salt and pepper and a dash of nutmeg. Stir over moderate heat about 3 minutes, adding more cream as needed for desired consistency; pour over chops. Top with toasted nuts.

143

Laurie's Stuffed Pork Chops

Yield: 6 servings

The special feature here is the sauce.

6 (1¼-inch) loin pork chops, split for pocket
salt and pepper
3 tablespoons butter
1 small onion, chopped
1 rib celery, chopped
½ 8-ounce package corn bread
   stuffing crumbs
½ cup hot water
¾ teaspoon poultry seasoning
½ cup mayonnaise
½ cup prepared mustard
1 teaspoon Worcestershire sauce
2 tablespoons teriyaki sauce
2 tablespoons brown sugar

1. Brown chops on both sides in large skillet. Remove from pan. Sprinkle with salt and pepper.
2. In skillet, melt butter and sauté onions and celery. Add to stuffing crumbs along with water and seasoning. Mix well.
3. Stuff chops with crumb mixture. Secure with wooden picks. Place in baking dish.
4. In a small bowl combine remaining ingredients. Spread over pork chops.
5. Bake at 350° for 50 to 60 minutes. If sauce begins to get dry, cover with foil during last 15 to 20 minutes.

Tourtiere (Pork Pie)

Yield: 8 servings

**A traditional French Canadian dish,
a legacy to New England from those who moved south.**

3 tablespoons vegetable oil
2 medium onions, minced
2 garlic cloves, minced
1½ pounds lean ground pork
2 medium tomatoes, peeled, seeded
   and chopped
¼ cup water
½ teaspoon cinnamon
½ teaspoon savory
¼ teaspoon celery seed
½ cup bread crumbs
1 tablespoon Dijon mustard
salt and pepper to taste
pastry for double-crust 9-inch pie

Glaze:
1 egg with 2 tablespoons heavy cream

1. Heat oil in skillet over medium heat; add onion and garlic, cover and cook for 10 minutes, stirring occasionally.
2. Add pork; stir to break up chunks of meat and cook until no longer pink. Mix in tomato, water, cinnamon, savory and celery seed. Reduce heat and simmer until most of liquid is absorbed, about 30 minutes.
3. Stir in bread crumbs, salt and pepper, cool.
4. Preheat oven to 425°. Line 9-inch pan with pastry; brush with mustard. Spoon in filling and cover with top crust. Brush with glaze.
5. Bake for 10 minutes; reduce heat to 350° and bake 35 minutes or until golden brown. Serve hot, warm or at room temperature.

Pork Roast Normandy

Yield: 6 to 8 servings

Celebrate autumn with this apple-filled, delicious entrée.

1 3-pound boned, butterflied pork loin roast
½ teaspoon dried thyme
¼ teaspoon salt
pepper to taste
1 large tart cooking apple, cored and
   sliced thin
2 tablespoons shortening
2 shallots, minced
¾ cup dry vermouth or chicken broth
½ cup apple cider
¾ cup heavy cream
12 ounces fresh mushrooms, quartered
1 tablespoon Calvados or apple brandy
   (optional)

1. Open up roast; sprinkle with thyme, salt and pepper. Distribute apples evenly along one side, near the center. Roll up roast; tie in several pieces with kitchen twine.

2. In Dutch oven, melt shortening; add meat and shallots. Brown meat well on all sides. Remove roast to platter and pour drippings into small skillet. Set both aside.

3. Stir wine into browned bits in Dutch oven; boil 2 to 3 minutes or until wine is reduced by half. Add cider; boil 3 to 5 minutes longer.

4. Stir in cream. Return roast to Dutch oven, reduce heat to low, cover and simmer about 45 minutes.

5. Meanwhile, heat reserved drippings in skillet; add mushrooms and cook about 5 minutes, stirring often. Add to roast; cook covered about 35 minutes longer or until pork is tender.

6. Let meat rest on cutting board 10 minutes before slicing into ½-inch thick slices. Skim fat from sauce; add Calvados, spoon over meat on serving platter. Pass extra sauce separately.

Baked Ham and Apples

Yield: 4 to 6 servings

An excellent way to use up ham. Serve for brunch at the ski lodge along with Johnnycakes and Mexican Coffee (see index).

3 cups cubed cooked ham
3 cooking apples, unpeeled, cut into wedges
⅓ cup brown sugar, packed
2 tablespoons flour
2 tablespoons lemon juice
2 teaspoons dry mustard
1 teaspoon grated orange rind

1. Preheat oven to 350°.

2. Combine all ingredients in a 2-quart baking dish. When thoroughly mixed, spread evenly over bottom of dish. Cover with foil and bake 25 to 30 minutes, until apples are tender; or cover with heavy-duty plastic wrap and microwave at 100% power (high) for 7 to 9 minutes, stirring once after 4 minutes.

Cider-Baked Ham

Yield: 12 servings

An easy way to glaze and sweeten ham. Accompany with Fried Sweet Potatoes (see index).

1 6-pound fully cooked, semi-boneless ham
1 to 2 cups light brown sugar, divided
1 32-ounce bottle apple cider
whole cloves
Glazed Apple Rings, optional (below)

If cooking smaller or larger ham, cook 20 minutes per pound, uncovering the last hour.

1. Preheat oven to 350°.
2. Place ham in roaster. Coat surface generously with half of brown sugar. Pour cider around ham; cover and bake for 1 hour, basting every 20 minutes.
3. Remove ham from cider; score fat in diamond pattern and stud with cloves.
4. Pour off half of cider. Return ham to pan, fat side up; coat top with remaining brown sugar. Continue baking, uncovered, for 1 hour, basting frequently with cider. Garnish with Glazed Apple Rings.

Glazed Apple Rings:

3 medium cooking apples, peeled and cored
¼ cup (½ stick) butter
2 tablespoons sugar

Glazed Apple Rings

1. Slice apples into ½-inch rings. Melt butter in large skillet over medium heat; sprinkle sugar over butter and stir.
2. Fry apple rings, a few at a time, until glazed and tender-crisp, about 4 minutes, turning once.

Apple Jack Turkey

Yield: about 12 to 14 servings

Johnny Appleseed's approach to the Thanksgiving bird?

1 15-pound turkey
salt and pepper
1 large onion, chopped
2 ribs celery, chopped
2 tablespoons butter
2 8-ounce bags herb-seasoned stuffing mix
1 cup (2 sticks) butter, melted
1 cup apple cider
1 cup Apple Jack or apple brandy
4 tart apples (Macoun or Rome), chopped
1 cup golden raisins
1 cup husked hazelnuts

Apple Glaze:

1 10-ounce jar crabapple jelly
Apple Jack or apple brandy

To use up turkey leftovers, try Curried Turkey Bites (see index).

1. Remove giblets from turkey; rinse bird and pat dry. Season inside and out with salt and pepper.
2. Prepare stuffing: sauté onion and celery in butter until tender. Mix well with stuffing mix, melted butter, cider, Apple Jack, apples, raisins and nuts.
3. Preheat oven to 325°. Stuff bird. Cook in roasting pan according to usual method for 4½ hours or approximately 18 minutes per pound. Baste frequently with Apple Glaze (below) during last hour of cooking.

Apple Glaze:

Melt jelly in saucepan over low heat. Remove from heat and stir in 10 ounces (fill empty jelly jar) of Apple Jack.

Turkey Cutlets with Cran-Raspberry Sauce   Yield: 6 servings

Glorious color and delicious taste starring a New England native.

1½ cups cranberries, picked over
2 tablespoons sugar
¼ cup water
½ cup cran-raspberry juice
1 12-ounce package frozen unsweetened
　red raspberries, thawed
1 tablespoon butter
1 tablespoon flour
1 teaspoon instant chicken bouillon
¼ cup sour cream
6 boneless turkey breast cutlets
½ cup milk
1 egg, lightly beaten
salt and pepper to taste
1½ cups fresh white bread crumbs
　(about 4 slices)
½ cup finely chopped walnuts
2 tablespoons olive oil
2 tablespoons butter
watercress (optional)

1. Simmer cranberries and sugar in water, stirring occasionally, for about 4 minutes, or until cranberries have popped. Purée in food processor or blender; pour into bowl and add juice.

2. Purée raspberries; force through a fine sieve and add to cranberries.

3. In a saucepan over moderately low heat, melt butter. Whisk in flour and cook for 3 minutes until roux is a rich caramel color. Remove pan from heat and gradually stir in berry mixture. Return to heat and add bouillon; stir and simmer the mixture for 5 minutes. Remove from heat; whisk in sour cream. Cover sauce and keep warm.

4. Flatten turkey pieces to ¼-inch thickness. Mix milk, eggs, salt and pepper in shallow bowl; mix bread crumbs and nuts in another. Dip turkey in egg mixture, then in crumb mixture, shaking off excess.

5. In a large skillet heat butter and oil over moderately high heat. In a single layer sauté turkey cutlets for approximately 3 minutes on each side, or until golden.

6. To serve: spoon sauce over turkey and garnish with watercress, if desired.

Chicken in Mexican Mustard Sauce   Yield: 6 servings

A spicy hot treat from Mexico.

1 2½- to 3-pound chicken, cut into pieces
½ cup lime juice
1 tablespoon mustard
1 tablespoon olive oil
3 tablespoons sugar
2 tablespoons Tabasco sauce
1 tablespoon chipolte chili sauce*
¼ cup water
¼ cup brandy

*available in food specialty shops

1. Preheat oven to 350°.

2. Place chicken in casserole dish. Combine remaining ingredients and pour over chicken.

3. Bake uncovered for 1 to 1½ hours, basting frequently with sauce.

Chicken and Sausage Rice

Yield: 6 to 8 servings

A poor man's paella without seafood.

3 slices bacon, diced
2 large onions, sliced
3 garlic cloves, minced
2 green peppers, cut in ½-inch strips
½ pound Spanish or Italian sweet sausage,
  in ½-inch pieces
½ pound Spanish or Italian hot sausage,
  in ½-inch pieces
4 cups chicken broth, or more
salt and pepper to taste
1 tablespoon capers
1 teaspoon saffron threads, crushed
3 pounds chicken pieces, breasts and legs
1 tablespoon paprika
3 tablespoons olive oil
2 cups uncooked converted rice
1 cup cooked green peas
pimento and green stuffed olives for garnish

1. Preheat oven to 400°.
2. Combine first six ingredients in a large skillet; cook, stirring occasionally, until onions are wilted. Spoon mixture into a large covered casserole and add ¼ cup broth, salt, pepper, capers and saffron.
3. Sprinkle chicken with salt, pepper and paprika. Brown in olive oil on all sides; add to casserole.
4. Add rice to casserole along with remaining 3¾-cups broth and cover. Bake 40 to 45 minutes, stirring once during baking and adding more broth if rice becomes too dry. When rice is tender, reduce oven to 300° and uncover casserole. Add peas; cook 10 minutes more.
5. Garnish with olives and pimento to serve.

Harvest Chicken Casserole

Yield: 8 servings

What does a mom feed her son, the chef?
"Family type food — a simple casserole with its delicious aroma."

3 pounds chicken thighs, skinned
¾ cup flour
1 teaspoon salt
1 teaspoon pepper
⅓ cup olive oil
⅓ cup butter
2 garlic cloves, crushed
juice of 1 lemon
1 large onion, sliced
2 ribs celery, sliced
1 tablespoon chopped fresh parsley
1 14½-ounce can Italian-style stewed tomatoes
1 tablespoon oregano
1 tablespoon basil
½ cup orange juice
⅔ cup hot water
1 tablespoon instant chicken-flavored
  bouillon powder
3 large yams, peeled and quartered

1. Toss chicken in plastic bag with flour, salt and pepper until coated.
2. In large skillet, brown chicken in hot oil, butter and garlic. Brown on all sides. Do not crowd pieces; allow room to turn.
3. Remove chicken to casserole dish; pour lemon juice over chicken and toss to coat.
4. Add onion, celery and parsley to pan drippings in skillet; sauté until tender.
5. Add tomatoes, herbs, orange juice and bouillon dissolved in hot water.
6. Pour vegetables over chicken in casserole; add yams. Toss to mix. Preheat oven to 375°.
7. Cover casserole and bake for one hour.

Wild Duck Supremes David

Yield: 6 servings

Delectable preparation of wild fowl, suitable for goose as well as duck.

6 duck supremes (breast halves), frozen

Overnight soak:

½ cup vinegar
1 tablespoon baking soda
1 tablespoon salt
water to cover

Marinade:

½ cup soy sauce
½ cup Marsala
2 tablespoons sherry
1 tablespoon vermouth
1 tablespoon Worcestershire sauce
1 teaspoon thyme
4 to 6 garlic cloves, minced

flour
salt and pepper
8 slices bacon
2 large onions, diced
6 peppercorns, crushed
10 juniper berries, crushed
½ cup Marsala or red wine
½ cup orange marmalade (Captain's Choice)
¾ cup sliced mushrooms

Garnish:

orange wedges
julienne orange rind
fresh parsley sprigs

Must be made ahead.

1. Allow 1 supreme per person if duck is large, or both halves from teal. (If using goose, each supreme will serve 2 persons.) While partially frozen, slice supremes diagonally into ¼-inch slices. Soak overnight in vinegar, soda, salt and water mixture. Remove supremes from soak; pat dry.

2. Combine all marinade ingredients. Marinate supreme slices for at least 4 hours.

3. Drain marinade; set aside. pat dry supremes; dust with flour, salt and pepper.

4. Cook bacon slices; crumble and set aside. Sauté onion in bacon drippings; set aside. Lightly brown supreme slices and place in casserole. Cover with onions.

5. Strain marinade, reserving solids and liquids.

6. To marinade solids add peppercorns, juniper berries, Marsala, marmalade and mushrooms. Add to casserole.

7. Preheat oven to 425°. Pour marinade around supremes. Bake at 350° to 400° for 30 to 45 minutes, basting thoroughly every 10 minutes.

8. To serve, sprinkle crumbled bacon on top of supremes and garnish with orange wedges, julienne orange rind and parsley. Accompany with wild rice, brown rice or fried rice, if desired.

DUCK AND GOOSE SUPREMES

If your family objects to the wild taste of duck or goose, try educating them by first serving supremes (breasts) only. When they start boasting of your gourmet expertise, then you can introduce the whole bird! — D.P., Naples, FL

Indian Summer Grilled Fish Steaks

Yield: 4 servings

Before putting the grill in winter hibernation, enjoy these unforgettable fish steaks.

2 pounds thick, firm-fleshed, white fish steaks
  such as cod or halibut
2 to 3 tablespoons chopped onion
2 to 3 tablespoons chopped green pepper
2 tablespoons vegetable oil
¼ cup soy sauce
½ cup dry white wine
½ cup chopped, peeled Italian tomatoes
1 large garlic clove, minced
2 tablespoons lemon juice
2 tablespoons grated fresh ginger root
  (DO NOT use powdered ginger)
½ pound mushrooms, thickly sliced
3 tablespoons butter

1. Sauté onion and green pepper in oil. Add remaining ingredients except fish, mushrooms and butter. Bring to a boil, reduce heat and simmer 1 minute.

2. Pour mixture over fish; marinate 2 hours in refrigerator or 1 hour at room temperature. Fish may be marinated longer but flavor will be stronger.

3. Reserve marinade and grill over hot coals for 10 to 15 minutes, turning once. Fish is done when it flakes easily. DO NOT OVERCOOK.

4. While fish is cooking, sauté mushrooms in butter. Add reserved marinade and heat through. Pour over cooked fish. Good served with rice pilaf or small red potatoes and a fresh steamed green vegetable.

Stuffed Baked Bluefish

Yield: 4 servings

Late summer vegetables enhance the flavor of this hearty native catch.

3 tablespoons butter
1 cup chopped celery
½ cup chopped fresh tomatoes
1 garlic clove, minced
2 leeks, chopped
¼ cup chopped green pepper
salt and freshly ground black pepper, to taste
1 4-pound bluefish, boned, whole or filleted
2 limes

1. Melt butter in skillet; add all ingredients, except fish and limes, and sauté until vegetables are tender and lightly browned, about 10 minutes.

2. Place fish in greased baking dish. Spoon sautéed vegetables into cavity of fish, or on top of one fillet, covering with other. Sprinkle fish with salt and pepper. Cover dish with foil and seal. (May be done ahead to this point and refrigerated several hours until ready to bake.)

3. Preheat oven to 350°; bake fish 1 hour. Remove foil for last 10 minutes to brown fish. Serve with lime wedges.

Brown-Bag Bluefish

Yield: 6 servings

In early fall, fishermen from all over the country come to lure bluefish in Long Island Sound.

6 bluefish fillets, about 8 ounces each
salt and pepper
1 teaspoon EACH dried tarragon, thyme
  and oregano
1½ teaspoons chopped fresh parsley
olive oil
6 brown paper bags

1. Preheat oven to 375°.
2. Sprinkle each fillet with salt and pepper.
3. Combine dried herbs and parsley; sprinkle mixture over fish. Sprinkle fish lightly with olive oil.
4. Place each fillet in a brown paper bag just large enough to hold it. Fold end tightly to close securely; place bags on baking sheet.
5. Bake for 20 minutes, or until fish flakes easily when tested with fork.

Scallops in Saffron Sauce

Yield: 6 to 8 servings

An outstanding seafood entrée.

2 pounds sea scallops
2 shallots, minced
½ teaspoon saffron threads
2 tablespoons butter
1 15- or 16-ounce can whole tomatoes,
  drained, seeded and chopped
  or 2 large tomatoes, peeled, seeded
  and chopped
8 ounces mushrooms, sliced
2 tablespoons brandy
2 tablespoons dry vermouth
1 cup heavy cream
4 tablespoons butter
salt and pepper
lemon slices
Yellow Rice (below)

1. Rinse scallops; pat dry.
2. In large skillet sauté minced shallots with saffron in melted butter over low heat until shallots soften. Add scallops, tomatoes and mushrooms along with brandy and vermouth. Cook, covered, over very low heat for 10 minutes.
3. Using a slotted spoon, transfer scallops to heated platter (containing cooked yellow rice, if desired). Cover with foil and keep warm.
4. Add heavy cream to skillet. Stirring frequently, reduce sauce over high heat to about ¾ cup.
5. Add 4 tablespoons butter, cut into pieces; stir to melt and blend. Season with salt and freshly ground pepper to taste; pour over scallops. Garnish with lemon slices.

Yellow Rice:

2 tablespoons butter
1 small onion, minced
½ teaspoon saffron threads
2 cups long grain rice
3 cups chicken broth

Yellow Rice:

1. Melt butter in saucepan; sauté minced onion with saffron. Add rice; stir to coat.
2. Add chicken broth; bring to a boil. Reduce heat, cover and simmer for 25 minutes.

VEGETABLES

Four Bean "Salad"

Yield: 10 to 12 servings

**A piquant baked bean dish rather than a salad,
as good at a big summer picnic as on a crisp fall night.**

8 slices bacon
1 cup chopped onion
1 large garlic clove, minced
1 1-pound can butter beans, drained
1 1-pound can lima beans, drained
1 1-pound can kidney beans, drained
2 15-ounce cans pork and beans,
  NOT DRAINED
¾ cup brown sugar
½ cup vinegar
½ teaspoon dry mustard
1 teaspoon pepper

1. Preheat oven to 350°.
2. Brown bacon in skillet; drain and crumble. Set aside.
3. Add onion and garlic to bacon drippings in pan; sauté until onion is soft.
4. Combine all ingredients in bean pot or covered ovenproof casserole. Bake 1½ hours.

Gingered Carrots

Yield: 6 servings

8 to 10 carrots, scraped and cut
  into 1-inch diagonal slices
¾ cup water
2 tablespoons butter
1 tablespoon honey
½ teaspoon ground ginger
1 tablespoon toasted sesame seeds

1. In saucepan, cover carrots with water and bring to boil. Cover, reduce heat and simmer 10 to 15 minutes or until crisp-tender. Drain well.
2. Stir in butter, honey and ginger; bring to boil, stirring often, and cook until sauce thickens. Sprinkle with sesame seeds.

Cranberry "Dressing"

Yield: 8 servings

**Not a traditional dressing as those used to stuff the bird,
but a good accompaniment.**

3 apples, unpeeled, chopped
2 cups fresh cranberries
1½ cups sugar
½ cup (1 stick) butter, melted
1½ cups quick-cooking oatmeal (not instant)
½ cup brown sugar
⅓ cup flour

1. Preheat oven to 350°. In a 9 x 13-inch glass baking dish, combine fruit and sprinkle with sugar.
2. In small bowl, combine remaining ingredients until crumbly. Evenly cover fruit with mixture. Bake for 1 hour. Serve warm.

Red Cabbage with Cranberries

Yield: 6 servings

A baked sweet 'n sour accompaniment — outstanding with pork or duck.

2 apples, grated
2 cups cranberries, washed
  and picked over
8 cups finely shredded red cabbage
½ cup brown sugar
1 teaspoon salt (or less to taste)
¼ cup (½ stick) butter
1 cup apple cider or apple juice
freshly ground black pepper

1. Preheat oven to 350°. Butter large casserole with lid.
2. Combine grated apple, cranberries and shredded cabbage with remaining ingredients. Place in buttered casserole; dot with butter.
3. Cover and bake for 1 hour until cabbage is tender. Serve hot.

Glazed Baby Onions and Cranberries

Yield: 8 servings

So attractive on the Thanksgiving Day table.

1 16-ounce bag frozen small whole onions
2 tablespoons butter
¼ cup sugar
2 cups cranberries
⅛ teaspoon salt
⅛ teaspoon white pepper
1 teaspoon grated orange zest (optional)
⅓ cup chicken broth

1. Cook onions according to package directions for 3 minutes only. Drain well.
2. Heat butter in large skillet. Lightly brown onions in a single layer over medium heat about 8 to 10 minutes; shake pan occasionally to prevent onions from sticking.
3. Add sugar; toss to coat. Add cranberries; toss again. Add remaining ingredients, stirring to scrape up any browned bits on bottom of skillet.
4. Preheat oven to 400°. Transfer onion mixture to 11 x 7-inch glass baking dish or oval au gratin dish. Bake about 30 minutes until onions and cranberries are tender and glazed.

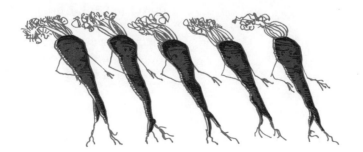

Crispy Oven Potatoes

Yield: 6 servings

¼ cup (½ stick) butter, melted
1 tablespoon scallions, chopped
1 tablespoon chopped fresh parsley
¼ teaspoon dried thyme
½ teaspoon salt
⅛ teaspoon pepper
4 large unpeeled potatoes, thinly sliced
1½ cups shredded Cheddar cheese (optional)

1. Preheat oven to 425°. Lightly grease 13 x 9 x 2-inch baking dish.
2. Combine melted butter with next five ingredients. Layer potatoes in baking dish, brushing each layer with butter mixture.
3. Bake for 40 minutes or until tender. Sprinkle with cheese, if desired, and bake 5 minutes more or until cheese is melted. (May also be baked at 350° for 1½ hours.)

Potato Mélange au Gratin

Yield: 8 servings

An easy, delicious addition to the Thanksgiving menu.

1 pound potatoes, pared
1 pound sweet potatoes or yams, pared
2 tablespoons flour
½ teaspoon salt
¼ teaspoon pepper
¼ teaspoon nutmeg
1 cup apple juice
1 cup shredded Jarlsberg cheese

1. Preheat oven to 400°. Slice potatoes into ⅛-inch thick slices. In a 9 x 13-inch glass baking dish, alternately layer slices of potato with sweet potato for a checkerboard effect.
2. Mix together flour, salt, pepper and nutmeg; slowly stir in apple juice, blending well. Pour over potatoes.
3. Cover and bake 45 minutes. Uncover, sprinkle with cheese and bake about 15 minutes more, until cheese melts and potatoes are tender.

Microwaving increases the intensity of flavor in certain seasonings.

Microwave instructions:

1. Proceed as in steps 1 and 2 above, reducing apple juice to ¾ cup and pepper and nutmeg to ⅛ teaspoon each.
2. Cover with plastic wrap and cook at 100% power (high) for 8 minutes. Give dish a half turn and cook 7 minutes. Sprinkle with cheese, cover and cook 2 to 4 minutes more, or until cheese melts and potatoes are tender. Let stand 10 minutes before serving.

Fried Sweet Potatoes

Yield: 8 servings

**Dipped in beer batter and deep fried,
these potatoes would make a unique hors d'oeuvre, too!**

4 medium sweet potatoes
¼ cup Cointreau or other orange liqueur
    (or orange juice)
¼ cup honey
1 teaspoon grated lemon rind
2 cups flour
2 cups beer
vegetable oil

1. Cook sweet potatoes, whole, in boiling water for 5 minutes; let cool. Peel and cut into ¼-inch slices. Place in large shallow dish.
2. Combine Cointreau, honey, and lemon rind; pour over potato slices. Marinate one hour.
3. Combine flour and beer, stirring until smooth. Dip sweet potato slices in beer batter; coat well.
4. Fry batter-coated slices in hot oil (390°) in saucepan or deep-fat fryer. When slices are golden, remove and drain on paper towels. Serve hot.

The sweet potato, one of the first vegetables imported to Europe from the New World, was highly touted as an aphrodisiac, while the white potato was thought to be poisonous.

Curried Apple Rice

Yield: 6 servings

**The apples and cider suggest autumn,
but you'll want to make this year 'round.**

2 tablespoons butter
2 to 3 teaspoons curry powder
1 Golden Delicious apple, cored,
    coarsely chopped
1 small onion, chopped
½ cup sliced celery
1 cup uncooked converted rice
⅓ cup raisins
2 cups apple cider or apple juice
1 teaspoon salt

Variation:
Add roasted cashews and cubed, cooked chicken for a main dish.

1. Melt butter in large skillet. Stir in curry powder, add chopped apple and gently sauté 2 minutes, stirring frequently. Remove apple with slotted spoon and set aside.
2. Add onion and celery to skillet; cook 1 minute, stirring constantly. Add rice, raisins, apple cider and salt. Bring to a boil; reduce heat, cover tightly and simmer about 20 to 25 minutes or until rice is tender and liquid absorbed. Gently stir in apples.

Butternut Squash and Apple Bake   Yield: 6 to 8 servings

**Traditional American foods in golden autumn colors
with old-fashioned good taste.**

1 large butternut squash,
  about 4 cups cubed
2 large tart cooking apples, cored
  and cut in ½-inch slices
½ cup raw, halved cranberries (optional)
½ cup brown sugar
¼ cup (½ stick) butter, melted
1 tablespoon flour
1 teaspoon salt
½ teaspoon mace

1. Preheat oven to 350°.
2. Slice and peel the squash; remove seeds. Cut squash into 1-inch cubes. Put into ungreased baking dish, roughly 7 x 11-inches. Arrange apple slices on top; sprinkle with cranberries.
3. Combine remaining ingredients in a small bowl. Sprinkle mixture over squash and apples. Cover with foil. Bake 50 to 60 minutes or until squash is tender.

Pumpkin Fritters   Yield: 1 dozen

May be served as side dish with roast pork or fowl, or as an hors d'oeuvre.

1 16-ounce can pumpkin
1 cup flour
1 teaspoon salt, or to taste
1 teaspoon baking powder
⅛ teaspoon cayenne pepper
½ teaspoon dry mustard
1 egg, slightly beaten
2 tablespoons milk
peanut oil

1. Mix all ingredients
2. Heat small amount of oil in skillet until very hot. Drop tablespoonfuls of batter into oil. Cook until browned on both sides. Serve at once.

Spinach-Cheese Bake   Yield: 8 servings

A vegetable side dish or main course for brunch or lunch.

1 pound chopped fresh spinach
  or 2 10-ounce packages frozen
  chopped spinach, thawed
8 ounces sharp Cheddar cheese, shredded
16 ounces small curd cottage cheese
4 eggs, beaten
3 tablespoons flour
3 tablespoons butter, cut into small pieces
salt, pepper and garlic to taste

1. If using fresh spinach, steam and drain well or drain thawed spinach.
2. Preheat oven to 350°. Lightly grease an 8-inch baking dish.
3. Mix together all ingredients until well blended. Pour into prepared dish.
4. Bake 45 to 60 minutes. Serve hot. Casserole freezes well once cooked.

Variation:
Substitute Swiss chard for the fresh spinach.

Saffron Risotto

Yield: 6 servings

2 tablespoons butter
2 garlic cloves, minced
½ cup chopped onion
½ cup sliced mushrooms
generous pinch saffron threads
2 cups rice
3 cups chicken broth
¼ teaspoon salt, or to taste
¼ cup minced fresh parsley
grated Parmesan cheese (optional)

1. Melt butter in medium saucepan. Add garlic, onion, mushrooms and saffron; cook until onion is tender.
2. Add rice to saucepan, stirring to coat with butter; cook, stirring, about 1 minute. Add broth, bring to boil; reduce heat, cover, and simmer 25 minutes.
3. Allow rice to sit about 5 minutes. Add parsley and cheese, if desired.

Zucchini with Pine Nuts

Yield: 6 to 8 servings

A nice accompaniment for Italian dishes.

½ cup pine nuts
¼ cup chopped onion
2 garlic cloves, minced
2 tablespoons butter
6 small zucchini, halved lengthwise
½ cup water
salt and freshly ground pepper
pinch oregano
⅓ cup chopped fresh parsley

1. Sauté pine nuts, onions and garlic in butter until nuts are browned and onion is tender. Set aside.
2. In a large covered skillet, cook zucchini in water about 5 minutes or until crisp-tender. Drain.
3. Sprinkle zucchini with pine nut mixture and cook, uncovered, a few minutes more. Season with salt, oregano and a generous amount of pepper. Sprinkle with parsley.

Green Tomato Mincemeat

Yield: 4 quarts

Just before the first frost, clean out the garden and make this filling for your holiday pies.

4 quarts green tomatoes
2 quarts tart apples, pared
1 pound raisins
4 tablespoons minced lemon or orange peel
1 tablespoon cinnamon
2 teaspoons salt
¼ teaspoon allspice
¼ teaspoon cloves
1½ cups packed brown sugar
2 cups granulated sugar
¾ cup vinegar
¼ cup lemon juice
1 cup water

1. Chop tomatoes in food processor; place in large pot or kettle. Chop apples in processor and add to pot.
2. Combine remaining ingredients with tomatoes and apples. Cook over low heat until mixture is tender and slightly thickened, stirring occasionally.
3. Freeze in four 1-quart containers and/or use to make four pies.

For a spicier mincemeat increase allspice and cloves to 1 teaspoon each.

SALADS

Beet and Walnut Salad

Yield: 6 servings

A salad for Blue cheese lovers.

10 medium beets, fresh or canned
¼ cup walnut oil
1½ tablespoons red wine vinegar
½ teaspoon salt
½ cup walnuts, toasted
1 cup sour cream
¼ pound Blue cheese
freshly ground black pepper
Boston or Bibb lettuce

1. Scrub fresh beets; cook in boiling water until tender, about 25 minutes. Drain, cool and peel.
2. Cut beets into pieces the size of matchsticks.
3. Combine oil and vinegar and salt; toss with beets. Cover and chill.
4. Allow beets to come to room temperature before serving; toss with walnuts and add sour cream.
5. Arrange mixture on lettuce leaves and crumble cheese over all. Grind black pepper over top to taste.

Fresh Fall Vegetable Salad

Yield: 8 servings

A mixture of crunchy, marinated vegetables. Tote them along on a tailgate picnic.

1 pound broccoli, separated into florets
1 small head cauliflower, separated into florets
2 medium carrots, scraped and thinly sliced
1 small purple onion, thinly sliced
1 green pepper, diced
½ cup sliced ripe olives
1 cup Italian dressing (commercial or favorite recipe)
generous pinch EACH thyme, oregano and basil crushed between fingers

Must be made ahead.

1. Cut florets into bite-size pieces, if necessary. Combine all ingredients in large bowl, or storage container; cover.
2. Chill at least 2 hours before serving.

Salad of Endive, Hot Bacon and Egg   Yield: 4 servings

A combination often used with spinach but surprisingly nice with endive too.

4 heads endive
4 slices bacon
1½ tablespoons balsamic vinegar
salt and freshly ground black pepper
1 hard-boiled egg, shelled and
   finely chopped

1. Slice endive leaves into narrow strips;
arrange on individual plates.

2. In a small skillet cook bacon over medium-
high heat until crisp; remove, drain and
crumble over endive.

3. Leave 3 tablespoons of bacon fat in skillet,
discarding the rest; stir in vinegar. Pour over
salad, season with salt and pepper and
garnish with chopped egg. Serve immediately.

Green Salad and Apples with Orange-Mustard Dressing   Yield: 8 servings

Delicious departure from Waldorf salad.

Orange-Mustard Dressing

1 large navel orange
⅓ cup olive oil
3 tablespoons red wine vinegar
1 teaspoon Dijon mustard
½ teaspoon salt
¼ teaspoon pepper

1 Golden Delicious apple
1 Red Delicious apple
1 head romaine lettuce
1 head curly lettuce
½ cup alfalfa sprouts (optional)

1. Prepare dressing: grate rind of orange and
add to remaining ingredients in large serving
bowl. Whisk together until creamy.

2. Remove all white membrane from orange,
separate into sections and add to bowl.

3. Core apples and dice into 1-inch pieces. Add
to bowl and toss to coat. Salad may be held
for 1 hour at this point.

4. Tear lettuce into bite-size pieces and add
to bowl with alfalfa sprouts. Toss gently
and serve.

Watercress and Apple Salad   Yield: 6 servings

A pleasant combination of tart flavors.

Dressing:

2 tablespoons white wine vinegar
½ teaspoon salt
⅓ cup olive oil
½ teaspoon Dijon mustard

2 bunches watercress
2 large tart apples
1 red onion, thinly sliced

1. Combine all dressing ingredients in jar with
tight-fitting lid. Cover and shake well.

2. Wash watercress; pat dry. Place in salad
bowl. Core apple; slice in thin rings and add
to salad bowl along with onion rings.

3. Toss salad with dressing, coating well.

Wild Rice Salad

Yield: 6 servings

Perfect for tailgates because it tastes best at room temperature.

1 13¾-ounce can chicken broth
1 6-ounce box long grain and wild rice
1 teaspoon sugar
¼ cup white rice vinegar
1 tablespoon dark Oriental sesame oil
2 tablespoons vegetable oil
⅛ teaspoon Tabasco sauce
2 to 3 ounces Prosciutto or Canadian bacon
  cut in slivers
1 6-ounce can water chestnuts, chopped
3 scallions, sliced

1. In saucepan, bring broth to boil; add rice, discarding seasoning packet. Lower heat, cover and cook for 25 minutes. Drain off any unabsorbed liquid; rinse rice in cold water and drain well. Place in bowl or plastic container.

2. Combine sugar and vinegar, stirring to dissolve sugar; pour over warm rice. Add sesame oil, oil and Tabasco; toss well. Let cool to room temperature, about 15 minutes.

3. Add Prosciutto or bacon, water chestnuts and scallions; toss. Serve at room temperature. If desired, cover and refrigerate up to 24 hours.

Zucchini and Tomato Salad

Yield: 6 servings

2 small zucchini, thinly sliced
2 medium tomatoes, cut into wedges
  or 1 cup cherry tomatoes, halved
1 medium green pepper, cut into thin slices
1 small onion, minced
lettuce

Dressing:
¼ cup vegetable oil
¼ cup white wine vinegar
2 tablespoons chopped fresh parsley
2 garlic cloves, minced
½ teaspoon salt
freshly ground pepper

1. Combine first four ingredients in bowl or plastic container; toss lightly.

2. Combine dressing ingredients in jar with tightly-fitting lid; shake well. Pour over vegetables. Cover and refrigerate several hours but not overnight.

3. Drain dressing from vegetables and serve on lettuce.

DESSERTS

Maple Baked Apples

Yield: 4 servings

Maple-flavored syrup may be substituted, but there's nothing like the real thing!

4 medium cooking apples
4 tablespoons raisins
4 tablespoons chopped pecans
1 teaspoon ground cinnamon
¾ cup maple syrup
¼ cup (½ stick) butter, divided
½ cup water

1. Preheat oven to 350°.
2. Core apples and peel top third of each. Place apples in shallow baking dish.
3. Combine raisins, pecans and cinnamon; fill apple cavities with mixture.
4. Pour maple syrup over apples; top each with 1 tablespoon butter.
5. Pour water into bottom of dish. Cover and bake 45 to 60 minutes. Serve warm.

Fresh Apple Cake

Yield: 12 to 16 servings

This cake will keep well, but you'll probably never get a chance to find out.

2 cups sugar
1½ cups vegetable oil
1 teaspoon vanilla extract
3 eggs
3 cups flour
1 teaspoon salt
1 teaspoon baking soda
1 tablespoon cinnamon
4 cups peeled, chopped apples
1½ cups chopped walnuts

1. Preheat oven to 350°. Grease and flour a 10-inch tube pan.
2. In a very large bowl, cream together first four ingredients thoroughly.
3. Sift together dry ingredients and add to creamed mixture, mixing well by hand.
4. Stir in apples and nuts. Spoon batter into prepared tube pan. Bake for 1¼ to 1½ hours, or until straw inserted in center comes out clean.
5. Cool 10 minutes on wire rack; remove from pan. Cool completely and cover top with Cream Cheese Glaze, if desired, or sprinkle with confectioners' sugar.

Cream Cheese Glaze:

1¼ cups confectioners' sugar
1 3-ounce package cream cheese, softened
1 tablespoon light corn syrup
½ teaspoon vanilla extract

Cream Cheese Glaze:

1. In small bowl of mixer, at low speed, beat together all ingredients until smooth and of spreading consistency.
2. Spread top of cooled cake letting excess drip down sides. Decorate top with walnut halves, if desired.

Apple Crisp

Yield: 8 to 10 servings

Whole wheat flour makes this a little different.

1½ cups quick-cooking oatmeal
  (NOT INSTANT)
1½ cups dark brown sugar
½ cup flour
½ cup whole wheat flour
2 teaspoons cinnamon
¾ cup chopped pecans or walnuts
1 cup (2 sticks) butter, softened
8 to 10 tart cooking apples, cored
  and sliced thin

1. Preheat oven to 350°. Grease 13 x 9-inch baking dish.
2. Combine oatmeal, sugar, flour, cinnamon and nuts; cut in butter.
3. Place apple slices in baking dish (should fill dish about three-quarters full). Sprinkle oatmeal mixture on top. Bake 30 to 35 minutes until light brown on top and bubbly in center.
4. Serve warm with cheese wedges, ice cream or whipped cream, if desired.

Applesauce Cake

Yield: 12 to 14 servings

A family favorite for 35 years, mailed to granddaughters away at college on their birthdays.

1 cup (2 sticks) butter, softened
2 cups sugar
2 eggs
3 cups sifted flour
1½ teaspoons nutmeg
1 tablespoon cinnamon
1 teaspoon cloves
1 tablespoon baking soda
2½ cups (20-ounce) jar applesauce
2 tablespoons corn syrup
1 cup raisins
1 cup chopped nuts

1. Preheat oven to 300°. Grease and flour tube pan.
2. Cream together butter and sugar. Add eggs, one at a time.
3. Sift together next five ingredients. Combine applesauce and corn syrup; add to creamed mixture alternately with dry ingredients. Fold in raisins and nuts.
4. Pour into prepared tube pan. Bake 1½ to 2 hours, until cake tests done when tester is inserted.
5. Cool cake in pan on wire rack 10 minutes, remove from pan and cool completely. If desired, serve with Caramel Sauce.

Caramel Sauce:

½ cup (1 stick) butter
1 cup brown sugar, packed
2 tablespoons light cream
2 teaspoons vanilla extract
confectioners' sugar
chopped nuts

Caramel Sauce:

1. Heat first four ingredients over low heat until melted.
2. Add vanilla; thicken with confectioners' sugar to sauce consistency. Pour sauce over cooled cake. Sprinkle with chopped nuts to decorate.

Apple Pound Cake

A family tradition at apple time.

Yield: 12 servings

3 cups flour
2 cups sugar
1 tablespoon baking powder
¼ teaspoon salt
1 cup vegetable oil
4 eggs
¼ cup apple juice or apple cider
1 teaspoon vanilla extract
3 to 4 tart apples, pared and sliced
3 tablespoons sugar
¾ teaspoon cinnamon

1. Preheat oven to 325°. Grease and flour a 10-inch tube pan.
2. Combine flour, sugar, baking powder and salt in large bowl of mixer.
3. Gradually beat in oil, eggs, juice and vanilla at medium speed just until smooth.
4. Pour half the batter into prepared pan. Arrange half the apple slices on top of batter. Combine sugar and cinnamon; sprinkle half over apples. Add remaining batter, top with remaining apple slices and sprinkle with remaining sugar mixture.
5. Bake for 1½ hours. Let cool in pan for 15 minutes. Invert and cool completely.

Apple Butter Cake

A dark, spicy tea cake. Grandma always made it with her own apple butter, but it's almost as good made with the store-bought kind.

Yield: 1 loaf cake

1 cup light brown sugar
½ cup (1 stick) butter, at room temperature
1 egg
2 cups flour
1 teaspoon EACH cinnamon, cloves, nutmeg and allspice
¾ cup buttermilk
2 teaspoons baking soda
1 cup apple butter

sweetened whipped cream,
   flavored with apple brandy (optional)

1. Preheat oven to 325°. Grease well a 9-inch loaf pan.
2. In bowl of electric mixer, cream together sugar and butter; beat in egg.
3. In another bowl mix flour and four spices.
4. In a one-cup measure, combine buttermilk and soda.
5. Add flour to sugar mixture alternately with buttermilk. Fold in apple butter by hand, stirring just until mixed.
6. Pour batter into prepared pan; bake for 5 minutes at 325°; increase oven to 350° and bake for 1 hour.
7. Let cake cool in pan for 5 minutes; turn onto wire rack. Cool completely. Serve topped with whipped cream sweetened and flavored with apple brandy, if desired.

Apple Cheesecake Torte

Yield: 8 to 10 servings

Cheesecake lovers' answer to apple pie.

Crust:

½ cup (1 stick) butter, softened
⅓ cup sugar
¼ teaspoon vanilla extract
1 cup flour

Filling:

1 8-ounce package cream cheese, softened
¼ cup sugar
1 egg
1 teaspoon vanilla extract

Apple topping:

⅓ cup sugar
½ teaspoon cinnamon
4 large apples, sliced
¼ cup sliced almonds

1. In large bowl, cream butter, sugar and vanilla; blend in flour. Pat dough into bottom and up sides of greased 9-inch springform pan.
2. Combine cream cheese and sugar; mix well. Add egg and vanilla. Pour over pastry.
3. Preheat oven to 375°. Combine sugar and cinnamon in large bowl. Toss apples in mixture; spoon over filling. Sprinkle with almonds.
4. Bake for 30 to 35 minutes. Cool before serving.

Sour Cream Apple Pie

Yield: 6 to 8 servings

An incredible apple indulgence.

Crust:

1½ cups graham cracker crumbs
¼ cup sugar
⅓ cup butter, melted

Filling:

2 tablespoon flour
⅔ cup packed light brown sugar
1 teaspoon cinnamon
pinch salt
1 egg
1 cup sour cream
½ teaspoon vanilla extract
¼ cup raisins
4 cups peeled apple slices

Topping:

½ cup light brown sugar
½ cup flour
½ teaspoon cinnamon
¼ cup (½ stick) butter, softened

1. Combine crust ingredients. Press mixture onto bottom and sides of 9-inch pan. Chill.
2. Preheat oven to 400°. Combine all filling ingredients except raisins and apples. Stir in raisins and apples and pour into chilled crust.
3. Bake pie for 15 minutes; reduce oven to 350° and continue baking for 30 minutes.
4. Prepare topping by combining ingredients until crumbly. Sprinkle evenly over pie and bake at 400° for 10 minutes. Serve warm or cold.

Fresh Pear Pie

Yield: 8 servings

**The combination of brown sugar, lemon and spices
produces a flavor reminiscent of mincemeat — a real old-time recipe.**

Pastry for double-crust 9-inch pie
½ cup firmly packed brown sugar
2 tablespoons flour
½ teaspoon cinnamon
½ teaspoon nutmeg
⅛ teaspoon cardamom
pinch of salt
6 cups peeled, sliced pears
juice and grated rind of one lemon
1½ teaspoons vanilla extract

1 tablespoon water
1 tablespoon milk
1½ teaspoons sugar

1. Preheat oven to 400°. Line a 9-inch pie plate with pastry.
2. In a large bowl combine brown sugar, flour, spices and salt. Add pear slices, lemon juice and rind, and vanilla extract; toss gently until well mixed.
3. Spoon fruit into pastry-lined pie plate, mounding in center. Brush rim of crust with water; cover with top crust. Flute edges and cut steam vents; brush with milk and sprinkle with sugar.
4. Bake 15 minutes. Reduce oven to 375°; bake 45 to 50 minutes or until crust is golden and juices bubbly.

Gilded Lily Pear Crisp

Yield: 6 to 8 servings

**Ever since their wedding in the classic Pears Hélène,
chocolate and pears have made a beautiful marriage.**

½ cup flour
½ cup packed light brown sugar
½ cup (1 stick) butter, divided
½ cup coarsely chopped walnuts
¼ cup golden raisins
¼ cup semisweet chocolate chips
5 Bartlett pears, peeled and sliced
2 tablespoons brandy

1. Preheat oven to 350°.
2. Combine flour, brown sugar and 6 tablespoons butter until mixture resembles coarse meal. Gently stir in nuts, raisins and chocolate, mixing thoroughly.
3. Place pear slices in a 2-quart baking dish (or 13 x 9 x 2-inch).
4. Melt remaining 2 tablespoons butter in small saucepan. Stir in brandy. Pour over pears; toss until coated. Sprinkle raisin-nut mixture over all.
5. Bake until pears are soft and topping lightly browned, about 30 to 35 minutes. Serve warm.

**The first Thanksgiving, a feast for approximately
145 colonists and Indians, lasted not a single day but
an entire week. With nary a dishwasher!**

Cranberry-Raisin Pie

Yield: 6 to 8 servings

**The tartness of this pie is complemented deliciously
by vanilla ice cream or Crème Fraîche.**

2½ cups cranberries
1 scant cup sugar
½ cup raisins
1 heaping tablespoon cornstarch mixed with
　cold water to make paste
boiling water (about ⅔ to ¾ cup)
1 teaspoon vanilla extract
pinch of salt
butter lump the size of a walnut
pastry for double-crust 10-inch pie
milk

1. Preheat oven to 350°. Line 10-inch pie pan
   with pastry. Reserve top pastry.
2. Make a small cut in each cranberry.
   (Best done accompanied by good conversa-
   tion or the TV Soaps!) Place in large bowl
   with raisins.
3. Add sugar, cornstarch paste to which ⅔ cup
   of boiling water has been added, salt and
   vanilla extract. Mix well.
4. Pour into bottom crust; crimp edges of top
   and bottom together. Cut steam vent in top
   crust; brush with milk. Bake for 1 hour, until
   crust is golden and filling bubbles.
5. Serve hot or cold, with vanilla ice cream or
   Crème Fraîche (see index).

Squash Pie

Yield: 6 to 8 servings

An alternative to traditional pumpkin pie for Thanksgiving.

1 cup sugar
1 tablespoon butter
1 teaspoon mace
3 eggs
1 cup milk
1½ cups cooked, mashed Hubbard
　or butternut squash
9-inch unbaked pie shell
whipped cream (optional)

1. Preheat oven to 425°.
2. In small bowl cream together sugar and
   butter; add mace.
3. In large bowl beat eggs; add milk,
   squash and sugar mixture. Pour into
   prepared pie shell.
4. Bake pie at 425° for 10 minutes; lower oven
   to 350° and continue baking for
   30 minutes, or until filling is set, except for
   a spot in the center about an inch in diameter.
   Remove pie from oven. It will continue to
   cook internally for a few minutes afterwards.
5. Serve warm or at room temperature, plain or
   with whipped cream.

Persimmon Pudding with Foamy Sauce

Yield: 18 servings

An old-fashioned favorite for fall.

2¼ cups flour
1 cup sugar
1 cup dark brown sugar
1 tablespoon baking powder
1 teaspoon baking soda
1½ teaspoons cinnamon
1 teaspoon allspice
½ teaspoon ginger
½ teaspoon salt
2 cups persimmon pulp
1 cup buttermilk
2 eggs

1. Preheat oven to 350°. Grease and flour two 9-inch square pans or one 13 x 9-inch baking pan.
2. In large bowl, measure all ingredients. With mixer at low speed, beat just until batter is smooth.
3. Pour batter into prepared pans; smooth batter with spatula. Bake 50 to 55 minutes or until wooden pick inserted in middle comes out clean. Serve warm with whipped cream or Foamy Sauce.

Foamy Sauce:

2 extra-large eggs
1 pound confectioners' sugar
1 pint heavy cream
2 tablespoons rum

Foamy Sauce: Yield: about 2 cups

1. In large bowl, beat eggs until well mixed.
2. Add sugar, a little at a time, until the eggs are too stiff to add more.
3. In another bowl whip cream. Fold whipped cream into sugar mixture; stir in rum.
4. Refrigerate if not serving immediately. If necessary, whisk to mix just before serving.

Chocolate Bread Pudding

Yield: 6 servings

A new twist for bread pudding? This recipe is at least 50 years old!

2 squares unsweetened chocolate
3 cups milk
1 cup sugar
½ teaspoon salt
3 eggs, slightly beaten
1 teaspoon vanilla extract
dash of mace
2 cups of ½-inch cubes day-old bread

1. Heat chocolate and milk together in top of double boiler over medium-low heat. When chocolate is melted, beat with mixer until blended.
2. In large mixer bowl, combine sugar, salt and eggs; slowly add chocolate mixture, beating well. Stir in vanilla and mace.
3. Preheat oven to 350°. Butter a 1½-quart baking dish. Place bread cubes in dish; pour chocolate mixture over them.
4. Place baking dish in pan of hot water; bake for 50 to 60 minutes.
5. Cool and serve with sweetened whipped cream, if desired.

Pumpkin Rum Bread Pudding

Yield: 10 servings

A far cry from granny's frugal use of day-old bread. This is fantastic!

8 to 10 slices day-old whole wheat bread, cubed
½ cup finely chopped nuts
3 eggs, slighly beaten
1 14-ounce can sweetened condensed milk
1 cup canned pumpkin
¾ cup packed brown sugar
2 teaspoons ground cinnamon
½ teaspoon ground nutmeg
2 cups milk
¼ cup rum
¼ cup butter, melted
2 teaspoons vanilla extract
Foamy Sauce (see index), or whipped cream (optional)

1. Preheat oven to 350°. Spread bread cubes and nuts in bottom of 12 x 7-inch baking dish.
2. In large bowl, combine remaining ingredients in order given, stirring gradually when adding milk. Pour over bread layer.
3. Place baking dish inside 9 x 13-inch baking pan. Pour hot water into larger pan to depth of one inch. Bake 50 to 60 minutes or until knife inserted comes out clean. Serve warm with Foamy Sauce or whipped cream, if desired.

Orange-Pumpkin Cake Squares

Yield: 12 to 15 servings

A great treat around Halloween time.

½ cup shortening
1½ cups sugar
1 cup cooked mashed pumpkin
2 eggs, beaten
⅓ cup frozen orange juice concentrate, thawed
1⅔ cups flour
1 teaspoon baking powder
½ teaspoon baking soda
½ teaspoon salt
1¼ teaspoons pumpkin pie spice

Spiced Whipped Cream:
1 cup heavy cream
¼ cup confectioners' sugar, or to taste
¼ to ½ teaspoon pumpkin pie spice
¼ teaspoon orange OR vanilla extract
red and yellow food coloring (optional)

1. Preheat oven to 350°. Grease and flour a 13 x 9-inch baking pan.
2. In large bowl of electric mixer, cream shortening and sugar; add pumpkin, eggs and orange juice concentrate and mix well.
3. In small bowl, combine all dry ingredients, mixing well; stir into pumpkin mixture.
4. Pour into prepared pan; bake 30 to 35 minutes.
5. To serve: cut into squares and top with Spiced Whipped Cream.

Spiced Whipped Cream.
Whip cream with sugar and flavorings until stiff and tint a light orange with food coloring, if desired.

Pumpkin Flan

Yield: 8 servings

Hate to make pie crust? Try this and you may never make pumpkin pie again!

¾ cup sugar
2 whole eggs
3 egg yolks
6 tablespoons sugar
1 cup cooked mashed pumpkin
2 teaspoons pumpkin pie spice
⅛ teaspoon ground cloves
½ teaspoon salt
1½ cups evaporated milk
  (or light cream), scalded
2 tablespoons orange-flavored liqueur

sweetened whipped cream, flavored with
  orange-flavored liqueur (optional)

1. Preheat oven to 350°. Lightly grease a 6-cup ring mold and place in a pan of hot water to warm.

2. Place ¾ cup sugar in small, heavy skillet and heat gently, stirring constantly with a wooden spoon, until sugar melts, is free of lumps and turns a pale golden brown. Pour immediately into warmed mold, rotating to coat bottom.

3. In small bowl of electric mixer beat eggs, yolks and 6 tablespoons sugar until foamy. Beat in pumpkin, spices and salt; gradually add milk and liqueur.

4. Pour mixture over caramelized sugar in mold; place mold in pan filled with enough hot water to come two-thirds up sides of mold. Bake flan for 1¼ hours, or until a silver knife inserted in the center comes out clean.

5. Let flan cool at room temperature for 20 minutes; loosen sides from mold with knife. Place serving plate over top of mold, invert and turn flan out onto plate. Serve with flavored whipped cream, if desired.

169

Cocoa-Mocha Torte

Yield: 8 to 10 servings

Delicious, light and fluffy dessert.

4 eggs, separated
1 cup sugar
½ cup cocoa
½ cup cold water
½ cup flour
1 heaping teaspoon baking powder

1 pint whipping cream
⅓ cup light brown sugar
2 tablespoons instant coffee crystals
grated chocolate

Variations:

For filling use cocoa-flavored whipped
cream, a favorite chocolate mousse recipe,
or Merry Cristmousse (see index).

1. Preheat oven to 350°. Butter two
   8 or 9-inch round cake pans and line
   bottoms with waxed paper.
2. Beat egg whites until stiff; set aside.
3. Mix egg yolks, sugar, cocoa, water, flour and
   baking powder thoroughly; fold in beaten
   egg whites.
4. Pour batter into prepared pans, dividing
   evenly. Bake 25 minutes.
5. Remove cakes from pans; cool completely
   and slice each cake in half to make 4 layers.
6. In medium bowl whip remaining ingredients
   until soft peaks form.
7. Spread whipped mixture between layers and
   on top and sides. Sprinkle grated chocolate
   on top to garnish.

Chocolate Chip Kudos Cookies

Yield: 2 dozen jumbo,
6 dozen regular

**Chocolate-chip cookies have become an
American classic. We include this variation as a salute
to their origin in New England at the Toll House
in Whitman, Massachusetts. (Kids love these baked up jumbo-size!)**

½ cup (1 stick) butter, softened
½ cup shortening
1 cup firmly packed brown sugar
½ cup sugar
2 eggs
2 teaspoons vanilla extract
2½ cups flour
1 teaspoon baking soda
½ teaspoon salt
1 12-ounce package semisweet
  chocolate chips
1 cup chopped pecans

1. Preheat oven to 350°.
2. Cream together butter and shortening;
   gradually add sugars, beating until light and
   fluffy. Add eggs and vanilla, beating well.
3. Combine flour, baking soda and salt; add to
   creamed mixture, mixing well. Stir in chips
   and nuts.
4. For jumbo cookies, drop onto cookie sheet
   using average-size ice cream scoop, flatten
   with palm of hand; bake about 10 to 12
   minutes. For regular cookies, drop by
   teaspoon onto cookie sheet; bake about
   8 to 10 minutes.

Old-Fashioned Hermits

Spicy and good.

Yield: 5 dozen

1½ cups shortening
(do NOT substitute butter or margarine)
2 cups sugar
2 eggs
½ cup molasses
4½ cups flour
4 teaspoons baking soda
½ teaspoon salt
1½ teaspoons nutmeg
2 teaspoons cinnamon
1½ teaspoons cloves
1 cup rasins
1 cup chopped walnuts

1. Preheat oven to 375°. Cover three cookie sheets with waxed paper.

2. In large bowl, cream shortening and sugar; beat in eggs and molasses. Add all ingredients, except raisins and walnuts, and beat well. (Batter will be stiff.) Stir in raisins and walnuts.

3. Divide dough into three equal parts; divide each part in half. Roll each half into a strip the length of cookie sheet. Place on cookie sheet, using two strips on each sheet and leaving space between strips for dough to spread as it bakes. Repeat for remaining sections of dough.

4. Bake for approximately 8 to 10 minutes or until bars are golden and beginning to crack. Slide waxed paper onto counter; let strips cool before cutting them into bars.

Rolled Molasses Cookies

Yield: 7 to 8 dozen 2-inch cookies

This is an OLD recipe from the days when every household had a steady supply of buttermilk from the weekly churning.

4¼ cups sifted flour
2½ teaspoons baking soda
1 teaspoon ground cinnamon
1½ teaspoons ground ginger
¼ teaspoon salt
½ cup sugar
1 cup molasses
½ cup vegetable shortening, melted
½ cup buttermilk

Must be made ahead.

1. Sift together first five ingredients into large bowl. In another large bowl combine remaining ingredients. Add dry ingredients about a third at a time, beating well after each addition. (Dough will be sticky).

2. Divide dough in half, wrap and refrigerate several hours or overnight. (May be frozen and thawed until soft enough to roll.)

3. Roll dough to about ⅛-inch thickness on a floured surface with floured, stockinette-covered rolling pin. Cut into desired shapes; space an inch apart on lightly greased cookie sheet.

4. Bake at 375° about 8 minutes, until edges brown. Let stand on baking sheets a moment before cooling on wire rack. Store airtight.

Carly's Peanut Butter Cookies

Yield: about 6 dozen

Back-to-school time requires batches of cookies for lunch boxes. Kids love these.

1 cup (2 sticks) butter or margarine
1 cup chunky peanut butter
1 cup granulated sugar
1 cup light brown sugar, firmly packed
2 large eggs
2 teaspoons vanilla extract
2½ cups flour
1½ teaspoons baking soda
½ teaspoon salt

1. Preheat oven to 375°. In large bowl of electric mixer at medium speed, cream together butter, peanut butter and sugars until light and fluffy. Beat in eggs and vanilla.

2. In small bowl combine flour, baking soda and salt. With mixer at low speed add dry ingredients to butter mixture until blended.

3. Roll heaping teaspoonfuls of dough into balls; place 2 inches apart on ungreased cookie sheets. Flatten with fork to form criss-cross pattern.

4. Bake 5 to 8 minutes until lightly browned. Cool cookies on wire rack.

Pumpkin Cookie Bars

Yield: 48 bars

A three-layer bar with cream cheese topping.

Crust layer:

1 cup flour
½ cup oats
½ cup packed brown sugar
¼ cup chopped nuts
1¾ teaspoons cinnamon
½ cup (1 stick) butter, melted

Pumpkin layer:

1 cup solid pack pumpkin
¾ cup undiluted evaporated milk
1 egg, slightly beaten
⅓ cup sugar
½ teaspoon allspice
¼ teaspoon salt

Cream Cheese topping:

1 8-ounce package cream cheese, softened
¼ cup orange marmalade (Captain's Choice)
finely chopped nuts for garnish (optional)

1. Preheat oven to 350°. Combine first five ingredients in medium bowl; add melted butter and mix until crumbly. Press into a 13 x 9-inch baking pan; bake 20 to 25 minutes.

2. Lower oven to 325°. Combine all pumpkin layer ingredients in bowl, mixing well. Pour over baked crust. Bake 25 to 30 minutes. Cool.

3. Make topping: beat cream cheese and marmalade until fluffy. Spread over cooled bars. Garnish with a dusting of finely chopped nuts, if desired.

Apple-Walnut "Brownies"

Yield: 4 dozen

A moist, fruity bar, delicious at tea time or for breakfast.

1 cup (2 sticks) butter, melted
2 cups sugar
2 eggs
2½ cups chopped, unpeeled apples
  (about 2 large apples)
1 cup chopped walnuts
2 cups flour
1 teaspoon baking soda
1 teaspoon baking powder
½ teaspoon salt
3 teaspoons cinnamon

1. Preheat oven to 350°. Lightly grease a 13 x 9-inch baking pan.
2. In large bowl, cream butter, sugar and eggs. Stir in apples and nuts.
3. Sift together dry ingredients; blend into creamed mixture.
4. Pour into prepared pan. Bake 45 to 50 minutes. Cool completely before cutting into squares.

Viennese Walnut Bars

Yield: 4 dozen

These may just waltz their way into your heart as a year 'round favorite.

Cream Cheese Crust:

½ cup (1 stick) butter
1 3-ounce package cream cheese
¼ cup sugar
1¼ cups flour

1½ cups walnuts, coarsely chopped, divided
1 cup (6 ounces) chocolate chips
1 cup flour
¼ teaspoon baking powder
¼ teaspoon salt
¼ cup (½ stick) butter
1½ cups packed brown sugar
2 large eggs
1 teaspoon instant coffee dissolved in
  1 teaspoon water

1. Preheat oven to 350°.
2. To make crust, combine butter, cream cheese and sugar with mixer or in food processor. Gradually stir in flour until blended. Pat evenly over bottom of 9 x 13-inch baking pan.
3. Sprinkle 1 cup nuts and chocolate chips over crust. Finely chop remaining nuts; set aside.
4. Sift together flour, baking powder and salt. With mixer cream butter and sugar; add eggs and dissolved coffee and mix well. Gently stir in dry ingredients. Spoon over chocolate chips and walnuts in pan and spread to cover.
5. Sprinkle top with reserved nuts. Bake 30 to 35 minutes, or until firm on top and lightly browned at edges. Cool completely on wire rack before cutting into 48 bars.

FAVORITE AUTUMN RECIPES

W I N T E R

WINTER

Winter dusts the Seaport with early snows and sends blustery river winds down cobbled streets, just as it did in the 1800's when Mystic was a noted center of New England shipbuilding. Blow as they may, the chilly breezes fail to dampen the spirit of community so evident there, and at no time more so than in December.

Christmas is, of course, the highlight of the winter season at Mystic Seaport. Visitors delight in seeing the traditional evergreen trees set atop ships' masts (a spot one would hardly expect to find a tree!) and in taking daily guided "Yuletide Tours" of selected exhibits depicting Christmas lore of bygone days.

Evening Lantern Light Tours, always sold out quickly, lead participants even deeper into the world of Christmas past with scenes peopled by costumed "personalities" of the 19th century, many of whom are recreated by local residents. Following the tour, area hostesses frequently invite people in for a congenial supper, where a guest might find such dishes as Rosemary Cream Chicken and Brussels Sprouts in Walnut Butter, accompanied by a savory Pecan Rice. And need we mention a seasonal Mincemeat Tart or an Eggnog Cheesecake for dessert?

Another event that encourages holiday get-togethers is the annual Carol Sing, held the Sunday afternoon before Christmas in the Seaport's Anchor Circle. Friends gather afterward to "thaw out" with such hearty buffet fare as Connecticut Cassoulet and Bean Pot Chicken or to sample robust soups like Granny's Beef and Vegetable or Split Pea with Kielbasa. It is this combination of season and sustenance that fills people with the camaraderie that makes Mystic a special place to live.

December melts into January, and the Seaport streets become hushed and peaceful as early twilights shroud the ships in wintery arms: a gearing-down time in anticipation of the busy season soon to come again. This is one of the nicest times to visit Mystic Seaport, especially if you have a small child. Tuck a few leftover Christmas cookies into your mittens and head for the Children's Museum. If you're lucky, you and your child will have it all to yourselves!

BEVERAGES

Old South Eggnog

Yield: 25 servings

12 eggs, separated
1½ cups sugar, divided
2½ cups bourbon
¼ cup rum
2 pints heavy cream
1 quart milk
nutmeg

1. Beat egg yolks until stiff and light yellow;
   slowly add 1 cup sugar, beating well.
   Add bourbon and rum; mix well. Pour into
   punch bowl.
2. Beat egg whites until stiff. Add remaining
   ½ cup sugar, 2 tablespoons at a time,
   beating well after each addition. Spoon into
   punch bowl. Do not stir.
3. Whip cream until it holds a peak. Add to
   punch bowl. Fold all together. Add milk; stir
   to blend.
4. Serve sprinkled with nutmeg.

EGGNOG AT THE MANSION

My former home was the Old Governor's Mansion in Milledgeville, Georgia, a beautiful setting for Christmas festivities. My mother, a devout Baptist who foreswore the imbibing of spirits at other times of the year, relented on Christmas Eve to serve eggnog frothed up with a few drops of bourbon. She also drenched the accompanying fruitcake with wine, which at any other time of the year would have been a wicked practice. My husband and I have happlily modified "Mother Wells" eggnog recipe to satisfy our more intemperate tastes! — A.B., Concord, MA

Icy Cranberry Slush

Yield: 14 6-ounce servings

Let's hope the name isn't descriptive of the weather conditions when you prepare this delicious crimson libation.

1 32-ounce bottle cranberry juice cocktail
1 28-ounce bottle ginger ale
1 12-ounce can frozen lemonade concentrate, thawed
1½ cups rum

Must be made ahead.

1. Mix all ingredients in a medium bowl. Freeze in several small airtight containers.
2. To serve, remove from freezer and thaw for 10 minutes. Scoop into stemmed glasses or place partially melted mixture in punch bowl.

Juanita's Tom and Jerry

Yield: 6 to 12 servings

This eggnog-like hot drink may be served with or without alcohol.

3 eggs, separated
¾ cup sugar
¹⁄₁₆ teaspoon baking soda
½ teaspoon vanilla extract
1 quart milk
nutmeg

1. In a large bowl, beat egg whites until frothy. Gradually beat in sugar; add soda and vanilla.
2. In a small bowl, beat egg yolks until thick. Fold yolks gently into egg white mixture.
3. Heat milk.
4. To serve: ladle ¼ cup egg mixture into mug. If desired, add 1 shot brandy, rum, or bourbon. Fill mug with hot milk; sprinkle with nutmeg.

Mexican Coffee

Yield: 25 to 30 servings

An elegant after-dinner drink or a tummy-warmer in a thermos for outdoor events.

24 (6-ounce) cups hot coffee
1 16-ounce can chocolate syrup
1 cup Kahlúa or other coffee liqueur
½ teaspoon ground cinnamon
whipped cream
cinnamon sticks (optional)

Mexican Coffee may also be served cold with ice cream instead of whipped cream.

1. In a large pot, combine coffee, chocolate syrup, liqueur and cinnamon; stir well over low heat, but DO NOT BOIL.
2. Ladle into mugs, topping each serving with a dollop of whipped cream. Garnish with a cinnamon stick stirrer, if desired.

Thanks to James Carrington of Wallingford, Connecticut, Americans were introduced to the first coffee mill in the spring of 1829 and no longer had to grind their beans unevenly by hand.

Nantucket Red

Yield: about 4 to 6 servings

Discovered on a Christmas stroll on Nantucket.

1 32-ounce bottle cranberry juice cocktail, chilled
1 750 ml bottle champagne, chilled
dash grenadine (optional)

1. Pour several tablespoons of cranberry juice into each champagne glass. The exact amount will depend on personal preference and the depth of color desired. (Refrigerate any leftover juice for another use.)
2. Fill glass with champagne. Add a dash of grenadine, if desired.

Scarlet Sipper

Yield: 8 servings

Refreshing and colorful non-alcoholic aperitif.

4 cups cranberry-apple drink
1 cup orange juice
¼ cup lemon juice
1 liter bottle orange-flavored seltzer water
ice cubes
orange slices for garnish (optional)

1. In large pitcher combine cranberry-apple drink, orange juice and lemon juice.
2. Slowly pour seltzer water down side of pitcher; stir gently.
3. Serve in wineglasses with ice. Garnish with orange slices, if desired.

Wassail Bowl Punch

Yield: about 1 gallon

This warm punch is delicious plain or spiked.

4 orange spice tea bags
1 quart boiling water
1 cup sugar
1 32-ounce bottle cranberry juice
1 32-ounce bottle apple juice
1 cup orange juice
¾ cup lemon juice
2 3-inch cinnamon sticks
24 whole cloves, divided
1 orange, sliced

2 cups rum or apple brandy (optional)

1. Brew tea bags in boiling water in large pot to make a quart of strong tea. Remove bags.
2. Add sugar to tea; stir in juices. Add cinnamon and 12 whole cloves.
3. Boil over medium heat about 2 minutes. Remove from heat and cool slightly.
4. Stud orange slices with remaining cloves. Pour wassail into punch bowl and float orange slices on top.
5. If desired, rum or apple brandy may be added after punch is removed from heat.

APPETIZERS

Clam Fondue Dip

Yield: 8 to 10 appetizer servings

Serve at a party with French bread, crackers or vegetables or on a cold winter's night for a family dinner with bread chunks and a big tossed salad.

1 8-ounce package cream cheese,
  cut into cubes
½ cup milk
1 small garlic clove, minced
⅔ cup grated Parmesan cheese
3 6-ounce cans minced clams, drained
2 tablespoons dry white wine
½ teaspoon Worcestershire sauce

1 loaf French bread, cubed

1. In a medium saucepan over low heat, combine cream cheese and milk, stirring until melted and smooth.
2. Stir in garlic, Parmesan, clams, wine and Worcestershire.
3. Cook over low heat 3 to 5 minutes or until heated through.
4. To serve: transfer to fondue pot or chafing dish to keep warm. Dunk bread cubes into fondue.

Boursin Quiche Tartlets

Yield: 2 dozen

Garlic and herb cheese makes these morsels terrific.

Cream Cheese Pastry:
½ cup (1 stick) butter
1 3-ounce package cream cheese
1 cup flour

Filling:
¾ cup shredded Swiss cheese
¼ cup chopped green onions
¼ cup chopped ripe olives
½ 7-ounce jar roasted peppers, chopped
3 eggs
4 ounces Boursin cheese, garlic and herbs
  (or Gournay)
½ cup heavy cream

Variation:
Make quiche in a 9-inch tart pan: roll out or press pastry into pan to fit; bake at 425° for 5 minutes before filling. Fill as in filling instructions; bake at 350° for about 30 minutes.

Pastry:
1. Cream butter and cheese together; add flour.
2. Mix well, roll into ball and chill about an hour.

Filling:
1. Preheat oven to 350°.
2. Press marble-size pieces of pastry into each of 1-inch muffin pan cups. Sprinkle each with shredded cheese.
3. Mix onions, olives, and roasted peppers together. Spread a teaspoonful over cheese in each tart.
4. Mix together eggs and Boursin; gradually add cream. Spoon over vegetables.
5. Bake for 25 minutes. Let cool 5 minutes before removing from pan. Serve warm or at room temperature.

Chafing Dish Crab Mornay

Yield: about 30 servings

Delicious and elegant for buffet party table.

1 small bunch green onions, chopped
½ cup (1 stick) butter
2 heaping tablespoons flour
1 pint half-and-half
2 tablespoons sherry (or more)
6 to 8 ounces grated Swiss cheese
¾ cup packed chopped fresh parsley
1 pound crabmeat
salt and pepper to taste

1. Sauté onions in butter; add flour and stir until smooth and lightly browned.
2. Gradually stir in remaining ingredients, carefully folding in crabmeat last.
3. Place in chafing dish and serve warm on toast points or in patty shells.

Charlestown Oysters

Yield: 12 first course servings
6 as main course

A rich, scalloped oyster dish to serve as a first course or as a light Sunday supper.

6 tablespoons finely chopped parsley
6 tablespoons finely chopped green onions
a good shake of Tabasco sauce
2 teaspoons Worcestershire sauce
1 tablespoon lemon juice
4 tablespoons melted butter
1 cup cracker crumbs
1 quart oysters, drained
1 teaspoon paprika
⅓ cup heavy cream

1. Combine first seven ingredients in bowl; mix well.
2. Place half of oysters in buttered large shallow baking dish. Cover with half the mixture. Repeat layers.
3. Sprinkle paprika over top.
4. Make six holes with tip of knife; pour cream into holes.
5. Bake 30 minutes, or until firm.

Oysters Rockefeller

Yield: 24 servings

A classic made easy.

2 dozen oysters on the half shell
½ cup (1 stick) butter, melted
3 ribs celery, minced
5 green onions, minced
1 10-ounce box frozen chopped spinach, cooked and drained
2 tablespoons lemon juice
3 tablespoons Worcestershire sauce
2 tablespoons bread crumbs
½ bunch parsley, minced
½ to ¾ cup grated Parmesan cheese

1. Preheat oven to 400°.
2. Place oysters in shells.
3. Combine remaining ingredients except Parmesan cheese. Top oysters with mixture. Sprinkle with Parmesan cheese.
4. Bake for 10 minutes.

Pecan-Stuffed Mushrooms

Yield: 2 dozen

**Better sample one in the kitchen
— there won't be any left once you've served them.**

24 medium mushrooms wiped clean
2 tablespoons butter
2 tablespoons chopped onion
2 slices fresh bread, preferably whole-wheat
⅓ cup pecans
1 teaspoon lemon juice
¼ teaspoon salt

1. Remove stems from mushrooms. Chop stems and set aside.

2. Melt butter; sauté chopped stems and onions until soft.

3. Combine bread slices and nuts in bowl of food processor; process until bread is crumbled and nuts finely chopped. Add to onions with remaining ingredients.

4. Spoon mixture into mushroom caps; place on cookie sheet. Broil 4 inches from element for 3 to 4 minutes. Serve hot.

Cranberry-Horseradish Sauce for Shrimp

Yield: about 2 cups

A delicious, colorful sauce for chilled cooked shrimp.

1 cup jellied whole-berry cranberry sauce
½ cup ketchup
¼ cup lemon juice
2 green onions, chopped
⅛ teaspoon celery seed
2 tablespoons prepared horseradish
1 tablespoon prepared mustard

Cooked, shelled shrimp

Must be made ahead.

1. Combine all ingredients except shrimp in container of blender or food processor; process until smooth.

2. Refrigerate until ready to serve. Serve with chilled cooked shrimp.

> "My family background is Danish and it is a sign of good luck and good health to eat herring around Christmas and especially on New Years. We always prepare at least one of these herring dishes for our holiday parties." P.S. — Grosse Point, MI

Tomato Herring

Yield: about 2 cups

4 tablespoons olive oil
2 tablespoons tomato paste
½ tablespoon Hungarian paprika
1 teaspoon ground cloves
1 teaspoon white pepper
½ teaspoon nutmeg
½ teaspoon allspice
½ teaspoon tarragon
1 medium onion, chopped
1 cup mayonnaise
1 12- or 15-ounce jar pickled herring, drained
red pepper slices, fresh dill for garnish

Must be made ahead.

1. Blend olive oil and tomato paste until smooth. Add spices; mix in mayonnaise and onion.
2. Cut herring into bite-size pieces; add to sauce. Refrigerate at least 24 hours before serving.
3. Decorate with red pepper strips and fresh dill. Serve on small triangles of pumpernickel bread.

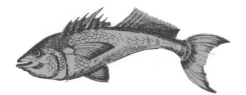

Golden Herring

Yield: about 2 cups

½ cup mayonnaise
1 egg yolk
1 teaspoon grated onion
1 small onion, chopped
¼ cup whipping cream, whipped
1 teaspoon curry powder
⅛ teaspoon cayenne pepper
½ teaspoon white pepper
1 teaspoon dried dill
1 tablespoon capers, drained
1 12- or 15-ounce jar pickled herring, drained

Must be made ahead.

1. Blend mayonnaise, egg yolk, onion, whipped cream and seasonings; add capers.
2. Cut herring into bite-size pieces and add to sauce. Refrigerate at least 24 hours.
3. Decorate with hard-boiled egg wedges and fresh dill; if desired. Serve on small triangles of pumpernickel bread.

Tangy Stuffed Tomatoes

Yield: about 36 appetizers

One-bite tomatoes with anchovy-flavored filling.

1 8-ounce package cream cheese, softened
½ teaspoon celery seed
2 teaspoons grated onion
1 tablespoon lemon juice
1½ tablespoons anchovy paste
1½ tablespoon cream
dash paprika
1 pint cherry tomatoes
parsley

Must be made ahead.

The filling mixture may be served as a spread on crackers. Try it on fish-shaped crackers!

1. In small bowl, blend all ingredients except tomatoes. Refrigerate overnight to blend flavors.
2. With small sharp knife, remove tops of tomatoes and scoop out insides. Spoon about ½ teaspoon anchovy mixture into each tomato, mounding slightly. Garnish top with bit of parsley. Refrigerate until ready to serve.

Curried Turkey Bites

Yield: about 4 dozen

Plan for enough turkey leftovers to make these yummy hors d'oeuvres for your holiday party.

1 8-ounce package cream cheese
3 tablespoons mayonnaise
3 tablespoons chutney
2 teaspoons curry powder
½ teaspoon salt, or to taste
2 cups finely chopped, cooked turkey
1½ cups finely chopped toasted almonds
2 cups flaked coconut

Must be made ahead.

Variation:

Mixture can also be used as a spread, if desired. Stir the coconut into the mixture before chilling in a serving dish or crock. Bring to room temperature and serve with McVitie's Wheatalo or Peak Freen's Sweet Meal crackers.

1. With mixer or in food processor, combine first five ingredients until smooth.
2. By hand stir in remaining ingredients except coconut. Refrigerate about 30 minutes.
3. Shape mixture into 1-inch balls; roll in coconut. Refrigerate several hours or until ready to serve.

Benjamin Franklin lobbied to have the turkey declared America's national bird!

SOUPS

Granny's Beef 'n Vegetable Soup
Yield: about 5 quarts

Five generations of kids have loved their vegetables served this way.

5 pounds beef shank, bone in
2 quarts water
1 tablespoon salt
1 garlic clove, minced
2 cups chopped onion
½ cup chopped celery leaves
⅓ cup pearl barley
1 28-ounce can tomatoes
1 tablespoon sugar
½ cup (1 stick) butter
1½ cups finely cut celery
1 cup diced carrots
1 cup diced green beans
1 cup finely shredded cabbage
1 10-ounce box frozen peas

Granny said, "It's better the next day!"

(Refrigerating overnight allows for easy removal of fat before reheating, too)

1. Place beef shanks in kettle with next six ingredients. Cover and simmer 3 hours or until meat is tender.

2. Remove meat and bones. Skim broth. Add tomatoes and 1 tablespoon sugar to the kettle.

3. Melt butter in large skillet. Add all remaining ingredients except peas. Cook about 7 minutes, stirring frequently.

4. Add vegetables to soup; simmer 20 minutes.

5. Add peas and meat cut into bite-size pieces. Correct seasonings.

Split Pea Soup with Kielbasa
Yield: 16 cups

Enough hearty soup to feed a crowd. Frozen foods add convenience and ease without detracting from the old-fashioned taste.

1 pound dried split peas
10 cups water
2 pounds kielbasa sausage,
  cut in 1-inch pieces (or meaty hambone
  or other smoked sausage)
1 12-ounce bag frozen chopped onion
1 20-ounce bag frozen sliced carrots
2 cups chopped celery
2 garlic cloves, chopped
¼ teaspoon freshly ground black pepper
pinch of dried thyme

1. Combine all ingredients in a large stock pot; bring to a boil. Reduce heat to low; partially cover and simmer 3 hours, stirring occasionally.

2. Remove pieces of sausage and set aside. In food processor or blender purée soup in several batches.

3. Return soup and meat to pot. Correct seasonings. Reheat uncovered about 5 minutes.

Choupy

Yield: 8 to 10 servings

A delicious, rich shrimp chowder.

¼ cup (½ stick) butter
2 large onions, sliced
4 medium potatoes, cubed
2 quarts whole milk
2 6½- or 7-ounce cans shrimp
1 3-ounce package cream cheese

Make soup several hours or a day ahead: the flavor improves with sitting.

1. Melt butter in top of double boiler over direct heat and sauté onions until limp but not browned; add cubed potatoes.

2. Place top of double boiler over simmering water; add milk, shrimp and cubed cream cheese and cook for 1½ hours until done. Do not allow to boil at anytime. Season to taste with salt and pepper.

Corn and Oyster Chowder

Yield: about 24 cups

A tummy satisfying chowder that's become a New Year's Day tradition for its chef.

¾ cup (1½ sticks) butter
8 ounces Ritz crackers, crushed
3 1-pound cans cream-style corn
2 1-pound cans whole kernel corn,
  drained and liquid reserved
1 quart whole milk
1 quart light cream or half-and-half
1 quart (or more) shucked oysters
white pepper, to taste

Recipe may be easily doubled or tripled: allow 3 to 4 oysters per person.

1. Melt butter in large saucepan; stir in cracker crumbs. Add both types of corn.

2. Add milk or cream and heat SLOWLY just to simmer. DO NOT BOIL.

3. When mixture is good and hot, add oysters with their liquid; cook just until their edges begin to curl. If soup is too thick, add some of reserved corn liquid. Season with white pepper to taste.

Donna Curried Turkey Soup

Yield: about 16 to 20 servings

A recipe for the cook who prefers not to have to do a lot of measuring.

1 meaty turkey carcass
water
6 to 8 BEEF bouillon cubes
cooked, cubed turkey leftovers
1 or 2 bay leaves
1 bunch celery, broken into ribs,
  washed and sliced
1 pound carrots, trimmed and sliced
1 large Spanish onion, chopped
1 7- or 8-ounce package curry rice mix
(such as R.M. Quiggs brand)

1. Place turkey carcass in large stockpot or Dutch oven; add water to cover completely and 6 bouillon cubes. Bring to boil; reduce heat, cover and simmer for 1 hour. Taste broth. If richer flavor is desired, add additional bouillon cubes. Cover and continue simmering for 1 hour.

2. Remove carcass from broth and pick all meat from bones. Return meat to broth along with leftover turkey, bay leaves and celery. Cook 10 minutes. Add carrots and simmer 10 minutes; add onion and cook until vegetables are almost tender.

3. Stir curry rice mix into soup; simmer 30 or 40 minutes more, until rice grains "pop" for fullest flavor. Remove bay leaves and serve hot.

Cream of Winter Vegetables Soup

Yield: 6 servings

The escarole adds a wonderful flavor and lots of nutrition!

2 medium leeks
2 tablespoons butter
1 pound butternut squash, pared
  and cut into 1-inch cubes
1 pound potatoes, pared and cut into
  1-inch cubes
3 cups coarsely chopped escarole, divided
2 cups chicken broth
1 teaspoon salt, or to taste
½ teaspoon thyme, crushed
1½ cups light cream
  OR evaporated milk, undiluted
2 tablespoons dry sherry

1. Wash and trim leeks; cut in half lengthwise and then crosswise into 1-inch pieces. Wash and drain. Melt butter in large saucepan over medium-high heat; add leeks and cook until lightly browned.

2. Add squash, potatoes, 2 cups of escarole, broth, salt and thyme. Bring to a boil over high heat; reduce heat to low and simmer covered, 30 minutes.

3. Purée vegetables in two batches in blender or food processor. Return to pot, add cream and sherry along with remaining cup of escarole. Heat through, but DO NOT ALLOW TO BOIL.

BREADS

Oatmeal Bread

Yield: 2 loaves

**A very old recipe which may have come from England via Canada.
working its way south into New England.**

2 cups boiling water
1 cup old-fashioned rolled oats
1 packet active dry yeast
½ cup warm water (110°)
½ cup pure honey (or ½ cup brown sugar)
1 tablespoon butter, softened
5 cups unbleached white flour

**Bread makes excellent stuffing for fowl.
When cool, cube and freeze in plastic bag
until needed.**

1. Pour boiling water over oats; let stand 1 hour.
2. When ready to proceed, dissolve yeast in warm water.
3. Add honey and butter to oatmeal, then add dissolved yeast.
4. Add flour a cup at a time, stirring thoroughly after each addition, until smooth.
5. Cover and let rise in warm, draft-free place until doubled in bulk.
6. Stir dough down with wooden spoon. Divide dough in half. With buttered hands, shape dough into two loaves and place in 2 buttered loaf pans. Cover and let rise again.
7. Preheat oven to 375°. Bake loaves 50 to 60 minutes.

Potato Dinner Rolls

Yield: about 8 dozen

**Make a batch of these tender, light dinner rolls before Thanksgiving
and put them in the freezer to have home-baked rolls ready for
all your special holiday meals.**

1½ cups mashed potatoes, fresh or instant
1 cup milk, scalded
⅔ cup shortening
½ cup sugar
1 teaspoon salt
1 package active dry yeast
½ cup warm water (110°)
2 eggs
7½ cups flour
melted butter

1. In bowl combine potatoes, scalded milk, shortening, sugar and salt; stir until shortening melts; let mixture cool to lukewarm.
2. In large bowl dissolve yeast in water; let stand 5 minutes. Add milk mixture and eggs, beating well. Gradually beat in 2 cups flour; add remaining flour to form a moderately stiff dough, beating well after each addition.
3. Knead dough on floured surface until dough is smooth and elastic (about 7 minutes). Place in greased bowl; turn to grease top.

Cover and let rise in warm, draft-free place, until doubled in bulk, about 1½ hours.

4. Punch down; shape into 1½-inch balls. Arrange on lightly greased jellyroll pan. Cover and let rise until doubled in bulk, about 1 hour.

5. Preheat oven to 350° and bake rolls for 20 to 25 minutes; brush tops with melted butter.

Hot Rolls Braman

Yield: 1½ dozen

This recipe was acquired during a vacation to Bermuda some fifty years ago.

First bowl:

1 yeast cake, crumbled or 1 envelope
  active dry yeast
¼ cup lukewarm water
¼ teaspoon sugar
½ teaspoon salt
2 egg whites, unbeaten

Second bowl:

¼ cup sugar
2 tablespoons shortening or margarine
1 cup warm water

4 cups flour

Must be made ahead.

1. Combine first five ingredients in a large bowl. Combine the next three ingredients in a small bowl. Add second mixture to first.

2. Stir in flour; mix until smooth.

3. Place dough in a large greased bowl; cover and refrigerate overnight.

4. Next morning form dough into small walnut-size balls, placing 3 balls into each of 18 greased muffin pans.

5. Cover and let rise in warm, draft-free place for 1½ hours.

6. Bake in preheated 350° oven for 15 to 18 minutes.

7. Remove from oven and brush crusts with butter, if desired. Serve warm.

Beer Bread

Yield: 1 loaf

**Even a non-baker can make a loaf of this bread
to accompany a hearty soup on a cold night.**

3 cups self-rising four
1 12-ounce can beer, at room temperature
3 tablespoons sugar
1 cup freshly grated Parmesan cheese

1. Preheat oven to 350°. Grease a 9 x 5-inch loaf pan.

2. Stir together all ingredients until well mixed. Pour into prepared pan. Bake for one hour, spreading butter on top of loaf during the last 15 minutes. Cool slightly before slicing.

Easy Pecan Sticky Buns

Yield: 9 rolls

A shortcut to delicious sweet rolls for breakfast or brunch.

1 loaf frozen white bread dough

Topping:
¼ cup (½ stick) butter
½ cup dark brown sugar
¼ cup light corn syrup
⅓ cup coarsely chopped pecans

Filling:
2 tablespoons dark brown sugar
2 tablespoons finely chopped pecans
1 teaspoon cinnamon

1. Thaw frozen bread dough as package directs.
2. Make topping: in small saucepan melt butter; add brown sugar and corn syrup. Heat, stirring, until mixture comes to a boil; boil for 1 minute. Pour into a greased 9-inch square pan. Sprinkle with chopped pecans. Set aside.
3. Roll out thawed bread dough on lightly floured surface, shaping into a 14 x 9-inch rectangle. Sprinkle brown sugar, pecans and cinnamon evenly over dough.
4. Roll from short end, jellyroll-style. Cut into 9 1-inch slices.
5. Arrange slices evenly in prepared pan, leaving space between slices.
6. Cover pan loosely with linen towel. Let rise in warm, draft-free place until dough fills pan, about 3 hours.
7. 10 minutes before baking, preheat oven to 350°. Bake buns for 20 to 25 minutes. Invert pan immediately onto large plate. Let cool slightly before serving.

May's Tea Biscuits

Yield: about 1 dozen

These tender biscuits are best served fresh from the oven. Delicious with Cider Baked Ham (see index).

2 cups flour
4 teaspoons baking powder
½ teaspoon salt
2 tablespoons butter
1 scant cup milk

1. Preheat oven to 450°.
2. Mix flour with baking powder and salt. Cut butter into flour mixture until fine particles form.
3. Stir milk into flour mixture until particles cling together.
4. Knead dough lightly; gently pat out dough on floured surface to ¾-inch thickness. Cut with biscuit cutter.
5. Place biscuits close together on ungreased baking sheet. Brush tops with milk.
6. Bake 12 to 15 minutes. Serve at once.

Boston Brown Bread

Yield: 2 loaves

A two-hundred-year-old recipe for the rich fragrant bread dear to the hearts of many New Englanders.

1 cup stone-ground rye flour
1 cup stone-ground corn meal
1 cup stone-ground graham flour
  (whole wheat)
½ teaspoon baking soda
4 teaspoons baking powder
1 teaspoon salt
¾ cup molasses
1¾ cups milk
1 cup raisins (optional)

1. Grease well two 1-pound coffee cans. Place a rack or trivet in bottom of large kettle. Fill kettle with water and bring to boil.

2. In large bowl combine dry ingredients. Combine molasses and milk; add to dry ingredients. Stir in raisins, if desired.

3. Fill coffee cans about two-thirds full; cover with foil secured with rubber band. Place cans on trivet in kettle. (Water should come about half-way up sides of cans.) Put lid on kettle; keep water at simmer and steam bread 3 hours.

4. Remove from kettle; remove foil covers and place cans in 300° oven for 10 minutes to "dry."

Holiday Fruit and Nut Bread

Yield: 1 loaf

A festive loaf for gift-giving or for breakfast, tea or snack. The secret ingredient? Eggnog!

2¼ cups flour
2 teaspoons baking powder
1 teaspoon salt
¾ cup sugar
½ teaspoon nutmeg
½ cup coarsely chopped pecans
1 cup diced mixed candied fruit
2 eggs, beaten
1 cup dairy eggnog
¼ cup (½ stick) butter, melted
Confectioners' Sugar Glaze (below)
glacé cherries (optional)

Confectioners' Sugar Glaze

¾ cup confectioners' sugar
2 tablespoons milk

1. Preheat oven to 350°. Grease well a 9 x 5 x 3-inch loaf pan.

2. Mix together first five ingredients in a large bowl. Add pecans and candied fruit. Mix until blended well.

3. Combine next three liquid ingredients in small bowl. Add to dry ingredients; mix just until moistened.

4. Pour into prepared loaf pan. Bake about 1 hour or until tester inserted in center comes out clean.

5. Cool then remove from pan. Combine confectioners' sugar and milk and glaze cooled bread. Decorate with glacé cherries, if desired.

Nana's Easy, Healthy Pancakes

Yield: 8 4-inch pancakes

Start with a box of corn muffin mix.

1 8½-ounce package corn muffin mix
¼ cup unprocessed bran
¼ teaspoon nutmeg
½ teaspoon cinnamon
2 eggs, lightly beaten
¾ cup milk
butter and maple syrup (optional)

1. Preheat lightly greased griddle.
2. In medium bowl combine muffin mix, bran and spices. In another bowl combine eggs and milk.
3. Add liquids all at once to dry ingredients, stirring until blended but still slightly lumpy.
4. Sprinkle a few drops of water on hot griddle to test temperature. (Water beads should dance on surface.) Pour about ¼ cup batter on griddle; cook over medium heat, 1 to 2 minutes per side, or until golden brown, turning pancakes when bubbles appear on surface and edges begin to brown. Serve hot with butter and syrup, if desired.

French Toast Surprise

Yield: 6 servings

A delightful breakfast/brunch dish which may be prepared ahead partially and served on a warming tray. Children adore it!

12 link sausages, cooked
12 slices good quality white bread
3 eggs, beaten
½ cup milk
pinch of salt
cinnamon sugar in shaker
butter

1. Remove crusts from bread and flatten slices with rolling pin.
2. Place one sausage on each slice of bread. Roll; secure with wooden pick.
3. Combine milk, eggs and salt. Dip rolls in mixture. Sprinkle with cinnamon sugar. Allow to sit 15 minutes or cover with plastic wrap and refrigerate overnight.
4. Heat butter in skillet and cook as you would French toast, browning on all sides over medium heat. Once seam side is browned, wooden picks may be removed.
5. Serve hot with maple syrup, if desired.

Marsh Indian Loaf

Yield: 8 servings

A dark crusted, thin pancake with the flavor of Indian Pudding.

2 cups corn meal
3 tablespoons rye flour
1 scant tablespoon salt
4 tablespoons molasses
6 cups milk

1. Preheat oven to 350°. Grease well a 2-quart cast iron pot or kettle with lid. Place inside a deep pan, such as a roaster, and fill with water half-way up sides of kettle. Place in oven.

2. Meanwhile, heat milk in large saucepan. Bring to a boil and pour hot milk into hot kettle; add molasses. Add dry ingredients and stir until mixture begins to thicken.

3. Put lid on kettle and cook at 350° for 2 hours. Add more water to deep pan if necessary.

4. Turn down oven to 200°; cook overnight. (Water may be added to deep pan if needed.)

5. At breakfast time, loaf should be thin with dark crust. Serve with butter and maple syrup and crispy bacon, if desired.

OLD LYME MARSH FAMILY INDIAN LOAF

This recipe is an old Marsh family Christmas tradition. Its preparation would begin Christmas Eve so as to be ready bright and early Christmas morning before presents were opened. We enjoy it today with butter and/or maple syrup and a "side order" of crispy bacon. Quite delicious, it sends everyone to the Christmas tree with a warm, contented tummy. — D.M.G., Andover, CT

MAIN DISHES

Venison Roast Forestiere

Yield: 6 to 8 servings

Mushroom-wine sauce enhances this game entrée.

1 3 to 5 pound venison roast
3 cups Zinfandel (or other red wine)
2 tablespoons minced shallots
12 black peppercorns
1 tablespoon juniper berries
1 teaspoon dried basil, crumbled
1 teaspoon dried thyme, crumbled

¼ pound bacon
2 cups sliced mushrooms
¼ cup minced shallots
3 tablespoons flour
¼ cup water
½ cup or more chopped, husked,
  roasted hazelnuts

Must be marinated ahead.

1. Remove any white membrane surrounding roast; place in shallow baking dish. Combine wine and next five ingredients; pour over roast. Cover roast and marinate overnight in refrigerator, turning occasionally.

2. Preheat oven to 350°. Drain marinade from roast and reserve. Brown roast in Dutch oven; add marinade and bake for 1½ hours or until meat thermometer registers 170°.

3. Meanwhile, in skillet cook bacon until crisp. Drain on paper towel, crumble and set aside. Add mushrooms and shallots to ¼ cup bacon drippings in skillet. Over medium heat, cook until brown, about 10 minutes.

4. When roast is done, remove from pan; strain marinade, returning to pan. In small bowl combine flour and water, stirring until smooth; gradually add mixture to marinade in pan. Cook over medium heat, stirring constantly, until thickened. Add mushroom mixture and bacon.

5. Serve a slice of roast with gravy and a sprinkling of hazelnuts. Add any remaining hazelnuts to remaining gravy and pass separately.

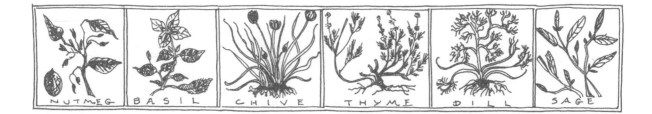

NUTMEG   BASIL   CHIVE   THYME   DILL   SAGE

Beef Filet Dijonaise

Yield: 4 servings

Steak topped with delicious mustard.

2 pound filet of beef
salt
Dijon mustard
fine bread crumbs
olive oil

Bérnaise Sauce (see index)
⅓ cup warm brandy

1. Cut a 1-inch deep gash down length of beef.
2. Rub meat with salt, coat with Dijon mustard, and roll it in bread crumbs.
3. In skillet slowly sauté filet in oil over medium-low heat until lightly browned on all sides and rare in center. Transfer filet to flameproof platter.
4. Cut filet into ½-inch slices and reassemble them. fill the lengthwise gash with béarnaise sauce. Pour warm brandy over beef; ignite and shake platter until flames die out.

Beef Bartholomew

Yield: 8 servings

A stew distinguished by its seasonings.

4 pounds boneless beef for stew, cubed
2 tablespoons olive oil
2 large onions, chopped (about 2 cups)
¼ cup flour
4 cups beef broth
2 14½-ounce cans whole tomatoes
½ cup orange juice
¼ cup chopped fresh parsley
2 tablespoons paprika
1½ teaspoons marjoram
1½ teaspoons thyme
1½ teaspoons salt
1 teaspoon caraway seeds
dash of pepper

1. In large heavy pot or Dutch oven, brown meat in olive oil; add onions and cook until tender.
2. Sprinkle flour over meat and onions; stir to blend into pan drippings. Slowly stir in beef broth.
3. Add remaining ingredients. Simmer for 2 to 3 hours, uncovered. Stir occasionally.
4. Serve with hot cooked noodles or rice.

Beef Stroganoff

Yield: 4 to 6 servings

An elegant classic in about thirty minutes.

½ pound fresh mushrooms, sliced
1 small onion, chopped fine
1 garlic clove, minced
¼ cup (½ stick) butter
1½ pounds boneless beef sirloin,
  cut into 3 x ½ x ¼-inch strips
2 tablespoons flour
1 10½-ounce can beef consommé, undiluted
1 teaspoon Worcestershire sauce
½ teaspoon Kitchen Bouquet
3 tablespoons dry sherry
¼ teaspoon pepper
¼ teaspoon dried dill
1 cup sour cream
hot cooked noodles (optional)

1. Sauté mushrooms, onion and garlic in butter in large skillet until onion is tender. Add beef and stir constantly, until browned.

2. Stir in flour and remaining ingredients except sour cream; bring to boil. Reduce heat and simmer 15 minutes, stirring occasionally.

3. Stir in sour cream; cook until heated through but DO NOT BOIL. Serve with hot noodles, if desired.

Slow-Cooked Beef Short Ribs

Yield: 4 to 6 servings

Although recently the microwave has superseded the slow cooker, the latter is still a blessing for those times when you want to eliminate any preparation after you come in the door — aprés ski or after work . . .

3 to 4 pounds beef short ribs
salt, pepper and paprika
¼ cup flour
1 cup chili sauce
1 cup beef
2 garlic cloves, minced
3 tablespoons brown sugar
1 tablespoon red wine vinegar
2 teaspoons prepared mustard
½ teaspoon Tabasco sauce
1 teaspoon salt
2 medium onions, sliced and
  separated into rings

1. Preheat oven to 450°. Season meat with salt, pepper and paprika; roll in flour and place on rack in roasting pan. Brown ribs on upper level of oven for 30 minutes.

2. Meanwhile, combine remaining ingredients, except onions. Pour one-third of the sauce into electric slow cooker (3½- to 5-quart size), or an ovenproof casserole. Arrange onion rings and short ribs in pot and pour remaining sauce over all.

3. Cover and cook on low setting for 7 to 10 hours, or on high for 4 to 6 hours, in slow cooker; or in oven for 2 hours at 350°. Serve with noodles, if desired.

Red, White and Green Lasagna   Yield: 12 servings

**Cream sauce and spinach distinguish this delicious pasta.
Pretty at Christmastime.**

1 pound extra-lean ground beef
1 tablespoon olive oil
2 garlic cloves, minced
1 10-ounce package frozen chopped spinach,
  thawed and squeezed dry
½ teaspoon dried basil
¼ teaspoon nutmeg
¼ teaspoon crushed red pepper
salt and freshly ground pepper to taste
Cream Sauce (see below)
12 ounces lasagna noodles, cooked
  according to package directions
10 ounces shredded mozzarella cheese
1 pound whole milk ricotta cheese
¾ cup freshly grated Parmesan cheese
1 7-ounce jar oil-packed sun-dried tomatoes
  drained

1. In skillet brown ground beef in oil with
   garlic. Remove from heat; stir in spinach,
   basil, nutmeg and crushed red pepper.
   Season to taste with salt and pepper;
   set aside.
2. Prepare Cream Sauce (see below).
   Add 1 cup to meat-spinach mixture.
3. Cover bottom of 13 x 9-inch baking dish
   with a thin layer of Cream Sauce. Place a
   layer of lasagna noodles over sauce. On top
   of noodles evenly spread meat mixture.
   Cover meat with about 4 ounces shredded
   mozzarella and ¼ cup Parmesan.
4. Make second layer of noodles. Cover with
   sauce, then ricotta. Top ricotta with
   4 ounces mozzarella, sun-dried tomatoes
   and ¼ cup Parmesan.
5. Make third layer of noodles. Cover with
   sauce and sprinkle with remaining cheeses.
6. Cover with foil and bake at 325° for about
   1 hour, or until hot and bubbly. Let stand
   10 minutes before serving.

Cream Sauce:

¼ cup (½ stick) butter
¼ cup flour
1 teaspoon salt, or to taste
¼ teaspoon pepper
¼ teaspoon nutmeg
3½ cups milk, heated
½ cup chopped parsley

Cream Sauce:

1. Melt butter in saucepan. Blend in flour, salt,
   pepper and nutmeg. Cook, stirring, until
   lightly golden.
2. Gradually add milk and stir until thickened.
   Boil about 1 minute. Add parsley. Makes
   about 3½ cups.

**Little did they imagine their far-reaching impact on
American culinary habits when the proprietors of
Louie's Lunch in New Haven presented an unsuspecting
American public with the first hamburger in 1895.**

Mexican Lasagna

Yield: 8 servings

A casserole layered with tortillas instead of noodles.

1½ pounds lean ground beef
1 1¼-ounce package dry taco seasoning mix
1 cup water
1 8-ounce can tomato sauce
2 cups sour cream
1 egg
½ cup sliced ripe olives (optional)
6 to 8 flour tortillas
8 ounces shredded sharp Cheddar cheese
8 ounces shredded Monterey Jack cheese
1 4-ounce can whole mild green chilies
Optional garnishes: sour cream,
   chopped tomato, shredded lettuce,
   avocado slices, extra taco sauce

1. Brown ground beef in skillet; drain excess fat. Add taco seasoning and water; simmer 5 minutes. Add tomato sauce, simmering until sauce thickens slightly.

2. In small bowl, beat egg and mix in sour cream; add ripe olives if using. Set aside.

3. Using a 13 x 9-inch baking dish, cover bottom of pan with small amount of sauce. Place a layer of overlapping tortillas on bottom of pan.

4. Continue layering with half the sauce, half the sour cream and a third of the cheese. Repeat these layers once more; top with green chilies, the final layer of tortillas and, lastly, the remaining cheese.

5. Bake in preheated 350° for 30 minutes or microwave at 100% power (high) for 10 to 15 minutes.

Greek Beef Stew (Stefatho)

Yield: 6 servings

**The Greeks are another group whose culinary contributions
have enriched New England cuisine.**

3 pounds lean beef stew meat,
   cut in 1½-inch cubes
salt and freshly ground pepper
2 tablespoons olive oil
2 tablespoons butter
1 16-ounce bag frozen whole small onions
1 cup tomatoe purée
⅓ cup red wine
2 tablespoons red wine vinegar
1 tablespoon brown sugar
1 garlic clove, minced
1 bay leaf
1 small cinnamon stick
pinch saffron
¼ teaspoon ground cumin
1 large onion studded with
   6 to 8 whole cloves
¼ cup raisins or currants

1. Season meat with salt and pepper. Heat oil and butter in Dutch oven; add meat, coat with oil but DO NOT BROWN.

2. Arrange onions over meat. Combine next five ingredients and pour over meat. Add remaining ingredients except raisins.

3. Cover pot and simmer about 3 hours until meat is very tender. Do not stir. Add raisins to stew the last 15 minutes of cooking time.

4. Stir sauce gently to blend. Discard bay leaf and clove-studded onion. Serve over saffron rice, if desired.

Connecticut Cassoulet

Yield: 8 servings

**A truly fine, classic cassoulet requires goose and a French chef.
This Americanized version uses chicken and a Polish Kielbasa!**

½ pound (1 cup) navy beans
4 cups water
1 pound pork loin country-style ribs
5 garlic cloves, minced
1 small onion, peeled and studded
  with 3 whole cloves
1 rib celery
2 bay leaves
¾ teaspoon thyme, divided
2 sprigs fresh parsley
½ teaspoon salt
2 tablespoons olive oil
8 chicken thighs
1 large onion, chopped
½ cup dry Vermouth
1 8-ounce can tomato sauce
½ pound Kielbasa or other smoked sausage
2 slices white bread, lightly toasted
  and crumbed
2 tablespoons chopped parsley

**May be made ahead through step 9 and held,
refrigerated, up to 24 hours.**

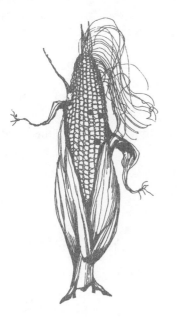

1. Wash and drain beans, picking over for stones or bad beans. In large saucepan bring beans and water to boil and boil for 2 minutes; remove from heat, cover, and let stand 1½ hours.

2. Into saucepan with beans place pork ribs, 2 minced garlic cloves, the whole onion with cloves, celery, 1 bay leaf, ½ teaspoon thyme, parsley sprigs and salt. Bring to a boil; reduce heat, cover, and simmer 1½ hours, until meat and beans are tender.

3. Remove pork ribs and set aside to cool. Discard celery, onion, parsley and bay leaf.

4. Bring beans to boil; cook, uncovered 5 to 10 minutes until liquid is reduced and just covers beans. Remove from heat.

5. Meanwhile, remove pork from ribs and cut into 1-inch chunks. Add to beans.

6. In large skillet, heat oil over medium heat. Add chicken; sauté 10 minutes or until brown on all sides. Place chicken in a 2-quart, deep casserole or baking dish.

7. Preheat oven to 375°.

8. Drain all but 2 tablespoons fat from skillet. Add chopped onion, remaining 3 garlic cloves, bay leaf and ¼ teaspoon thyme to skillet. Cook over medium heat, stirring often, until onion is tender. Stir in wine and tomato sauce; boil 5 minutes. Stir sauce into beans.

9. Assemble cassoulet: split sausage lengthwise, cut into 1½-inch pieces and place in casserole with chicken. Add beans and sauce to casserole.

10. Combine bread crumbs and parsley; sprinkle over top of casserole. Bake 1 hour, until sauce is bubbly and crumbs are browned.

Pastitsio

Greek lamb and macaroni with saffron custard.

Meat layer:

2 pounds lean ground lamb (or ground beef)
2 cups chopped onions
2 teaspoons minced garlic
1 teaspoon salt, or to taste
¾ teaspoon freshly ground black pepper
½ teaspoon cinnamon
½ teaspoon dried thyme
1 cup tomato purée
½ cup dry red wine

Macaroni layer:

8 ounces elbow macaroni
2 tablespoons butter, melted
¾ cup (about 3 ounces) freshly
   grated Parmesan cheese
¼ teaspoon salt
¼ teaspoon freshly ground black pepper

Custard layer:

3 tablespoons butter
⅓ cup flour
pinch saffron threads
2 cups milk
1 teaspoon salt, or to taste
½ teaspoon freshly ground black pepper
⅛ teaspoon nutmeg
1 cup ricotta cheese
1 egg, lightly beaten

1. In a large skillet over medium-high heat cook lamb, onion and garlic until onions are translucent and meat is browned. Break up meat as it cooks. Drain or spoon off excess drippings. Stir in salt, pepper, cinnamon and thyme; cook 1 minute more. Add tomato purée and red wine; simmer 5 minutes more. Spread evenly over bottom of 13 x 9-inch or 2-quart baking dish. Set aside.

2. Cook macaroni in boiling salted water according to package directions until tender, about 8 minutes. Drain; return to saucepan and toss with melted butter, ½ cup of Parmesan cheese and salt and pepper. Spread macaroni evenly over meat in baking dish.

3. In a medium saucepan melt butter over medium-high heat. Whisk in flour; cook 1 minute. Add saffron and gradually whisk in milk, salt, pepper and nutmeg; cook, stirring constantly, until sauce thickens and begins to boil. Reduce heat and simmer 5 minutes. Remove from heat; stir in ricotta cheese and egg. Pour custard over macaroni; sprinkle with remaining ¼ cup Parmesan cheese. (May be covered and refrigerated up to 8 hours; bring to room temperature before baking). Preheat oven to 350°.

4. Bake 35 minutes or until bubbly. Let stand 10 minutes before serving.

The farmers of Cheshire, Massachusetts, each contributed the milk from one day's milking to produce the largest single cheese ever made in New England. Weighing in at 1,450 pounds, the finished "Big Cheese" was presented on New Year's Day, 1802, to President Thomas Jefferson, who promised to "cause this auspicious event to be placed on the records of our nation."

Baked Ham with Cranberry Cumberland Sauce   Yield: 20 to 24 servings

Perfect for a holiday buffet table.

1 16-pound smoked, uncooked ham
¾ cup Dijon mustard
1 cup red currant jelly (Captain's Choice)
1 cup cranberry juice cocktail
2 teaspoons whole cloves
Cranberry Cumberland Sauce

1. Preheat oven to 325°.
2. Tightly wrap ham in foil, fat side up. Place in shallow roasting pan and bake 2½ hours.
3. Remove ham from oven and unwrap. Score fat in diamond design and stud with cloves. Insert meat thermometer, being careful that it does not touch fat or bone.
4. Combine mustard; jelly and cranberry juice in a small saucepan, stirring until jelly dissolves. Pour over ham; bake, covered, for 2½ to 3 hours, or until meat thermometer reads 160°. Remove cover the last hour, basting ham every 15 minutes. If ham begins to brown too much, cover with foil. Serve hot or cold with Cranberry Cumberland Sauce.

Cranberry Cumberland Sauce:

2 green onions, finely chopped
1 tablespoon butter
2 cups fresh cranberries
½ cup sugar
¾ cup red currant jelly (Captain's Choice)
¼ cup orange juice
3 tablespoons lemon juice
1 tablespoon EACH grated lemon rind and orange rind
1 teaspoon Worcestershire sauce
2 teaspoons Dijon mustard
1 teaspoon dry mustard
½ cup port wine

Sauce preparation: Yield: 2 cups

1. Sauté green onion in butter in medium saucepan over low heat. Add cranberries, sugar and jelly; cook until jelly dissolves and cranberries pop, stirring occasionally, about 15 minutes.
2. Place cranberry mixture and remaining ingredients in bowl of food processor; process until smooth. Return to pan and heat over low heat, stirring often. Serve warm with ham. Sauce may be made up to one week ahead and stored in a covered container in refrigerator. Reheat gently before serving.

Pork Carnitas con Chilies

Yield: 6 to 8 servings

**Slow-cook this spicy dish while you're on the ski slopes and have a
hot meal waiting, or serve in the summer with a big pitcher of Margaritas.**

3 pounds boneless pork, cut into
    1-inch cubes
2 large onions, coarsely chopped
1 large red pepper, seeded and chopped
1 large green pepper, seeded and chopped
3 garlic cloves, minced
1 fresh jalapeño pepper, seeded,
    if desired, minced
¼ teaspoon cayenne pepper
½ teaspoon dried oregano
¾ teaspoon ground cumin
1½ teaspoons salt, or to taste
2 tablespoons cornstarch
1 tablespoon red wine vinegar
1 tablespoon water
1 4-ounce can chopped mild green chilies,
    drained
½ cup minced fresh cilantro (coriander)

1. Place all ingredients, except chopped green chilies and cilantro, in slow-cooker, mixing cornstarch with water and vinegar before adding. Cover and cook on high setting for 5 hours.

2. After 5 hours, setting can be turned to low and left several hours longer.

3. Just before serving, stir in chopped chilies and cilantro. Serve with flour tortillas, lime, sour cream and avocado slices, if desired.

Rosemary Cream Chicken

Yield: 8 servings

**Sooo delicious and sooo easy — it's sure to become one of your favorite
company dishes if your family doesn't demand that you make it more often.**

3 tablespoons butter
6 pounds chicken pieces, skinned
    (2 chickens, cut up)
2 large garlic cloves, minced
1 small onion, minced
⅓ cup white wine vinegar
2½ cups heavy or whipped cream
3 generous pinches rosemary,
    crushed between fingers
½ teaspoon salt
2 bay leaves
fresh bay leaves for garnish, if available

1. In large skillet melt butter; add chicken and brown on all sides. Drain chicken on paper towels and place in 13 x 9-inch baking dish.

2. Pour off excess drippings. Add garlic and onions and cook, stirring up any browned bits in bottom of pan, for about 3 minutes.

3. Add vinegar; stir to dissolve brown bits in bottom of skillet. Cook, stirring often, until vinegar evaporates. Add cream, rosemary, salt and bay leaves. Boil rapidly about 10 minutes, until reduced to about 2 cups.

4. Preheat oven to 350°. Pour sauce over chicken; bake 40 minutes.

5. To serve: transfer chicken to serving platter and spoon over the remaining sauce. Garnish with bay leaves, if available.

Bean Pot Chicken with Vegetables

Yield: 4 to 6 servings

Grandmother actually prepared this recipe in her bean pot with fresh cream.

1 3- to 4-pound chicken, cut in pieces
5 medium onions, sliced
½ cup (1 stick) butter, melted
salt and pepper, to taste
paprika
2 green peppers, cut in strips
4 to 6 small potatoes, pared
1 12-ounce bag baby whole carrots, trimmed
1 12-ounce package mushrooms, washed, trimmed, and sautéed
1 cup half-and-half, warmed

1. Preheat oven to 325°. In clay pot (or Dutch oven) place chicken, onions, butter and seasonings. Cover and cook for 1½ hours. DO NOT ADD WATER.
2. Add green pepper, potatoes and carrots to pot. Cook 1½ hours more.
3. At the end of 3 hours, remove chicken meat from bones except legs and wings. Return meat to pot; add mushrooms. Stir in warm half-and-half. Corrrect seasonings and serve.

Recipe may be doubled or tripled to serve a large crowd.

Poulet Jacqueline

Yield: 4 to 6 servings

Roasted peppers and <u>herbes de Provence</u> make this an exceptional chicken dish.

1 sweet red pepper
1 sweet green pepper
1 yellow pepper
1 green Italian frying pepper
2 tablespoons olive oil
6 to 8 whole small white onions, peeled
1 14-ounce can artichoke hearts, drained and rinsed
½ pound fresh mushrooms, sliced or left whole if small
2 garlic cloves, minced
1 cup dry white wine
1 tablespoon <u>herbes de Provence</u> (OR 1 teaspoon thyme, 1 bay leaf, 1 teaspoon basil, few sprigs Italian parsley)
generous pinch saffron (optional)
⅛ teaspoon cayenne pepper

1 3-pound broiler-fryer chicken, cut in pieces and boned (use carcass for soup or stock, if desired)
flour
salt and pepper
1 tablespoon butter
1 tablespoon olive oil

1. Wash, dry and split peppers in half lengthwise. Place under broiler until they begin to char and blister; remove from heat and close up in paper bag until cool. Peel, seed and cut into thin slices. Set aside.
2. Heat olive oil in skillet until hot but not smoking; add onions, peppers, artichoke hearts, mushrooms, garlic, wine and herbs. Cook over low heat about 15 minutes.
3. Meanwhile, in another larger skillet, brown chicken, which has been dredged in seasoned flour, in butter and oil until chicken is golden brown.
4. Add contents of first skillet to chicken; cook over low heat for 30 to 40 minutes or until sauce is reduced and chicken is tender. Serve on a bed of rice or with saffron rice if saffron was not added to vegetables.

Apricot Chicken Breasts

Yield: 4 servings

Dried fruits are a boon in the winter when fresh varieties aren't available.

1 cup diced dried apricots
1 cup apple juice or cider
2 boneless, skinless chicken breasts, halved
salt to taste
paprika
1 tablespoon oil
1 tablespoon butter
3 tablespoons chopped shallots
¼ cup dry vermouth
¼ teaspoon mace
⅓ cup chopped toasted almonds

1. About 30 minutes before preparing chicken, soak apricots in apple juice.

2. Sprinkle chicken with salt and paprika. Heat oil and butter over medium-high heat in large skillet. Add shallots; sauté about 2 minutes. Add chicken; cook until lightly browned, 2 to 3 minutes per side.

3. Drain apricots reserving ½ cup apple juice. Add the juice, vermouth and mace to skillet. Reduce heat to low; simmer covered about 10 minutes. Stir in apricots; simmer covered 5 minutes longer.

4. Sprinkle with almonds; serve. Good with rice or couscous.

Swiss Enchiladas

Yield: 6 servings

A mildly seasoned Mexican favorite.

3 small whole chicken breasts
3 cups chicken broth
¼ cup canned chopped green chilies
1½ cup or more Chili Sauce (recipe below)
vegetable oil
12 corn tortillas
2 cups light cream
1½ cups shredded Monterey Jack cheese
½ cup Parmesan cheese
2 tablespoons chopped fresh cilantro
  (coriander)

Chili Sauce:

1 large onion, minced
2 tablespoons oil
1 10-ounce can tomatoes and green chilies
¾ cup chicken broth
salt to taste
1 teaspoon sugar
¼ cup chopped fresh cilantro (coriander)

1. In saucepan cover chicken breasts with broth and bring to boil; simmer until tender, 20 to 25 minutes. Cool in broth; remove and discard skin and bones, straining and reserving ¾ cup broth. Shred meat.

2. Prepare Chili Sauce below using reserved broth. Combine shredded chicken, chopped chilies and Chili Sauce. Set aside.

3. Heat a quarter-inch of oil to medium-hot (375°) in skillet. Add tortillas, one at a time, cooking briefly on each side and turning once, just until soft but not crisp or brown.

4. After passing each tortilla through oil, dip each into cream which has been poured into shallow dish.

5. Spoon chicken-chili mixture into center of each tortilla and roll them, dividing mixture as evenly as possible between 12 tortillas.

Arrange rolled tortillas side by side in large rectangular baking dish. At this point the tortillas may be covered and held several hours until ready to cook. Also cover and refrigerate cream until ready to use.

6. Preheat oven to 400°. Pour the cream, into which the tortillas were previously dipped, over tortillas; sprinkle with shredded cheese and Parmesan. Bake 20 to 25 minutes, slightly longer if previously refrigerated. Serve hot, garnished with additional cilantro.

A Mexican dish called "Swiss Enchiladas"?? Some suggest that a European chef created the entrée while visiting Mexico City; others speculate that the name derives from the cream used in the dish — an atypical ingredient for Mexican cuisine.

Chicken Breasts with Roasted Peppers on Fettuccine

A delicious herb-blended marinade flavors the chicken.   Yield: 4 servings

4 chicken breast halves, boned, skinned
  and pounded thin
2 large red peppers
2 garlic cloves

Marinade:

½ cup olive oil
¼ cup Raspberry Vinegar (see index)
½ teaspoon fennel seeds, chopped
2 teaspoons basil
2 teaspoons tarragon
freshly ground black pepper

1 cup broccoli florets, steamed crisp-tender
8 or 9 ounces fresh fettuccine

Must be made ahead.

Variation:

If you have a favorite recipe for polenta, substitute that for the fettuccine, adding only the broccoli to the peppers and marinade, and serving polenta alongside chicken with the vegetables.

1. In 400° oven, roast peppers with garlic, turning occasionally, until peppers turn black. Place peppers in brown bag and close; set aside for 15 minutes. Peel and slice in thin strips.

2. Prepare marinade: combine all ingredients; add roasted peppers and garlic. Marinate chicken in shallow baking dish, covered, at least two hours, turning occasionally.

3. Remove chicken, reserving marinade; pat dry. In a large skillet, heat butter and oil; sauté chicken until browned on both sides. Remove to platter, cover with foil and keep warm.

4. Meanwhile, cook fettuccine in large amount of boiling water until al dente. Drain.

5. Add reserved marinade with peppers to skillet; heat through. Add broccoli and fettuccine; toss to coat pasta with marinade.

6. To serve: mound pasta mixture on platter, place chicken breasts on top and arrange red pepper slices attractively over chicken.

Sunshine Chicken Cutlets

Yield: 4 servings

When fresh oranges are in season, add some sunshine to a winter menu.

1 tablespoon butter
1 tablespoon oil
4 chicken breast halves, skinned, boned and slightly flattened
1 bunch green onions
¾ cup orange juice
½ cup heavy cream
salt to taste

1 cup couscous
1½ cups chicken broth
1 tablespoon butter

1 orange, thinly sliced

1. Heat together butter and oil in large skillet. Add chicken and sauté, turning once, until golden and firm to touch, about 5 to 6 minutes. Remove chicken to heated plate, cover with foil and keep warm.

2. Slice green onions, separating green part from white. Add white part, orange juice, cream and salt to skillet. Cook over high heat for about 2 minutes to reduce sauce, stirring up browned bits from bottom of pan.

3. Meanwhile, prepare couscous in boiling broth with butter according to package directions.

4. Stir green part of onions into couscous. Spoon onto serving platter, arrange chicken breasts on top, cover with sauce and garnish with orange slices.

New England Clam Pie

Yield: 4 to 6 servings

There are almost as many variations for pie as there are for chowder with debate ranging from the type of clams used, quahogs or steamers, to the kind of crust, biscuit or pastry.

2 strips bacon
3 tablespoons unsalted butter
1 large onion, minced
1 small celery rib, minced
3 cups finely chopped raw clams
⅔ cup cracker crumbs
¼ teaspoon freshly ground black pepper
⅛ teaspoon Tabasco sauce
⅛ teaspoon nutmeg
salt to taste
2 eggs
1 cup milk
pastry for one-crust 10-inch pie
1 egg white, lightly beaten

1. In heavy saucepan, cook bacon over medium heat until brown and crisp, 3 to 5 minutes. Drain on paper towel; crumble.

2. Pour off all but 1 tablespoon bacon drippings; add butter and melt. Add onion and celery; cook over low heat until tender but not brown.

3. Drain clams well, reserving ½ cup clam liquor. Add chopped clams to pan along with cracker crumbs. Remove from heat; season mixture with pepper, Tabasco, nutmeg and salt to taste.

4. In bowl beat eggs with milk and reserved clam liquor; gradually stir into crumb mixture.

5. Cook over low heat 3 to 4 minutes, stirring

in additional milk if mixture seems too thick. Add crumbled bacon.

6. Preheat oven to 350°. Pour clam mixture into buttered 10-inch glass or ceramic quiche dish or deep-dish pie plate. Cover top with pastry, thinly rolled. Crimp pastry securely around edges, brush with beaten egg white, slash in several places and bake 40 to 45 minutes until golden brown. Serve hot.

Easy Lobster Casserole

Yield: 4 servings

One of life's simple pleasures, this casserole makes the "Best Dressed" list.

1 pound lobster meat
1½ cups (3 sticks) butter, melted

Dressing:
1 10-ounce box fine dry bread crumbs
¼ teaspoon dry mustard
½ teaspoon garlic salt, or to taste
chopped fresh parsley (or parsley flakes)

Recipe may be divided or expanded easily; allow approximately ¼ pound lobster meat per person.

1. Preheat oven to 350°.
2. Cut lobster meat into bite-size pieces and line casserole dish with it.
3. Melt butter. Pour one-fourth of this over lobster meat. Reserve rest.
4. Combine dressing ingredients with reserved butter, using some or all of melted butter depending on consistency desired for dressing. Spoon dressing over lobster meat in casserole.
5. Bake 15 to 20 minutes.

Shrimp Kathleen

Yield: 4 servings

A hint of curry sparks this dish.

½ cup (1 stick) butter, melted
4 bay leaves
1 large onion, chopped
2 tablespoons flour
2 cups milk
2 teaspoons curry powder
1 to 1½ pounds cooked shrimp, shelled and deveined
8 ounces sliced mushrooms, sautéed
½ pound Swiss cheese, shredded

1. Melt butter in large skillet. Sauté onion with bay leaves. When onion is tender, remove bay leaves; stir in flour until thick and bubbly. Slowly stir in milk; cook until thickened. Add curry powder; set aside.
2. Preheat oven to 350°. Grease a 2-quart au gratin baking dish or 13 x 9-inch dish.
3. Line dish with cooked shrimp; sprinkle with sautéed mushrooms. Cover with cream sauce. Top all with Swiss cheese.
4. Bake about 25 minutes or until cheese melts. Serve hot.

Creamy Oysters and Crabmeat

Yield: 6 servings

A deluxe duo for the "R" months.

½ cup (1 stick) butter
3 to 4 green onions, chopped
2 cups chopped fresh parsley
½ cup flour
1½ cups water
½ cup dry white wine
1 teaspoon salt
¼ teaspoon pepper
⅛ teaspoon Tabasco sauce

3 dozen fresh select oysters, undrained
  (1 to 1½-pounds)
½ pound fresh crabmeat, drained and flaked
6 tablespoons soft bread crumbs
paprika

1. Melt butter in heavy saucepan; add green onion and parsley and sauté until onion is tender. Stir in flour; cook over low heat 1 minute, stirring constantly. Gradually add water and wine; cook over medium heat, stirring constantly, until thickened and bubbly. Add salt, pepper and Tabasco.

2. In another saucepan, cook undrained oysters over medium heat 8 to 10 minutes, or until edges of oysters begin to curl. Drain.

3. Preheat oven to 350°. Lightly grease six 10-ounce ramekins or custard cups. Place 6 oysters in each ramekin and cover with 2 tablespoons crabmeat. Spoon about ¼ cup sauce over crabmeat; sprinkle with a tablespoon of bread crumbs and paprika. Bake for 20 to 25 minutes or until hot and bubbly.

Cod Gumbo

Yield: 4 to 6 servings

Accompany with hot corn bread.

2 slices of bacon, chopped
  (or 2 tablespoons oil)
1 large green pepper, seeded and chopped
1 large onion, peeled and chopped
1 large garlic clove, minced
1 16-ounce can stewed tomatoes
1 cup chicken broth
¾ teaspoon salt, or to taste
⅛ teaspoon freshly ground black pepper
½ teaspoon dried basil leaves
¼ teaspoon Tabasco sauce
1 pound fresh or frozen cod fillets
  (or other white fish such as sole or perch)
1 10-ounce package frozen sliced okra
1 tablespoon chopped fresh parsley
2 cups hot cooked rice

1. In a large skillet over medium heat, cook bacon. As fat is released add green pepper, onion and garlic and cook 3 to 4 minutes, stirring occasionally, until onion is tender.

2. Add tomatoes, broth, salt and pepper, basil and Tabasco; cover and simmer 10 minutes.

3. If fish is frozen, remove from freezer, unwrap and let stand at room temperature 5 to 10 minutes. Using a sharp knife, cut fish into 1½-inch cubes. Stir fish and okra into tomato mixture. Cover and simmer 15 minutes longer, or until fish flakes easily with a fork and okra is tender; stir in parsley. Serve in deep dishes over rice.

VEGETABLES

Grammy's Baked Lima Beans
Yield: 2 quarts

**A natural partner to Boston Brown Bread (see index),
these beans are gently seasoned the old-fashioned way.**

1 pound dried lima beans
½ pound lean salt pork
½ pound dark brown sugar
1 medium onion, cut up
1 teaspoon dry mustard
dash of pepper (no salt)

Must be made ahead.

Variation:
Zippy Baked Limas

1. Wash and pick over beans; soak them overnight in water to cover completely.
2. Dice salt pork into ½-inch pieces; add to beans and parboil 15 minutes, using water beans were soaked in.
3. Add remaining ingredients. Pour into baking pan or bean pot; bake, uncovered in 350° oven for about 3 hours, stirring throughly when half done. Adjust sugar to taste.

Zippy Baked Limas:
Proceed as above but leave onion whole and stick with 3 whole cloves. Add ½ teaspoon ginger and ½ teaspoon curry powder along with dry mustard. Add 3 or 4 good shakes of Worcestershire sauce. Stir well. Increase brown sugar to ¾ pound and add to beans along with ¼ cup ketchup. Bake as above for 3 hours.

Brussel Sprouts with Walnut Butter
Yield: 6 servings

A pinch of sugar neutralizes any bitterness in the sprouts.

1 pound fresh brussel sprouts
1 cup water
½ teaspoon salt
½ teaspoon sugar
¼ cup (½ stick) butter
½ cup coarsely chopped walnuts
⅛ teaspoon ground pepper

1. Wash and trim brussel sprouts by removing any discolored leaves and cutting off stem ends. Cut an X in the bottom of each sprout.
2. Place sprouts in large saucepan, add water, salt and sugar; bring to a boil. Cover, reduce heat and simmer 15 to 20 minutes or until tender. Drain. Place in serving bowl.
3. Melt butter until lightly browned. Add walnuts and cook until lightly browned, stirring constantly. Pour over brussel sprouts and sprinkle with pepper.

Easy Broccoli Casserole

Yield: 4 servings

Fresh cauliflower also may be prepared this way.

1 large bunch broccoli (or medium head
   cauliflower)
½ cup mayonnaise
½ cup (2 ounces) shredded
   sharp Cheddar cheese
½ teaspoon dry mustard
¼ teaspoon salt
⅛ teaspoon cayenne pepper

Variation:

For a large crowd, use both broccoli and
cauliflower and double the remaining
ingredients

1. Wash and trim broccoli or cauliflower; cook
   covered, in small amount of boiling salted
   water, about 10 minutes, or until crisp-
   tender. Drain.
2. Preheat oven to 400°. Place vegetable in
   1-quart casserole.
3. Combine remaining ingredients, stirring well.
   Spoon evenly over vegetable. Bake,
   uncovered, for 8 to 10 minutes or
   until bubbly.

Cauliflower Soufflé

Yield: 6 to 8 servings

Sure to convert any non-cauliflower eater!

2 cups (1 small head) cauliflower florets,
   cooked and drained
½ cup (1 stick) butter
¼ cup plus 2 tablespoons flour
1½ cups milk
4 eggs, separated, at room temperature
1 3-ounce package cream cheese,
   cubed and softened
½ teaspoon salt
¼ teaspoon white pepper
⅛ teaspoon nutmeg

1. In container of food processor, purée
   cauliflower until smooth. Set aside.
2. Melt butter in saucepan over low heat, stir in
   flour and cook 1 minute. Gradually add milk;
   stir over medium heat until thickened
   and bubbly.
3. Beat egg yolks until lemon colored.
   Gradually stir ¼ cup hot white sauce into
   yolks; add to remaining white sauce, stirring
   constantly.
4. Add cream cheese, stirring until melted. Add
   cauliflower purée, salt, pepper and nutmeg;
   mix well. Preheat oven to 350°.
5. Beat egg whites until stiff but not dry.
   Gently fold into cauliflower mixture. Spoon
   into 2-quart soufflé dish.
6. Bake for 45 to 60 minutes or until golden
   brown. Serve immediately.

Green Beans and Red Peppers

Yield: 6 servings

A colorful, make-ahead side dish for a holiday buffet.

1 pound green beans, trimmed (or
   1 16-ounce box frozen whole green beans)
2 sweet red peppers
½ cup finely chopped onion
1 teaspoon Dijon mustard
1 tablespoon red wine vinegar
⅓ cup olive oil
½ teaspoon ground cumin
salt and pepper to taste
¼ cup finely chopped parsley

1. Boil enough water to cover beans; add beans; return water to boil and cook 8 minutes or until tender. Drain well. Place in large serving bowl.

2. Broil peppers, turning frequently, until skins are burned all over. Place peppers in brown paper bag; close and let stand at least 10 minutes or until cool enough to handle. Remove peppers from bag; peel and cut in half, discarding stem, seeds and membranes. Cut each half into very thin strips, about ¼-inch wide. Add to beans. Add chopped onion.

3. In a screw-top jar combine mustard, vinegar, oil and seasonings; shake well to blend. Pour over bean mixture; toss well to coat. Refrigerate until needed. Serve at room temperature.

Onion Rings Schaefer

Yield: 4 servings

The ones to have when you're having more than one!

1 large Bermuda onion
1 12-ounce can or bottle cold Schaefer beer
12 ounces sifted flour
2 teaspoons salt
1½ teaspoons baking powder
1 egg, separated
1 tablespoon vegetable oil

shortening

1. Peel onion; cut into ¼-inch slices, separating into rings. Place in deep bowl, cover with beer and let stand 30 minutes, stirring once or twice. Drain, reserving ⅔ cup beer.

2. Sift together flour, salt and baking powder; set aside.

3. Beat egg yolk slightly; stir in reserved beer and salad oil. Pour beer mixture into flour mixture; stir until smooth.

4. Beat egg white until peaks form. Fold into batter.

5. Heat shortening, 1-inch deep in skillet, to 375°. Dip onion rings in batter, letting excess batter drip back into bowl. Drop several rings at a time into hot fat; fry until golden. Drain on paper towels. Keep hot in oven until all rings are fried.

Roasted Potatoes

Yield: 6 to 8 servings

In England, a traditional accompaniment for roasted meats, particularly for Christmas dinner.

6 to 8 large potatoes
oil or pan drippings.

Variation: Roasted Potatoes and Fennel

Cut one bulb of fennel (about ¾ pound), into 1 x ½-inch strips. Add to potatoes for the last 30 minutes of roasting. Stir to coat with oil; sprinkle with ½ teaspoon rosemary. Continue baking until fennel is soft and potatoes are crisp.

1. Preheat oven to 400°. Generously grease a metal roasting or baking pan.
2. Peel and quarter potatoes; boil about 10 minutes. Do not overcook. Potatoes should be just softened on outside for proper crisping when roasted. Drain potatoes.
3. Preheat pan in oven. Add potatoes. Using basting brush, coat potatoes well with oil or fat drippings from meat. Roast for 1 hour, turning over after 30 minutes. Serve immediately.

Scalloped Potatoes and Turnips

Yield: 6 servings

Good served with ham or pork.

2 cups peeled, thinly sliced potatoes
2 cups peeled, thinly sliced turnips
¼ cup chopped onion
¼ cup chopped green pepper
¼ cup chopped red pepper
2 tablespoons butter
¼ teaspoon salt
¼ teaspoon white pepper
2 tablespoons chopped fresh parsley
¾ cup half-and-half
½ cup (2 ounces) shredded Cheddar cheese
½ cup crushed buttery rich cracker crumbs
¼ cup (½ stick) butter, melted

1. Preheat oven to 350°. Grease a 1¾-quart baking dish.
2. Mix potatoes and turnips; layer half of mixture in prepared dish.
3. Sauté onion and peppers in 2 tablespoons melted butter until tender. Stir in salt, pepper, 1 tablespoon parsley; add half-and-half, stirring until blended.
4. Pour half of onion mixture over potatoes and turnips. Repeat layers. Top with cheese. Cover and bake for 45 minutes.
5. Combine cracker crumbs, 1 tablespoon parsley and melted butter. Sprinkle over vegetables. Bake, uncovered, 15 minutes more.

Pecan Rice Mélange

Complements chicken or turkey nicely.

Yield: 6 servings

1 6-ounce box long grain and wild rice
2⅓ cups chicken broth
1 tablespoon butter
½ teaspoon salt, or to taste
¾ cup toasted pecans

1. Prepare long grain and wild rice as package directs, using chicken broth and butter but OMITTING seasoning package included in box. Bring rices to boil in salted broth, cover, reduce heat and simmer 25 minutes.
2. Pour off any excess broth. Toss rice with toasted pecans just before serving.

Spinach Rice Ring

This colorful combination can also be used as a stuffing for chicken or turkey (double recipe to fill turkey).

Yield: 6 to 8 servings

2 cups chicken broth
1 cup uncooked rice
3 tablespoons butter
½ pound mushrooms, sliced
1 small onion, diced
2 10-ounce packages frozen spinach, thawed and drained or ½ pound fresh spinach chopped
2 tablespoons dry sherry or vermouth

Rice may be prepared also in a regular casserole.

1. In saucepan, heat broth to boiling; add rice, reduce heat to low, cover and cook 25 to 30 minutes.
2. Meanwhile, sauté mushrooms and onion in butter in skillet. Remove from heat; add spinach, cooked rice and sherry.
3. Place in greased 6-cup ring mold; cover with foil. (May be made ahead several hours to this point.)
4. When ready to cook, place in 300° pre-heated oven and heat for 30 minutes.
5. Unmold on large platter.

Spinach Timbales

Popeye wears his tuxedo for this!

Yield: 6 servings

3 eggs
½ cup shredded Cheddar cheese
¼ cup half-and-half
½ teaspoon prepared horseradish
¼ teaspoon salt
dash pepper
dash Tabasco sauce
1½ cups well-drained cooked, chopped spinach (about 2 10-ounce packages frozen)
fresh spinach leaves for garnish, if desired

1. Preheat oven to 325°. Butter well six 6-ounce custard cups, ramekins, or molds.
2. Beat eggs slightly in mixing bowl; add cheese, cream, horseradish and seasonings. Stir in spinach.
3. Spoon mixture equally into custard cups. Place cups in a 13 x 9 x 2-inch baking pan and add one inch hot water to pan. Bake uncovered 20 to 30 minutes or until set. Unmold and serve immediately, garnished with fresh spinach leaves.

Scalloped Tomatoes

Yield: 6 servings

**Even better than you remembered,
especially if made with home-canned tomatoes.**

1 28-ounce can good quality tomatoes
4 slices bread
1 small onion, chopped and sautéed in
  2 tablespoons butter
½ teaspoon salt
½ teaspoon sugar
1 egg
butter, softened

1. Preheat oven to 350°. Butter well a
   1½-quart casserole.
2. Pour tomatoes into casserole and cut into
   bite-size pieces.
3. Break up bread and add to tomatoes,
   using 2 or more slices depending on
   juiciness of tomatoes.
4. Add sautéed onion, salt and sugar. Break
   egg directly into casserole and mix well.
5. Butter remaining bread squares and cover
   top of tomatoes with them.
6. Bake 25 to 35 minutes, or until hot and
   bubbly and bread is golden brown.

Winter Vegetable Sauté

Yield: 6 servings

Colorful and quick, this may be prepared in a skillet or a wok.

3 medium yellow squash
3 ribs celery
2 medium carrots
1 garlic clove, minced
2 tablespoons vegetable oil
1 pound bunch broccoli, stems and florets
  separated
1 tablespoon lemon juice
½ teaspoon thyme
¼ teaspoon salt
⅛ teaspoon pepper
¼ cup minced fresh parsley

1. Cut squash, celery, carrots and broccoli
   stems into 3 x ¼-inch strips. Sauté with
   garlic in hot oil in skillet or wok for
   6 minutes or until crisp-tender; add broccoli
   florets during last 3 minutes.
2. Sprinkle vegetables with lemon juice, thyme,
   salt and pepper; toss well to coat. Add
   parsley and mix well.

SALADS

Winter Green Salad

Yield: 8 to 10 servings

This one's a little different and VERY good.

Dressing:

2 tablespoons red wine vinegar
¼ cup extra-virgin olive oil
¼ cup salad oil
1½ teaspoons Dijon mustard
1 garlic clove, minced
1 teaspoon anchovy paste (optional)
2 teaspoons drained capers
salt and freshly ground pepper

¼ pound fresh mushrooms, cleaned, trimmed and thinly sliced
1 small head romaine lettuce, cleaned and torn into bite-size pieces
1 small fresh fennel bulb, thinly sliced
2 to 3 endives, trimmed, cut lengthwise into julienne slivers
2 to 3 cups fresh spinach, cleaned and torn into bite-size pieces
2 scallions, sliced thinly

1. Make dressing: in a small jar with lid, combine vinegar, oils, mustard and garlic. Cover tightly and shake jar until dressing is smooth and mixed. Add anchovy paste, capers, salt and pepper.

2. Place dressing in bottom of large bowl. Add mushrooms; let stand.

3. In another bowl mix together all greens and scallions.

4. To serve: add greens to bowl with mushrooms and toss gently. Season with salt and pepper, if desired.

Cranberry Fruit Mélange

Yield: 8 servings

A colorful fruit salad, ideal for the holidays.

1 cup (4 ounces) fresh cranberries
½ cup water
⅓ cup sugar
¼ cup raisins
1 teaspoon lemon juice
1 teaspoon grenadine syrup
4 plums, peeled, halved and sliced (about 3 cups)
6 kiwi fruit, peeled, halved and sliced (about 3 cups)
2 carambola (star fruit), sliced crosswise
mint sprigs (optional)

Must be made ahead.

1. In small saucepan combine cranberries, water, sugar, raisins, lemon juice and grenadine syrup. Cook, stirring, over medium heat for 5 to 7 minutes or until mixture is the consistency of thin syrup. Remove from heat; cool slightly.

2. Mix cranberry mixture with plums in a large glass serving bowl. Cover with plastic wrap; marinate in refrigerator overnight, stirring occasionally.

3. Just before serving add kiwi fruit and carambola (this preserves their distinctive color). Garnish with mint, if desired.

Salad Italiano

Yield: 6 servings

**A classic Italian "insalata" with a light lemon vinaigrette.
The croutons are worth the extra effort.**

Basil Croutons:

10 ½-inch thick slices of Italian bread
2 garlic cloves, sliced
¼ cup extra-virgin olive oil
1 tablespoon minced fresh basil,
  or ¼ teaspoon dried basil

1 medium head romaine lettuce
1 medium head radicchio
1 bunch arugula
4 ounces Parmesan cheese (NOT GRATED),
  at room temperature
oil-cured olives or ripe black olives
  (about ¾ cup)

Dressing:

⅓ cup extra-virgin olive oil
2 tablespoons lemon juice
2 tablespoons white wine vinegar
1 tablespoon sugar
¼ teaspoon salt
⅛ teaspoon pepper

1. Make croutons: Preheat oven to 350° and line cookie sheet with foil. With 1¾-inch biscuit or cookie cutter, cut 2 rounds from each slice of bread (reserve crusts and trimmings for crumbs another time). Place rounds on cookie sheet.

2. Heat oil over moderate heat; add garlic and cook until brown. Remove from heat; discard garlic and add basil. With pastry brush, brush each bread round on both sides. Bake bread 10 minutes; turn and bake 10 minutes more, or until crisp and golden.

3. Meanwhile, tear washed salad greens into bite-size pieces and combine in large bowl.

4. With a cheese slicer or vegetable peeler, cut across Parmesan cheese to make thin, wide slices. Arrange cheese slices and olives over greens.

5. Make dressing: combine all ingredients in a jar with screw-top lid and shake vigorously. Pour dressing over salad; toss gently to coat greens well. Serve with Basil Croutons.

Orange-Avocado Salad with Cilantro Dressing

Yield: 6 servings

**Serve this salad with a favorite Tex-Mex entrée,
such as Pork Carnitas (see index).**

Dressing:

¼ cup fresh lime juice
¼ cup chopped fresh cilantro (coriander)
2 tablespoons vegetable oil
2 tablespoons chopped green onion
½ teaspoon salt
½ teaspoon sugar
¼ teaspoon freshly ground pepper

3 ripe avocados, sliced
3 oranges, peeled and sectioned
Boston lettuce

1. Make dressing: combine all ingredients in blender; mix well.

2. Arrange avocado and orange slices on a bed of lettuce leaves. Drizzle with dressing.

Tossed Hearts and Love Apples
Yield: 8 servings

A salad for Valentine's Day or any special occasion.
Cherry tomatoes are the old-fashioned "love apples."

2 avocados, peeled and coarsely chopped
lemon juice
1 14-ounce can hearts of palm, drained
  and sliced
1 14-ounce can artichoke hearts, drained
  and coarsely chopped
½ pint cherry tomatoes, halved

1 tablespoon lemon juice
¼ cup olive oil
2 garlic cloves, minced
½ teaspoon marjoram
½ teaspoon oregano
1 teaspoon salt, or to taste
¼ teaspoon pepper

leafy lettuce such as Boston or Bibb

Bottled Italian dressing may be substituted
for lemon/olive oil.

1. Sprinkle avocado with lemon juice; toss to coat well. Combine with next three ingredients; toss gently and refrigerate until serving time. (Do not prepare more than 2 hours ahead or avocado may become mushy.)
2. Combine remaining ingredients, except lettuce, in jar with tightly fitting lid. Shake well; chill.
3. Toss salad with dressing just before serving on bed of lettuce leaves.

Spiced Fruit Salad Mold with Ginger Dressing
Yield: 4 to 6 servings

This piquant gelatin salad is nice with holiday ham or turkey.

1 17-ounce can fruit cocktail
¼ cup cider vinegar
½ cup sugar
12 whole cloves
1 cinnamon stick
dash of ginger
1 3-ounce package orange, cherry
  or strawberry gelatin
¾ cup cold water

1. Drain fruit cocktail, measuring ¾ cup syrup. Bring syrup, vinegar, sugar and spices to a boil; simmer for 10 minutes.
2. Strain syrup and discard cinnamon stick and cloves. Add boiling water to make 1 cup, if necessary. Dissolve gelatin in hot syrup.
3. Add cold water; stir. Chill until slightly thickened; fold in fruit. Pour into lightly greased 4-cup mold; chill until firm.
4. Unmold on serving plate and serve with Ginger Dressing, if desired.

Ginger Dressing: (optional)
⅓ cup mayonnaise
⅓ cup sour cream
2 tablespoons crystallized ginger chopped

Dressing:
Combine all ingredients. Store in refrigerator until needed.

217

DESSERTS

Black Midnight Mocha Cake with Fluffy Mocha Frosting

Yield: 12 servings

Dark, moist, chocolatey, yummy — the quintessential birthday cake! And so easy, it will make you wonder why you ever use a cake mix.

2 cups flour
2 cups sugar
¾ cup unsweetened cocoa powder
2 teaspoons baking soda
1 teaspoon baking powder
½ cup vegetable oil
1 cup boiling coffee, preferably French Roast
2 eggs
1 cup milk
Fluffy Mocha Frosting (below)

1. Preheat oven to 350°. Grease and flour a 9 x 13-inch baking pan or two 8-inch round layer cake pans.
2. In large bowl of electric mixer, combine all ingredients. Mix well. Batter will be very thin.
3. Pour batter into prepared pan or divide evenly between layer pans. Bake 35 minutes or until done. Cool on wire rack; remove layers from pans after 10 minutes. Frost with Fluffy Mocha Frosting.

Fluffy Mocha Frosting:

½ cup (1 stick) butter, softened
1 cup confectioners' sugar
1 egg, lightly beaten
2 teaspoons instant coffee crystals
¼ cup cream or milk
¼ teaspoon vanilla extract
dash of salt
2 ounces unsweetened chocolate, melted

Fluffy Mocha Frosting:

1. In small bowl of mixer, cream butter and sugar until fluffy.
2. Add egg, coffee crystals and milk. Beat slowly to mix.
3. Add vanilla, salt and melted chocolate. Beat well.

Walnut Cake with Butter Cream Frosting
Yield: 9-inch layer cake

Owner Lois M. Moore herself moves into the kitchen to bake this outstanding cake for her guests at the 1784 Inn of Franklin, CT.

1½ cups (3 sticks) butter, softened (no substitute)
1½ cups sugar
2 cups flour
1 teaspoon cream of tartar
½ teaspoon baking soda
¾ cup milk
1 teaspoon vanilla extract
4 egg whites
pinch of salt
¾ cup coarsely chopped walnuts
Butter Cream Frosting (below)

1. Preheat oven to 350°. Butter two 9-inch layer pans, line with waxed paper; butter paper.
2. In large bowl cream butter and sugar until fluffy.
3. In another bowl sift together flour, cream of tartar and baking soda; stir into butter mixture alternately with milk mixed with vanilla.
4. In large bowl of electric mixer, beat egg whites with salt until they hold peaks.
5. Stir one-fourth of whites into batter, then

gently but thoroughly fold in remaining whites. Fold in walnuts.

6. Pour batter into prepared pans, dividing evenly. Bake 40 to 45 minutes, until cake tester comes out clean.

7. Cool cake in pans for 5 minutes. with knife release cake from pans onto wire racks. Remove waxed paper and cool cake completely.

Butter Cream Frosting:

½ cup (1 stick) butter, softened
2 cups confectioners' sugar, sifted
2 tablespoons light cream, plus more
  if needed for spreading consistency
½ cup chopped walnuts for garnish

Frosting:

Combine all ingredients until smooth and of good spreading consistency. Chill for 15 minutes. Use for filling and top and sides of cake. Garnish with walnuts.

Marzipan Pound Cake

Yield: 16 servings

If the Magi had brought homemade gifts, they probably would have included this cake.

8 ounces almond paste
½ cup light cream
¼ cup dark rum
½ cup slivered almonds

½ cup (1 stick) unsalted butter, softened
1 cup sugar
2 eggs, lightly beaten
2 cups flour
¼ teaspoon salt
1 teaspoon baking powder
1 teaspoon baking soda
1 cup sour cream
1 teaspoon vanilla extract

4 tablespoons milk
4 tablespoons confectioners' sugar

Warning: do NOT use bundt pan!

1. In a small bowl, mix together almond paste, cream, rum, and slivered almonds. Set aside.

2. Preheat oven to 350°. Grease and flour a 9- or 10-inch tube pan.

3. In a large bowl, cream together butter and sugar; add eggs, mixing until smooth.

4. Sift together flour, salt, baking powder and baking soda.

5. Add dry ingredients to butter mixture alternately with sour cream; stir in vanilla. Mix well.

6. Pour half of batter into prepared pan. Reserving ½ cup of almond paste mixture, spread remainder over batter in pan. Spoon remaining batter over and spread to cover.

7. Bake cake 35 minutes.

8. Meanwhile, add milk and confectioners' sugar to reserved ½ cup almond paste mixture. Spread over partially baked cake; cook cake 25 minutes longer.

9. Cool cake 10 minutes on wire rack; remove outer pan. Cool at least 10 minutes more before carefully removing tube.

The Ultimate Fruitcake

Yield: 2 8-inch loaves

Very rich and very colorful.

1 pound dates, cut
2 3½-ounce cans flaked coconut
1 pound pecans, coarsely chopped
½ pound candied cherries, red and green mixed, halved
½ pound candied pineapple, chopped
1 14-ounce can sweetened condensed milk
1 teaspoon salt
3 tablespoons rum

1. Preheat oven to 275°. Line two 8-inch loaf pans with waxed paper, bottom and sides.

2. Mix chopped dates with coconut until dates are coated. Add remaining ingredients; mix thoroughly.

3. Place a pan of water on bottom rack of oven while cakes are baking. DO NOT PLACE CAKES IN WATER.

4. Bake 1½ hours. Remove cakes from pan and cool on wire rack. When almost cool, strip off waxed paper.

5. Wrap cakes in foil; refrigerate or freeze. Serve thinly sliced as cake is very rich.

Eggnog Cheesecake with Cranberry Glaze

Yield: 12 to 16 servings

What a magnificent dessert for the holidays!

Crust:

¼ cup butter
2 tablespoons sugar
½ teaspoon vanilla extract
½ cup flour

Filling:

20 ounces cream cheese, softened
⅓ cup half-and-half
¼ cup whipping cream
¾ cup sugar
1½ teaspoons vanilla extract
3 eggs
2 egg yolks
2½ tablespoons dark rum
2 tablespoons Cognac
1 teaspoon ground nutmeg

Glaze:

½ cup sugar
1 tablespoon cornstarch
¾ cup fresh cranberries
⅔ cup cranberry juice cocktail or water

1. Make crust: preheat oven to 400°. Combine crust ingredients in bowl of processor. Process until mixture forms ball of dough. With floured fingertips press dough evenly over bottom of ungreased 9-inch springform pan. Bake until golden, 10 to 12 minutes. Cool completely.

2. Make filling: lower oven temperture to 350°. In bowl of food processor place cream cheese; process until cheese is smooth. Add remaining ingredients and process until smooth and well blended. Pour into prepared crust. Bake 50 to 60 minutes.

3. Make glaze shortly before serving. Combine all ingredients in a saucepan. Cook just until berries pop. Cool to room temperature. Spread over cheesecake just before serving.

Slovakian Walnut Torte

Yield: one 9-inch layer cake

Spectacular!

Torte:

12 eggs, separated
2 cups sugar
1 cup fresh bread crumbs
1 teaspoon baking powder
pinch of salt
2 cups ground walnuts
1 teaspoon vanilla or rum extract

1. Preheat oven to 300°. Grease and flour three 9-inch cake pans.
2. In large bowl of mixer, combine egg yolks and sugar. Beat until smooth and lemon-colored. Add bread crumbs, baking powder, salt, ground walnuts and flavoring. Continue mixing until well blended.
3. In a clean large bowl, beat egg whites until stiff peaks form. DO NOT UNDER MIX.
4. Gently but thoroughly fold egg yolk mixture into beaten egg whites.
5. Pour batter into prepared cake pans. Bake for 1 hour. Cool completely on wire rack before removing from pans.

Filling:

½ cup (1 stick) unsalted butter, softened
¾ pound confectioners' sugar
1 egg
2 teaspoons instant coffee powder
1 teaspoon vanilla or rum extract
milk, if needed
walnut halves

Filling:

1. Place all filling ingredients in small bowl of mixer and blend to spreading consistency, adding a few teaspoons of milk if frosting is too thick.
2. Frost top of each layer, placing one on top of another, allowing filling to ooze over side. Use remaining filling to frost top of torte. Decorate top with walnut halves.

SLOVAKIAN WALNUT TORTE

My maternal grandmother, who served this torte every Christmas before midnight mass, brought the recipe with her when she came to America early in this century. The original recipe called for walnuts picked in the High Tatras near her childhood home. When I recently shared the torte with relatives in Kezmarok, Slovakia, this marvelous dessert had not been altered one iota in the 50 years since it first passed my lips! — D.W.D., Honey Brook, PA

Jessica's Chocolate Brownie Cheesecake

Yield: 12 to 16 servings

**Jessica won a cooking contest with this original recipe when she was only 10.
It's easy enough for a kid to make but the taste is R-rated!**

1½ cups prepared brownies, cubed or
  crumbled in 1-inch chunks

20 chocolate wafer cookies, crushed
  to make 1 cup
3 tablespoons butter, melted

1 12-ounce package chocolate chips
3 8-ounce packages cream cheese, softened
1 cup sugar
3 eggs
pinch of salt
1 teaspoon vanilla extract
1 8-ounce carton sour cream
whipped cream (optional)

Must be made ahead.

1. In small bowl, or food processor, combine crushed wafers and melted butter. Press into bottom of 9-inch springform pan.
2. Place chocolate chips in top of double boiler over pan of simmering water. Heat, stirring occasionally, until melted.
3. Preheat oven to 350°. In bowl of food processor, process cream cheese until smooth. Add sugar, eggs, salt, vanilla and sour cream; process until smooth. Stir in melted chocolate; process to blend. (At this point you may wish to transfer mixture to a larger bowl.)
4. Fold brownie chunks into cheese mixture. Pour into prepared crust. Bake 55 to 60 minutes or until firm. (Center may be soft but will firm up when chilled.)
5. Cool cheesecake completely in pan on a wire rack. Refrigerate overnight. Remove springform sides and serve with whipped cream, if desired.

Steamed Chocolate Pudding

Yield: 8 servings

For those who don't care for traditional Christmas steamed puddings.

2 tablespoons butter, softened
½ cup sugar
1 egg, at room temperature
2 squares (2 ounces) semisweet chocolate,
  melted
1 cup flour
1½ teaspoons baking powder
¼ teaspoon salt
½ teaspoon cinnamon*
½ cup milk
1 teaspoon vanilla extract
Spiced Hard Sauce

***Up to 1 teaspoon cinnamon may be used.
This will give pudding a spicy character.**

1. Cream butter and sugar; add egg and melted chocolate, stirring until smooth.
2. Combine all dry ingredients; add to creamed mixture alternately with milk. Stir in vanilla.
3. Pour into well-greased pudding mold or 1-pound coffee can, filling two-thirds full; cover with lid to mold or foil held in place with rubber band.
4. Place pudding mold in covered pot or kettle on a rack or trivet; steam for one hour. Boiling water should come up sides of mold at least 2 inches.
5. When done, unmold. Serve warm. (Or wrap in foil and reheat later in warm oven.)

Spiced Hard Sauce:

½ cup (1 stick) butter, softened
2 cups confectioners' sugar
¼ cup brandy or sherry
dash nutmeg and cinnamon

Spiced Hard Sauce:

1. Using mixer or food processor, combine all ingredients until smooth.
2. Place in serving dish; chill until firm.

Snow Pudding with Crimson Sauce

Yield: 10 to 12 servings

A molded coconut cream with raspberry sauce.

2 envelopes unflavored gelatin
1 cup sugar
½ teaspoon salt
1¼ cups milk
1 teaspoon vanilla extract
3½ ounces flaked coconut
1 pint whipping cream, whipped

1. In large saucepan combine first three ingredients; add milk slowly. Let stand 5 minutes to soften gelatin.
2. Cook milk mixture over medium heat until sugar and gelatin dissolve. Chill until thickened like egg whites.
3. Stir vanilla and coconut into chilled gelatin. Fold in whipped cream. Pour into lightly oiled 6-cup mold.
4. Chill 4 hours or until firm. Unmold and serve with Crimson Sauce.

Crimson Sauce:

1 10-ounce package frozen raspberries, with syrup, thawed
½ cup hot water
1 tablespoon lemon juice
⅓ cup sugar
1 tablespoon cornstarch
pinch salt
2 tablespoons framboise or Kirsch (optional)

Must be made ahead.

Variation:

Prepare Snow Pudding in a heart-shaped mold for Valentine's Day, either 1 large or 6 individual. Unmold heart on plate and surround with Crimson Sauce.

Sauce:

1. Purée raspberries in food processor or blender. Press through sieve.
2. Place raspberry purée in saucepan with all remaining ingredients except liqueur. Bring to boil; reduce heat to medium and cook, stirring constantly, until mixture thickens.
3. Remove from heat; cool and stir in liqueur. Refrigerate until ready to serve.

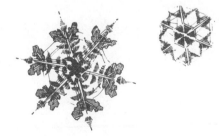

Merry Christmousse

**Flavored with crushed peppermint sticks
and garnished with chocolate curls: Yum!**

Yield: 6 to 8 servings

1 envelope unflavored gelatin
1 cup milk
2 eggs, separated, at room temperature
⅓ cup sugar
1 cup whipping cream
¾ cup finely crushed peppermint stick candy

Garnish:

whipped cream, chocolate curls,
  additional crushed candies

Must be made ahead.

1. Lightly oil a 5-cup mold. A star mold is ideal, if you have one.

2. In large heavy saucepan combine gelatin and milk; let stand 5 minutes. Stir in egg yolks. Cook over medium heat, stirring constantly, until smooth. Remove from heat; cool.

3. Beat egg whites until foamy. Gradually beat in sugar a tablespoon at a time, beating until stiff peaks form. Fold into cooled gelatin mixture.

4. In large chilled bowl, beat whipping cream until stiff peaks form. Fold cream, along with candy, into egg white mixture.

5. Spoon mousse into prepared mold. Chill several hours.

6. To serve: unmold onto platter and garnish with crushed candy, whipped cream and/or chocolate curls. Or melt 2 ounces semisweet chocolate, spread on waxed paper, allowing to harden slightly. Using small Christmas cookie-cutters, cut shapes in chocolate; chill. Use to garnish mousse.

Mocha Coeur à la Crème

A Valentine for your chocolate-loving lover!

Yield: 10 to 12 servings

1 cup heavy or whipping cream
1 8-ounce package cream cheese, softened
⅓ cup sugar
dash salt
4 teaspoons Kahlúa or coffee-flavored liqueur
1 teaspoon vanilla extract
1 6-ounce package semisweet chocolate chips
  melted
chocolate curls for garnish
confectioners' sugar

Must be made ahead.

1. Line a 7-inch coeur à la crème mold or heartshaped basket with single layer damp cheesecloth, allowing 4-inch overhang all around.

2. In large mixer bowl whip cream until soft peaks form; set aside.

3. In food processor or another large mixer bowl, combine cream cheese, sugar and salt. Process until light and fluffy. Add liqueur and vanilla; process until blended. Add melted chocolate; process until thoroughly blended, scraping down sides as necessary.

4. Fold whipped cream into chocolate mixture.

5. Spoon mixture into prepared mold, spreading evenly to edges. Fold cheesecloth over top. Set mold inside shallow pan; refrigerate overnight.

6. To serve: unfold cheesecloth; invert onto serving platter. Remove mold and cheesecloth. Garnish with chocolate curls and sprinkle with confectioners' sugar, if desired.

Frozen Cranberry Silk

A favorite holiday dessert.

Yield: 8 to 10 servings

1¼ cups crushed vanilla wafers
6 tablespoons butter, melted
2 3-ounce packages cream cheese, softened
¼ cup sugar
pinch salt
½ teaspoon almond extract
1 cup heavy cream, whipped
1 16-ounce can whole cranberry sauce
additional whipped cream (optional)

Must be made ahead.

1. Combine crumbs and melted butter; press firmly on bottom of 8-inch square baking pan. Chill while preparing filling.

2. With mixer or processor combine cream cheese, sugar, salt and almond extract until fluffy. Fold mixture into whipped cream. Add cranberries, gently folding into mixture. Spoon into chilled crust.

3. Freeze until firm. Remove from freezer 10 minutes before serving; cut into squares. Garnish with additional whipped cream, if desired.

Mincemeat Tart with Walnut Crust

Yield: 8 servings

**This is the kind of recipe we like — a little creativity
and a little help from pre-packaged foods. If homemade mincemeat is desired,
see Christmas Memories Cookbook, p. 227.**

Walnut Crust:

½ cup walnuts
1 ¼ cups flour, spooned and leveled
2 tablespoons sugar
¼ teaspoon salt
6 tablespoons very cold butter
3 to 4 tablespoons very cold whipping cream

Filling:

1 20½-ounce jar ready-to-use mincemeat
½ cup chopped walnuts
2 tablespoons brandy (may be fruit-flavored)
2 canned pear halves

Topping:

¼ cup flour
2 tablespoons light brown sugar
2 tablespoons butter, softened

1. Grind walnuts medium-fine in food processor. Blend in flour, sugar and salt; add butter, cut into chunks, processing just until mixture resembles coarse meal.

2. With processor running, slowly add cream through feed tube to moisten dough; DO NOT form a ball. By hand form ball and flatten.

3. With hands press dough into a 9-inch tart pan with removable bottom. Using fingertips, work dough evenly across bottom and against sides. Chill about 30 minutes before filling.

4. Combine mincemeat with walnuts and brandy; pour into crust.

5. Slice pear halves vertically, being careful not to slice completely through. Carefully place halves in center of tart and fan out slices.

6. Prepare topping: combine all ingredients until coarse crumbs form. Sprinkle topping over mincemeat and pears.

7. Bake at 350° for 40 minutes. Cool on wire rack 30 minutes. Remove sides of pan before serving tart.

Almond Macaroons

Yield: about 3 dozen

**Similar to the Italian ones in the red tin,
but made at home in a flash in the food processor.**

1 8-ounce can almond paste
1 cup sugar
3 large egg whites
¼ teaspoon vanilla extract
½ teaspoon almond extract
3 tablespoons sifted flour
⅓ cup confectioners' sugar, sifted
pinch of salt

1. Using food processor fitted with steel blade, break up almond paste into fine particles, pulsing 6 to 8 times (may have to do in two batches).

2. Combine almond paste, sugar, egg whites and flavorings in processor bowl and process 30 seconds. Add remaining ingredients and process about 1 minute or until completely blended.

3. Cover baking sheets with brown paper. Drop almond mixture by rounded teaspoonful onto pan. Dampen fingers and flatten dough. Let stand for an hour, uncovered.

4. Preheat oven to 300°. Bake 25 to 30 minutes.

5. Remove from oven; place brown paper on damp towel and remove macaroons with spatula to cool on wire rack.

Dundee Tea Bars

Yield: 24 bars

Little Dundee fruitcake bars, yummy and Christmasy.

½ cup (1 stick) butter, softened
½ cup sugar
1 teaspoon vanilla extract
2 eggs
1⅓ cups flour
1 teaspoon baking powder
¼ teaspoon salt
½ teaspoon nutmeg
¾ cup chopped candied mixed fruit
¼ cup currants or raisins
Lemon Glaze (below)

Lemon Glaze:

¼ cup sifted confectioners' sugar
1 teaspoon water
½ teaspoon lemon juice

1. Preheat oven to 325°. Grease a 9-inch square baking pan and line bottom with waxed paper.

2. Cream first three ingredients; beat in eggs.

3. Add sifted dry ingredients and fruit; mix well. Pour into prepared pan.

4. Bake 25 to 30 minutes. Turn out onto rack and peel off paper.

5. Turn right side up and brush with Lemon Glaze, made by mixing together all glaze ingredients until smooth.

6. When cool, cut into bars.

Here's My Heart Cookies

Yield: about 2½ dozen

A special chocolate-dipped shortbread Valentine.

1 cup (2 sticks) unsalted butter, softened
½ cup brown sugar, packed
2½ cups flour
1 teaspoon vanilla extract

4 or 5 squares semisweet chocolate, melted
½ cup finely chopped nuts

1. Using mixer or food processor, cream butter and sugar until smooth. Add flour and flavoring. When dough is well mixed, pat into a ball and chill for 2 hours.

2. Preheat oven to 300°. Roll dough on floured board to ¼-inch thickness. Cut with dusted heart-shaped cutters. Place on ungreased cookie sheets.

3. Bake 20 to 25 minutes, until brown around edges. Cool for 15 minutes.

4. When cooled, dip HALF of heart into melted chocolate; sprinkle immediately with nuts. Set cookies on wire rack or on waxed paper to harden chocolate.

Here's My Heart

Valentine Cookies

Yield: 2½ dozen

Heart-shaped cookies sandwiched with raspberry jam.

1 cup shortening
1 cup confectioners' sugar
½ cup light brown sugar
2 egg yolks
3 tablespoons light cream
2 teaspoons vanilla extract
2½ cups flour
2 teaspoons cream of tartar
1 teaspoon baking soda
½ teaspoon salt
seedless raspberry jam (Captain's Choice)

1. Using food processor, thoroughly combine first six ingredients. Add dry ingredients; mix well. Chill dough at least one hour.

2. Preheat oven to 350°. Roll out half of dough on floured surface to ⅛-inch thickness. Cut with heart-shaped cookie cutter. Repeat with remaining dough. Bake on ungreased cookie sheets for about 10 minutes or until lightly browned. Cool cookies on wire rack.

3. Heat about ⅓ cup raspberry jam until evenly melted. Brush back of one cookie with warm jam and sandwich with another cookie. Continue with all cookies. For variety, drizzle melted bittersweet chocolate over some cookies.

Half-Way-to-Heaven Bars

Yield: 4½ dozen bars

A brown-sugar meringue crowns these chocolate chip bars, transforming them from the mundane to the ethereal. Perfect for holiday gift-giving.

½ cup (1 stick) butter
½ cup sugar
½ cup brown sugar
2 egg yolks
1 tablespoon water
1 teaspoon vanilla extract
2 cups flour
¼ teaspoon salt
¼ teaspoon baking soda
1 teaspoon baking powder
1 12-ounce package chocolate chips

Topping:
2 egg whites
1 cup brown sugar

1. In large bowl, cream together butter and sugars; add egg yolks, water and vanilla. Mix well.
2. Mix together flour, salt, baking soda and baking powder. Add to butter mixture.
3. Preheat oven to 350°. Lightly grease 15-inch jellyroll pan. Pat dough into pan. Sprinkle evenly with chocolate chips.
4. Make topping: in small bowl of mixer, beat egg whites until stiff. Gradually beat in brown sugar. Spread mixture over top of chocolate chips.
5. Bake 20 to 25 minutes. Cool, then cut into bars.

Toffee Bar Cookies

Yield: 2 dozen bars

Wonderful for gift-giving — a candy-like cookie.

Crust:
⅓ cup butter, softened
⅓ cup brown sugar, firmly packed
1 egg yolk
1 teaspoon vanilla extract
½ cup flour
⅓ cup oats, old-fashioned
   or quick cook BUT NOT INSTANT

Topping:
5 squares semisweet chocolate
2 tablespoons butter

¾ cup chopped pecans

1. Preheat oven to 375°. Grease 9-inch square baking pan.
2. Combine first four ingredients using food processor or mixer. When smooth, add flour and oats; combine well.
3. Press mixture into bottom of prepared pan and bake about 15 minutes or until golden brown.
4. Meanwhile, make topping: melt chocolate squares and butter over hot water in double boiler. Spread over baked crust; sprinkle with nuts. Cut into bars when cool.

Maple Creams

**Flex your biceps and get out the saucepan;
it takes lots of beating but the end product is divine.**

1½ cups PURE maple syrup
½ cup heavy cream
¼ teaspoon salt
approximately 2 dozen pecan halves

1. In saucepan over low heat, mix all ingredients, except nuts; cook until candy thermometer registers 236°, or until a soft ball forms in cold water. DO NOT STIR during cooking.
2. Pour candy mixture onto clean platter; let stand until lukewarm.
3. Here comes the hard part: beat mixture with a spoon until it lightens in color and begins to set.
4. Taking a teaspoonful at a time, roll mixture into balls in palms of hands; place on greased cookie sheet. Press a nut half into each and flatten. Let cool; refrigerate in tin or airtight container.

Savannah Pralines

Yield: about 4 dozen

The Southern cousin to the Maple Creams.

4 cups sugar
2 cups light brown sugar
1 cup (2 sticks) butter
2 cups milk
4 tablespoons light corn syrup
8 cups pecan halves

1. In large heavy saucepan, combine all ingredients except pecan halves and cook for 20 minutes, stirring constantly until mixture boils.
2. Add pecan halves and continue cooking and stirring until mixture forms a soft ball when dropped in cold water, or 236° on candy thermometer.
3. Stir praline mixture very well; drop by tablespoonsful onto cookie sheets covered with parchment or waxed paper. Allow to cool.
4. Stack pralines in an airtight tin or container, using waxed paper between layers.

FAVORITE WINTER RECIPES

Index

Z

Also Available:

Christmas Memories Cookbook

A collection of outstanding Holiday suggestions inspired by the private recipe files of the Members of the Mystic Seaport Museum. 350 refreshing ideas for festive year-round entertaining and personal gift giving. You will discover a rich array of imaginative variations on classic New England cooking; based on the lasting traditions of Victorian festivities. Delightfully illustrated by artist Lynn Anderson, with additional pages for recording your own memorable Family Recipes and Christmas Menus. The Christmas Memories Cookbook is an excellent resource for both the beginner and the adventurous cook. Such distinctive fare as:

MEMORABLE MAIN COURSES

Roast Goose with Apple-Prune Stuffing
Block Island Turkey
Crabapple Glazed Ham with Raisin Sauce
Shrimp Etouffé

FANCIFUL DESSERTS

Captain Cooke's Plum Pudding
Blackberry Jam Cake
Chocolate Mousse Cake in Hazelnut Meringue
Nantucket Cranberry Dumplings
with Cinnamon Sauce

IMAGINATIVE APPETIZERS

Gingerbread Muffins with Smoked Turkey
Herbed Spirals
Curried Chutney Spread
Caviar Mousse
Mushroom Paté

INVENTIVE GIFT IDEAS

Chocolate Chip Meringues
Cranberry Almond Coffee Cake
Lemon Snow Bars
Plum Conserve
Cranberry-Pear Relish

Send Orders to:
Mystic Seaport Museum Stores
Mystic, CT 06355

Credit Card Telephone Orders: Call (203) 572-8551

ORDER BLANK

Please send me:

_____ copies of **Mystic Seaport All Seasons Cookbook**   @ $13.95 ea. _____
_____ copies of **Christmas Memories Cookbook**
                                    @ $13.95 ea. _____
Add $3.00 each for packing and shipping $3.00

Total: _____

Ordered By:
Name _____

Address _____

City _____ State _____ Zip _____

Ship To:
Name _____

Address _____

City _____ State _____ Zip _____

☐ Check ☐ VISA ☐ AMEX ☐ MC [MC Bank No. _____]

Credit Card No. [| | | | | | | | | | | | | | | | |]

Signature _____ Exp. Date _____

ORDER BLANK

Please send me:

_____ copies of **Mystic Seaport All Seasons Cookbook**   @ $13.95 ea. _____
_____ copies of **Christmas Memories Cookbook**
                                    @ $13.95 ea. _____
Add $3.00 each for packing and shipping $3.00

Total: _____

Ordered By:
Name _____

Address _____

City _____ State _____ Zip _____

Ship To:
Name _____

Address _____

City _____ State _____ Zip _____

☐ Check ☐ VISA ☐ AMEX ☐ MC [MC Bank No. _____]

Credit Card No. [| | | | | | | | | | | | | | | | |]

Signature _____ Exp. Date _____